A GIRL'S CHILDHOOD

A Girl's Childhood

Psychological Development,
Social Change, and
The Yale Child Study Center

Edited by
LINDA C. MAYES &
STEPHEN LASSONDE
Foreword by DEBORAH WEINSTEIN

Yale UNIVERSITY PRESS/NEW HAVEN & LONDON

Published with assistance from the foundation established in memory of
Calvin Chapin of the Class of 1788, Yale College.

Yale University Press books may be purchased in quantity for educational, business, or
promotional use. For information, please e-mail sales.press@yale.edu (U.S. office) or
sales@yaleup.co.uk (U.K. office).

Designed by Mary Valencia.
Set in Minion and Fournier MT types by Newgen North America.
Printed in the United States of America.

Library of Congress Cataloging-in-Publication Data

A girl's childhood: psychological development, social change, and The Yale Child Study
Center / edited by Linda C. Mayes and Stephen Lassonde ; foreword by Deborah Weinstein.
    pages cm
Includes bibliographical references and index.
    ISBN 978-0-300-11759-2 (cloth : alk. paper)   1. Child development—United States—
Longitudinal studies.   2. Children—United States—Longitudinal studies.   3. Parent and
child—United States—Longitudinal studies.   I. Mayes, Linda C.   II. Lassonde, Stephen.
    HQ792.U5L664 2014
    305.231—dc23
                                                                                        2014005822

A catalogue record for this book is available from the British Library.

This paper meets the requirements of ANSI / NISO Z39.48–1992 (Permanence of Paper).

10 9 8 7 6 5 4 3 2 1

To Bill Kessen, Marion Mayes, Alex Lassonde, and Jonathan Lassonde

CONTENTS

FOREWORD

DEBORAH WEINSTEIN

In the introduction to the edited volume *Biographies of Scientific Objects*, historian of science Lorraine Daston juxtaposes the "solid, obvious, sharply outlined, in-the-way things of quotidian experience" with the "elusive and hard-won" status of scientific objects.[1] In contrast to everyday objects that require "neither effort nor ingenuity nor instruments" for their detection, scientific objects require significant effort to be recognized as such and rendered observable, measurable, and/or subject to experimentation. As Daston and the other contributors to *Biographies of Scientific Objects* contend, phenomena as diverse as dreams, atoms, monsters, economic value, and the self had a reality prior to becoming the target of scientific investigation, but there is a historicity to their status as scientific objects per se, and scientific attention has affected them in important ways.

One might similarly consider the biography of "child development" as a scientific object that came into being during the twentieth century. A biographical heuristic is particularly suggestive for framing one mid-century psychoanalytically informed study of child development, the Yale Longitudinal Study (YLS), whose archive has provided the inspiration for this book. The YLS bore the traces of its genesis and implementation in a moment of scientific optimism and changing views of childhood (as the chapters that follow amply demonstrate), and its records are an astonishing set of materials for scholars interested in any of the many dimensions of postwar American life that informed the project. In the psychic life and childhood experiences of Evelyn, the young girl whose analysis is at the heart of this book, we can see crucial dimensions of postwar American history. Beyond the life story of any individual person, the biography of the YLS as an interdisciplinary research project contributed to the biography of child development as a scientific object.

Scientific studies of child development had roots in the first half of the twentieth century. The early twentieth-century efforts of child guidance professionals, mental hygienists, child welfare advocates, and child psychologists, such as Arnold Gesell, established the child as a legitimate subject of psychological research.[2] During the same period, pediatricians and other childhood experts became increasingly invested in measuring children's physical growth and standardizing those measurements in height and weight charts. Such charts contributed not only to increased clinical attention to well child care and preventative screening efforts, but also to the more widespread emphasis on measurement and standardization that characterized the Progressive era. Growth charts also shaped the framework of several longitudinal studies of the 1930s and 1940s that focused on variability in developmental growth rates among healthy individuals, thereby challenging the normative view of progressive developmental stages based on chronological age advocated by Gesell and others and highlighting the important distinction between average and healthy in the multiple meanings of "normal." While such studies were primarily concerned with somatic growth patterns, they also set important precedents for child development studies by including the relationship between physical and psychological development in their purview and contributing to the establishment of longitudinal studies as a model for developmental research.[3]

The post–World War II proliferation of interdisciplinary child study research, including the YLS, and the emergence of child psychiatry as a discipline, were crucial to the subsequent fortunes of child development as an object of scientific investigation, as was the consolidation of the "developmental paradigm" characterized by Linda Mayes and Stephen Lassonde in their introduction to this volume. Several dimensions of mid-century American life contributed to shaping the contours and salience of the Yale project and child development studies more generally.

The postwar ascendance of psychoanalysis and psychology, expansion of interdisciplinary social scientific research, and cultural investments in family life and child rearing synergistically fostered scientific attention on children's psychological development. Indeed, these seemingly distinct trends were deeply intertwined in ways that were not unique to the YLS but that the project nonetheless made vividly apparent.[4]

One dimension of postwar America, the growth of psychology and psychoanalysis during the 1940s and 1950s, itself had multiple facets. The number of psychologically oriented clinicians, including clinical psychologists, psychiatric social workers, and professionals in the new field of child psychiatry, grew sharply after World War II. Psychiatrists in general increasingly advocated their mission of promoting the mental health of the general population, not just treating mental illness among institutionalized patients. Psychoanalysis was well suited to this framing of psychiatry, given its interest in the unconscious drives and instincts of all people. Buoyed by their perceived success treating psychoneurotic casualties among soldiers during World War II, psychoanalytic psychiatrists such as William Menninger became influential leaders in their profession. Furthermore, the passage of the National Mental Health Act in 1946 and the ensuing establishment of the National Institute of Mental Health in 1949 were significant both for institutionalizing federal support for psychologically oriented research and clinical care and for their designated names highlighting "mental health" rather than neuropsychiatric disorders, a choice that was emblematic of psychiatry's postwar emphasis on normalization.[5] The attention to mental health also had broader cultural implications, particularly through the popularization of psychoanalysis in arenas as disparate as the childrearing manuals of Dr. Spock, Hollywood films such as *Spellbound* or *Lady in the Dark*, the advice columns of women's magazines, and what Vance Packard in *The Hidden Persuaders* described as the "mass psychoanalysis" of subliminal messages in postwar advertising.[6]

The influence of psychoanalysis went beyond the realms of the clinic or popular culture, infusing many of the intellectual currents of the 1950s. In the social sciences, prominent scholars such as the sociologist Talcott

Parsons and anthropologists in the culture and personality movement drew on psychoanalysis in their work. Psychoanalysts simultaneously turned to the expertise and research ambitions of social scientists in order to address some of their more socially minded questions. The social sciences of the Cold War were part of a mid-century moment of interdisciplinary vision that was manifest institutionally in university settings such as the Institute of Human Relations at Yale and the Department of Social Relations at Harvard. Postwar social sciences embodied the period's optimistic investment in scientific objectivity and scientific solutions to social problems, and they included psychological experts in their interdisciplinary efforts.[7]

The psychologization of parenting and child rearing echoed the turn to psychoanalysis and psychology in the social sciences. Postwar views of motherhood increasingly framed the importance of upbringing in terms of the psychological formation of future democratic citizens.[8] From studies that located the source of the "authoritarian personality" responsible for fascism in family life, to the polemical critiques of "momism" that attributed soldiers' psychological breakdowns and weakened American character to poor mothering, commentators of varying political and disciplinary stripes pinned the health of the nation to the psychological stability of properly reared children. The domestic ideology and familialism of the 1950s also intersected with contemporary concerns about mass society and conformity, debates about which were themselves framed in psychoanalytically informed terms, such as in David Reisman's widely read 1950 book *The Lonely Crowd.* Concurrent discussions of race relations in the early years of the civil rights movement also turned on claims about upbringing and psychological damage, in this case attributed to so-called matriarchal black families, in ways that underscored the psychological rather than the structural bases for the perpetuation of racial inequality. For example, in *The Mark of Oppression,* psychoanalysts Lionel Ovesey and Abram Kardiner claimed that the effects of slavery on the structure of the black family contributed to the upbringing of ongoing generations of black Americans afflicted with self-hatred, impaired personalities, and other signs of psychological distress.[9] The common thread through these diverse postwar views of motherhood and child rearing was the shared psychoanalytic attention to the role of the family in shaping the link between personality and society, psyche and politics.

Psychoanalytic interest in mother-child interactions was particularly relevant for child development research. The work of John Bowlby and Anna Freud, among others, contributed to intensified postwar interest in the mother-child dyad among British and American psychoanalysts. The wartime observations by Anna Freud and Dorothy Burlingham of British children living at the Hampstead Nurseries while separated from their families during the Blitz underscored the importance of children's attachment to their mothers for healthy psychological development. Historian Eli Zaretsky has argued that, in the United States, the psychoanalytic mother-child paradigm was filtered through American ego psychology, in which it "tended to devolve into a straightforward developmental psychology" rather than address drives, self-reflection, or other Freudian concerns.[10] Psychoanalysts exhorted American mothers to navigate between the Scylla of emotional deprivation, characterized vividly by psychoanalyst René Spitz's studies of hospitalism among institutionalized infants who received adequate physical care but lacked emotional attention from a consistent caregiver, and the Charybdis of maternal overprotection, which according to David M. Levy and other mid-century analysts could have similarly detrimental effects.[11] Such studies tended to reinscribe traditional gender roles for mothers as well as their children. They also underscored the dynamic relationship between the pathological and the normal since investigations of detrimental environmental conditions and poor psychological outcomes were used to formulate theories of normal childhood development and prescribe normative childrearing practices.

These intellectual, social, and cultural contexts of the YLS informed the study, and the archives of the project offer historians and other scholars a novel, valuable set of sources with which to analyze those contexts anew. As several of the authors in this volume note, the architecture and genre of the archival materials inevitably affect any scholarship that uses them as evidence. The contents of the process notes reproduced here offer a window into the inner life of a young girl, while the structure of those notes and the institutional records of the research project are indicative of the methods of child psychoanalysis and the fraught professional politics of psychoanalytic institutes during the period.

The question of how to read the materials in the YLS archives is not a straightforward one, however, and it surfaces multiple times in the essays that follow in ways that are suggestive for theories of the archive more generally. Scholars from a range of disciplines engaged with questions of the archive have problematized any straightforward notion of the link between archival collections and the production of knowledge.[12] In a 1925 essay on the inscription of traces in human memory, Sigmund Freud drew a connection between writing and the operations of the psyche that seems apropos in the context of theorizing about an archive of notes for a psychoanalytic research project. He wrote,

> If I distrust my memory . . . I am able to supplement and guarantee its working by making a note in writing. In that case the surface upon which this note is preserved, the pocket-book or sheet of paper, is as it were a materialized portion of my mnemic apparatus, which I otherwise carry about with me invisible. I have only to bear in mind the place where this "memory" has been deposited and I can then "reproduce" it at any time I like, with the certainty that it will have remained unaltered and so have escaped the possible distortions to which it might have been subjected in my actual memory.[13]

Freud subsequently in the essay rejected the initial promise of a deposited memory, a materialized portion of his mnemic apparatus unaltered by time and other distortions, by arguing that human memory operates not like a note on a piece of paper but rather in a manner akin to a multilayered mystic writing pad on which inscriptions can be erased, like a chalkboard, but nonetheless leave an imprint on a deeper layer. Beyond the intriguing question of the relationship between memory and the archive, this digression into Freud's writing underscores a set

of issues about the status of psychoanalytic records as a type of historical evidence, given that they are themselves based on the analyst's own
memory and framing of the analytic encounter. The archives of the YLS
seem more, rather than less, significant given these conditions of their
production, for they have the potential to provoke reflection on the
conditions of the archive itself.

Lavish, extraordinary, massive, textured, intimate—these are some
of the adjectives that commentators have used to describe the YLS archives that inspired this volume. The essays that follow are significant,
original contributions to multiple areas of scholarship; they are also an
evocative invitation to engage with the archival materials themselves.

NOTES

1. Lorraine Daston, "The Coming into Being of Scientific Objects," in Daston, ed., *Biographies of Scientific Objects* (Chicago: University of Chicago Press,
2000), 2.

2. Kathleen Jones, *Taming the Troublesome Child* (Cambridge, MA: Harvard University Press, 1999); and Alice Boardman Smuts, *Science in the Service
of Children, 1893–1935* (New Haven: Yale University Press, 2006).

3. Heather Munro Prescott, "'I Was a Teenage Dwarf': The Social Construc-
tion of 'Normal' Adolescent Growth and Development in the United States," and
Jeffrey P. Brosco, "Weight Charts and Well Child Care: When the Pediatrician
Became the Expert in Child Health," both in Alexandra Minna Stern and
Howard Markel, eds., *Formative Years: Children's Health in the United States,
1880–2000* (Ann Arbor: University of Michigan Press, 2002), 153–82, 91–120.

4. See Deborah Weinstein, *The Pathological Family: Postwar America and
the Rise of Family Therapy* (Ithaca, NY: Cornell University Press, 2013) for more
on the mutually influential history of therapeutic culture and the history of the
family and childhood in the postwar period.

5. Deborah B. Doroshow, "Emotionally Disturbed: Residential Treatment,
Child Psychiatry, and the Creation of Normal Children in Mid-Twentieth
Century America," Ph.D. diss., Yale University, 2012; Gerald Grob, *From Asy-
lum to Community: Mental Health Policy in Modern America* (Princeton, NJ:
Princeton University Press, 1991); and Ellen Herman, *The Romance of American
Psychology: Political Culture in the Age of Experts* (Berkeley: University of Cali-
fornia Press, 1995).

6. Quoted in Eva S. Moskowitz, *In Therapy We Trust: America's Obsession with Self-Fulfillment* (Baltimore: Johns Hopkins University Press, 2001), 157. On the American popularization of psychoanalysis, see also Nathan Hale, *The Rise and Crisis of Psychoanalysis in the United States: Freud and the Americans, 1917–1985* (New York: Oxford University Press, 1995); Martin Halliwell, *Therapeutic Revolutions: Medicine, Psychiatry, and American Culture, 1945–1970* (New Brunswick, NJ: Rutgers University Press, 2013); and Eli Zaretsky, *Secrets of the Soul: A Social and Cultural History of Psychoanalysis* (New York: Vintage Books, 2004).

7. Herman, *Romance of American Psychology*, 124–73; and Mark Solovey and Hamilton Cravens, eds., *Cold War Social Science: Knowledge Production, Liberal Democracy, and Human Nature* (Basingstoke, Eng.: Palgrave Macmillan, 2012).

8. Rebecca Jo Plant, *Mom: The Transformation of Motherhood in Modern America* (Chicago: University of Chicago Press, 2010).

9. Abram Kardiner and Lionel Ovesey, *The Mark of Oppression: A Psychosocial Study of the American Negro* (New York: W. W. Norton, 1951). See also Herman, *Romance of American Psychology*, 174–207; and Daryl Michael Scott, *Contempt and Pity: Social Policy and the Image of the Damaged Black Psyche* (Chapel Hill: University of North Carolina Press, 1997).

10. Zaretsky, *Secrets of the Soul*, 297.

11. Lisa Cartwright, "'Emergencies of Survival': Moral Spectatorship and the 'New Vision of the Child' in Postwar Child Psychoanalysis," *Journal of Visual Culture* 3 (2004): 35–49; Denise Riley, *War in the Nursery: Theories of the Child and Mother* (London: Virago Press, 1983); Marga Vicedo, *The Nature and Nurture of Love: From Imprinting to Attachment in Cold War America* (Chicago: University of Chicago Press, 2013); and Zaretsky, *Secrets of the Soul.*

12. See, for example, Anjali Arondekar, *For the Record: On Sexuality and the Colonial Archive in India* (Durham, NC: Duke University Press, 2009); Jacques Derrida, *Archive Fever: A Freudian Impression* (Chicago: University of Chicago Press, 1998); Carolyn Steedman, *Dust: The Archive and Cultural History* (New Brunswick, NJ: Rutgers University Press, 2002); and Ann Laura Stoler, *Along the Archival Grain* (Princeton, NJ: Princeton University Press, 2010).

13. Sigmund Freud, "A Note upon the Mystic Writing-Pad," 1925, reprinted in Charles Merewether, ed., *The Archive* (London: Whitechapel Gallery, 2006), 20.

ACKNOWLEDGMENTS

The idea for this book belongs to William Kessen, distinguished developmentalist and historian of psychology in Yale's Psychology Department from 1952 to 1997. One day in 1988, Bill took us to lunch hoping to convince us to look at the materials produced by the Yale Longitudinal Study and fashion some kind of book out of it. Bill had known everyone involved in the study and was instrumental in salvaging the mountain of documents it generated so it could be preserved by the Yale University Library. Of course, Bill's persuasive devotion to the many stories hidden among these documents made us very curious. And as we began wading through the stories of Evelyn and the other children who were the study's subject, we were hooked almost immediately, fascinated by what we read.

Neither of us is a historian of science "by day" and so we had to fit our visits to the archives around the edges of our professional lives. Bill's shorthand description of the study was that it had "swallowed up its investigators by its massiveness." Indeed, the thought of wading through all the process notes and the study's scaffolding was daunting. More than once, we too believed we would suffer the same fate, echoing the investigators' voices calling out from the hundreds upon hundreds of pages of their observations. But we pushed through, year after year, with many pauses along the way. Grant and book deadlines, the necessary but disruptive migration of more of the YLS papers from Al Solnit's closet at the Yale Child Center to Manuscripts and Archives, and the daily demands of each of our jobs put the project on the back burner

too many times. When Bill passed away in 1999 we recommitted ourselves to seeing this book to fruition. Now, with more than two decades
in the rearview mirror, we take enormous satisfaction in completing it
and savor the opportunity to acknowledge both Bill's influence on each
of us, and his desire for these materials to be shared more widely.

Many other debts accrued along the way. Donald Cohen, Albert
Solnit, and William Sledge each intervened at various points to grant
us access to the study during the long pauses between its acquisition
and its processing by Manuscripts and Archives. Laura Baum, Nikki
Hunter, Ivy Nally, and Margaret Sledge read and summarized sections
of the process notes for us. John Modell advised us and helped to secure
support for our work between 1995 and 1998 from The John D. and
Catherine T. MacArthur Foundation's Research Network on Successful
Pathways through Middle Childhood. Drs. Anna Wolff and Tony Kris,
the daughter and son of Ernst and Marianne Kris, provided important
background for our consideration of the context of the YLS. And Frank
Kessel gave helpful advice and insightful commentary along the way.
One of the most interesting features of this effort, we think, is the perspective our contributors have brought to it—each offering his or her
own view of their "part of the elephant"—differing points of entry into
the study's depth and richness.

Our anonymous reviewers provided critical guidance in refram-
ing and reorganizing the book. We thank them and believe the book is
much improved by their suggestions. Sara Hoover and later Samantha
Ostrowski at Yale University Press offered timely assistance with details
of the manuscript's production. Julie Carlson's sharp editorial eye saved
us from the inaccuracies and oversights that inevitably attend the birth-
ing of a manuscript whose gestation is so protracted, and we want to acknowledge the importance of her contribution here. Finally, this work
wouldn't have seen the light of day if Jean Thomson Black, executive
editor for science and medicine at the press, hadn't believed in its inherent value and championed its revival. For this we are deeply grateful.

Each of us owes a debt of gratitude to members of our own families
who in their own ways have nurtured our interest in family stories told

over many years and many generations. We each dedicate the book to not only Bill Kessen, then, but also to members of our families: to Marion Mayes, who as the mother of Linda Mayes encouraged her daughter from a very early age to listen to the stories swirling around her and whose courage and curiosity has sustained a vital and generous spirit—and to Stephen's two sons, young children when we got this project under way and now both wonderful young men. The lives of these children growing up demonstrate (again) just how important temperament and endowment are to happiness and "success" in its many forms.

Introduction

LINDA C. MAYES AND STEPHEN LASSONDE

A Girl's Childhood examines the history of a unique longitudinal study during the 1950s—a time when the boundaries between childhood and adulthood crisply, if briefly, came into focus across the U.S. social spectrum for the first time. Somewhat implausibly, Milton Senn, director of the Yale Child Study Center, assembled a team of psychoanalysts, developmentalists, pediatricians, and educators to initiate an intensive observational study of children and their parents. This eclectic group produced a remarkably detailed record of children's developmental trajectories from infancy through middle childhood. Their ambition was to devise a general psychoanalytic theory of child development based on careful, skilled observations. The narratives they created in weekly or biweekly sessions in multiple venues were recorded on audiotape and transcribed, then summarized, interpreted, and distributed for weekly and monthly group discussions by the team. The process notes from these sessions and the team's discussions would form an extraordinarily rich archival record. The project was singular in the expanse of the description it offered, for the depth and vintage of its analysis, and for the insights it still provides into early and middle childhood material in the post–World War II era. But it was also remarkable in its anticipation of many aspects of the contemporary scholarly landscape in developmental studies. As developmentalist-historian Frank Kessel has observed of the study, its emphasis on "widespread discourse and institutional action surrounding 'inter'- and even 'trans-disciplinarity'" was precocious in its integration of mental health, pediatrics, psycho-analysis, and social science. The coalescence of the study's investigators represented a historic convergence of U.S. psychoanalytic, behavioral, and pediatric science under the guiding influence of Ernst Kris, a rising star among the intellectual émigrés fleeing Nazi Europe. Kris's group exemplified the kind of "team science" that was to become the mark of innovation in psychological research toward the end of the twentieth century. Similarly, remarks Kessel, the study exhibits "current moves towards 'mixed methods,' [or] greater openness to qualitative methods (for example, ethnography) in social science disciplines where those had been until quite recently taboo." In what would become known as the "Yale Longitudinal Study" (YLS), such divergent approaches were well, if unevenly, represented. The study's methods of data collection, corpus of documents, and process notes, specifically, represent a unique "scien-tific" and humanistic contribution by an unprecedented collaboration of psychoanalysts at the peak of their intellectual and professional influ-ence in American academic research and medicine.[1]

Yet the study was hampered in a number of ways. Kris, who was its leading light and who was recruited by Senn to organize the study, died suddenly only a few years after its launch. In addition, its protocol was not laid out in the manner of experimental developmental science that was typical of the time or thereafter. It was, as Andrew Fearnley has pointed out, "action research," in which experiment and therapy were iterative and open-ended—a research design that would be unrecogniz-able today. How the researcher-clinicians related to one another is also unclear. Kris was their guiding force, but Anna Freud consulted with the group periodically and it remains for a future scholar to assess her influence on the orientation and conduct of each researcher-clinician. Certainly Anna Freud's interest in the mother-child bond and the concept of "lines of development" are evident throughout, but each staff member brought his or her own psychoanalytic preoccupations (and particular theoretical emphasis from his or her training) to bear on the material. Samuel Ritvo, the psychiatrist who saw the primary subject of this book ("Evelyn") over the course of a decade, pursued in their weekly sessions his career-long interest in the resolution of aggression, which he believed to be universal and fundamental to human developmental work. The role of aggression, as any reader of the process notes will see, guided both his interactions with Evelyn and his interpretation of her path through childhood.[2]

The field of psychoanalysis was both at high tide as an intellectual force in North American intellectual life and approaching the peak of its popularity with the U.S. public. This no doubt had its own shaping, even sometimes distortive, effect on the interests of its chief players and the character of their interactions as researcher-clinicians.[3] But it also undoubtedly played a part in the way that therapists utilized and leaned on the rest of the YLS staff: preschool teachers, social workers, and the group's pediatricians. Earlier in the century, the medical profession had yielded to the authority of educational psychologists and public school officials in determining the care and destiny of so-called feeble-minded children (children with special needs). But even if the educational and therapeutic custodianship of the "feeble-minded" had been resolved by the 1920s, the landscape of expertise on the health and development of children shifted dramatically during the interwar years. The field of child health and welfare became at once more medicalized and increasingly concerned with the trajectory of children's psychological, emotional, and cognitive growth. Academic psychology was ascendant, in general, but within psychology departments in the United States, research, whether funded by foundations or by the federal government, needed to be justified scientifically. Breakthroughs in American medicine during the interwar period and just after had enhanced the prestige of the American medical profession and in turn the "mental sciences," such as psychiatry and psychoanalysis, since both required their practitioners to receive medical training.

The orientation of the physicians in the YLS had been etiological. Their domain was mental disease and health in individuals. The
YLS, moreover, was their project and it was underwritten by the major private foundation concerned with juvenile health at that time, the
Commonwealth Fund, which poured millions of dollars into Yale University between 1921 and 1982. Since the medical school was the primary
recipient of its largesse at Yale, and the locus of the YLS was the medical
school's Child Study Center, we can safely assume that the contributions of YLS staff members were framed in terms familiar to the professional hierarchies and jealousies of the day. Educators involved with
the study, then, were likely to have yielded to the medical authorities in
these discussions even though the group's method was supposed to be
interdisciplinary and collaborative.

A half century later, we the authors of *A Girl's Childhood* have set
out to show how "the concept of 'the child,' the status of developmental
studies of children, and the nascent methodology of longitudinal sampling are historical, sociocultural constructions that reflect contextual-
ly-grounded assumptions, values, interests, and ideas."[4] It is our hope,
therefore, that despite the limitations of the Yale Longitudinal Study,
this book will be of interest to historians of contemporary America, historians of childhood and family life, and specialists in the history of
child psychiatry and developmental psychology. Similarly, the nature of
the material as well as the combined historical and clinical analysis of
this study and its documentation will make the volume useful for sociologists and anthropologists examining changes in the American family
during the second half of the twentieth century. But we also expect that
practicing child therapists, child psychoanalysts, and developmentalists interested in observational accounts of children's imaginary play, as
well as mental health clinicians-in-training, who have few opportunities
to discuss the work of experienced clinicians, will find it uniquely useful too—and will be sufficiently intrigued to want to access the archival
material for use in their clinical teaching and writing.

The purpose of this book, then, is twofold. The foremost is to highlight the extraordinary character of the records of the YLS, which

document the early and middle childhood years of a dozen children in New Haven County as they interacted weekly with a team of therapist-researchers at the Yale Child Study Center between the mid-1950s and mid-1960s. The "raw" transcripts of their visits offer extraordinary views into the unfolding capacities of children's cognitive, emotional, and social growth at a time in the United States when white, middle-class family life was held up as an ideal both in the dominant culture of postwar America and as a significant component of Cold War ideology abroad. Two-parent, nuclear families living in single-family dwellings, with stay-at-home-mothers, breadwinning fathers, and evenly spaced children born early in their mother's child-bearing years, imbued a pervasive cultural aspiration with sufficient truth to impugn anyone whose race, sexual orientation, or marital status deviated from the new norm.[5] But "the family" of this era and the childhood it promised its children were the short-lived culmination of peculiar, converging historical circumstances. The childhood touted by 1950s-style families was a fragile construct, subject to long-term demographic, economic, and social forces that eventually relegated this newly fabricated cultural ideal to the realm of historical mythmaking.[6]

Our second purpose is to reflect on, analyze, and contextualize the intellectual worldview of the therapist-researchers involved in the study as a window on the history of post–World War II child-development, child-psychiatric, and child-psychoanalytic theory. One of our authors offers an insightful assessment of the history of developmentally oriented longitudinal studies, and another illuminates the context of psychoanalytic practice in postwar western New England and New Haven, but we do not offer a comprehensive history of developmental science generally in the mid-twentieth century. Instead what we present here is intended to supplement a probing, provocative literature that extends back to the work of Ellen Herman twenty-five years ago and contributions more recently by Nikolas Rose, Elizabeth Lunbeck, Eva Moskowitz, Barbara Beatty, Emily Cahan, and Julia Grant. Deborah Weinstein's compelling look at the role of psychiatry in pathologizing American family life during the post–World War II period offers a complementary and much more thorough examination of the sibling field of family therapy over the same years.[7]

The domains of children's mental health and developmental science grew in complementary directions after mid-century. Until then, as Fearnley notes, developmental issues (specifically cognitive development and endowment) and pathology were viewed by child psychiatry as distinct domains. But after World War II, two shifts occurred. The ascendance of psychoanalysis in American psychiatry heightened attention to children's development, particularly in light of work by Anna Freud, John Bowlby, and others on the significance of the mother-child relationship in shaping normal as well as disturbed psychological outcomes. At the same time as this "developmental paradigm" was taking form, child welfare advocates and those in the emerging multidisciplinary field of child development were increasingly focusing on the mental health of children.

The emerging developmental paradigm had several defining features: a declining faith in children's innate resiliency and preprogrammed constitutional strength in favor of a view of children as fragile and highly sensitive to their environments; a scheme of children's development as stage-like with consequential outcomes—which thus reinforced the importance of intervention at earlier ages; the rise of a corps of professionals (academic, research-oriented psychologists, psychiatrists, pediatricians, and educators) who stressed the need for parental vigilance and the influence of parental care; and finally and perhaps most significantly, an expanded cohort of middle-class mothers conversant in childrearing literature, who zealously applied the lessons of the most contemporary parenting techniques.[8] The group assembled at the Yale Child Study Center was decidedly focused on the problem of identifying developmental outcomes and the sources of mental health and pathology in the child's interaction with her or his environment. The orientation of their observations dovetailed well with claims made by family therapists about psychiatric disorders, since the field was moving away from an exclusive concentration on pathology to an emphasis on the healthy development of the individual child and to understanding pathology through the lens of normal development.[9]

We think of the rich, multifaceted material in *A Girl's Childhood* as a kind of "meta" case study, and so have organized the book around a selection of YLS process notes, which appears at its center. We invite readers, then, to wade midstream into young Evelyn's middle childhood years with their own questions and purposes.

The book is divided into three parts: historical, documentary, and interpretive. In the first section, Stephen Lassonde qualifies the meaning of "the child" as a historically constructed subject. He reminds us that the boundary between child and adult in its now-familiar form was only recently delineated, that its acceptance and enforcement across the social spectrum even within specific societies is even more novel, and that the definition, use, and experiences of children have varied widely across the world.

In the same vein, Andrew Fearnley places the Yale Longitudinal Study in the context of other longitudinal studies during the middle decades of the twentieth century. Fearnley observes that the longitudinal study filled a gap: in the absence of systematic ways to study children's cognitive, social, and emotional development and the later emergence of sub-specialist residency programs, it became the "method of choice" for many child psychiatrists from the 1950s through the mid-1970s because it fit their "interest in epidemiological techniques, preventative forms of intervention, and new ideas about disease etiology." More important, Fearnley asserts, the YLS reflected a signal moment in the study of children within the mental sciences. Before the middle decades of the twentieth century, he points out, "most mental-health professionals associated childhood with mental deficiency, rather than mental illness, posing questions about children inspired by the recapitulation perspectives of an earlier generation of natural scientists." In the post–World War II era, he writes, children's "capacity for intellect, an independence of action and thought, autonomy and rationality" became fundamental to the study of children as objects of scientific inquiry and of "childhood" itself.

David Carlson's essay recreates the institutional history of the YLS within its regional intellectual and disciplinary environment: the so-called "New Haven–Stockbridge Group," represented by the Austen

Riggs Center in Stockbridge, Massachusetts, and New Haven's Western New England Psychoanalytic Society. Carlson skillfully limns a network of psychoanalytically oriented behavioral and social scientists ranging from John Dollard, Erik Erikson, and Anna Freud to Jules Coleman and August B. Hollingshead. He locates these figures in a professional landscape that includes the New York Psychoanalytic Institute, the Austen Riggs Center, and New Haven's fledgling Western New England Institute for Psychoanalysis. Their shared affiliations and jealous rivalries resemble the narratives of dynastic feuds nested within some of the preeminent research incubators of the day, such as the Commonwealth Fund, Yale's Institute of Human Relations, and Yale's formidable medical and law schools.

Viewed from one angle, the YLS can be seen as a kind of microenvironment constituted by the personalities and collective expertise of Yale Child Study Center staff. Linda Mayes's chapter offers a complement to Carlson's, a prosopography, if you will, of the Yale Child Study Center from Arnold Gesell to young clinician and future head Albert Solnit. Mayes shows how the YLS was confected from a unique concoction of fate, historical contingency, and the savvy recruiting instincts of its director, Milton Senn.

Clinical and developmental psychologist Virginia Demos of the Austen Riggs Center and John Demos, renowned U.S. historian, collaborate to examine the methodology of the YLS. In their concluding chapter to the first part, they explore the idiosyncrasy, genius, and blind spots in the conception and execution of the study while describing the merits of its process notes as historical documents.

In the second part of the book, Diane Kaplan from the Manuscripts and Archives division of the Yale University Library undertakes a more literal examination of the documents as archival records, discussing their provenance and preservation (or neglect), as well as the difficulties of offering access to a wider audience. She also illustrates how important it is for archivists to understand the context and history of the documents they are responsible for preserving and cataloguing. To this end and expanding on Mayes's chapter, Kaplan begins with a closer examination of how the YLS began, focusing on what the study and the resulting documents were expected to provide. The responsibilities of professional archivists often include a description of the "architecture," purpose, and constraints of a body of documents, but Kaplan also offers a very useful discussion of the archivists' efforts to preserve the anonymity of the study's subjects while helping make these enormously rich documents accessible. Rounding out the book's second part is a sampling of the process notes from Ritvo's sessions with Evelyn, a sampling that is intended to allow the reader to interpret for her- or himself this little girl's emergence into personhood. These are, we think, a highly evocative set of records, the centerpiece of this book and the very reason for bringing these materials to light.

In part three, Mayes and Lassonde interpret Evelyn's process notes, focusing on her awakening interest in how her status as a female relates to the male-dominated social hierarchy that she encounters at every stage of her growth. Evelyn, as noted elsewhere, had the most enduring involvement with the study, which makes her transcripts an unusually rich source of information about children's development at this time. Ritvo and members of the Yale Child Study Center contribute contemporaneous observations of Evelyn's therapy from 1954 to 1963 that were reworked for this volume by Ritvo just months before he died.[10] Finally, Wayne Downey, clinical professor at the Yale Child Study Center, offers his own reflections on the process notes of another child in the study whose involvement was of briefer duration and certainly more tumultuous than Evelyn's. Downey's analysis provides an intriguing contrasting approach and the materials of the child he writes about offer an interesting counterpoint to Evelyn's interactions with Ritvo. Downey, we hasten to note, worked as a bursary student at the Child Study Center while an undergraduate at Yale during the study and was tasked with transcribing tapes to text in triplicate. His own contribution to the YLS, then, spans his entire career and the existence of the process notes is owed quite literally to his laborious efforts.

The accumulated day-to-day records and weekly summaries of the observations of the children and parents in this study provide a massive, granular accounting of the moment-to-moment interactions among therapists, children, and parents. Evelyn's case study presents an

arresting view into the way one child came to understand herself in relation to the world around her. Interactions with family, friends, neigh-
bors, church members, and teachers reveal an unfolding sense of self
across the decade of her involvement in the study—against the backdrop
of a highly gendered social order and the rapidly changing configuration of social class in post–World War II America.[11] Our collaboration
as historians and developmentalists explores the sociocultural context
of the Yale Longitudinal Study in Eisenhower's America—one in which
heightened awareness of gender roles, a rapidly expanding middle class,
the acceleration of migration from cities to suburbs, and rising levels of
education prepared the ground for a social and cultural revolution that,
within the decade, contributed to the civil rights and feminist movements, the contraceptive pill, zero population growth efforts, pacifism,
and a "youth revolt." By bringing these materials to light and reflecting on their value to historians and developmentalists, we hope to contribute to a clearer understanding of the fascinating contradictions that
emerged during these years.

NOTES

1. Frank Kessel, draft of commentary on manuscript for Mayes and Lassonde, August 24, 2010.

2. See Chapter 4. Note that "Evelyn" is the pseudonym that Ritvo and
other members of the YLS team used to refer to "Beth," their study's subject.
The process notes refer to her as one or the other, but published manuscripts
from the study often refer to her as "Evelyne," but occasionally as "Cathy." A
family name of "Olsen" was also assigned to Beth's/Evelyn's family but it was
just as common to refer to them as "Parr" in the process notes, or just as commonly "Mrs. P.," for Evelyn's mother, and published articles at times referred
to her as "Mrs. L." Apart from the many "flavors" of psychoanalytic theory that
differentiated this group of clinicians, pervasive was the importance of maternal love and the sway of the mother-child bond above all others. See Marga
Vicedo's illuminating discussion of concepts of "mother love" during this period in *The Nature and Nurture of Love: From Imprinting to Attachment in Cold
War America* (Chicago: University of Chicago Press, 2013), esp. chap. 5.

3. On the popularity of psychoanalysis during the first few decades after
World War II, see Deborah Weinstein, *The Pathological Family: Postwar Amer-*

ica and the Rise of Family Therapy (Ithaca, NY: Cornell University Press, 2013), 24; also see Nathan Hale, *The Rise and Crisis of Psychoanalysis in the United States: Freud and the Americans, 1917–1985* (New York: Oxford University Press, 1995); Jonathan Freedman, "From *Spellbound* to *Vertigo*: Alfred Hitchcock and Therapeutic Culture in America," in Jonathan Freedman and Richard Millington, eds., *Hitchcock's America* (New York: Oxford University Press, 1999), 77–98; and Michael Sulman, "The Humanization of the American Child: Benjamin Spock as a Popularizer of Psycholanalytic Thought," *Journal of the History of Behavioral Science* 9 (1973): 258–65, all cited in Weinstein, *Pathological Family*.

4. Kessel commentary, August 24, 2010.

5. The classic formulation of this is Elaine Tyler May, *Homeward Bound: American Families in the Cold War Era* (New York: Basic Books, 1988).

6. "Family and Demography in Postwar America: A Hazard of New Fortunes?" in Jean-Christophe Agnew and Roy Rosenzweig, eds., *A Companion to Post-1945 America* (Malden, MA: Blackwell, 2002), 3–19.

7. See Chapters 2 and 3. On the history of psychoanalysis, the rise of "therapeutic culture," and developmental science in twentieth-century America, see Nikolas Rose, *Governing the Soul: The Shaping of the Private Self* (London: Free Association Books, 1989); Elizabeth Lunbeck, *The Psychiatric Persuasion: Knowledge, Gender, and Power in Modern America* (Princeton, NJ: Princeton University Press, 1994); Ellen Herman, *The Romance of American Psychology: Political Culture in the Age of Experts* (Berkeley: University of California Press, 1995); Eva S. Moskowitz, *In Therapy We Trust: America's Obsession with Self-Fulfillment* (Baltimore: The Johns Hopkins University Press, 2001); Barbara Beatty, Emily Cahan, and Julia Grant, eds., *When Science Encounters the Child: Education, Parenting, and Child Welfare in 20th-Century America* (New York: Teachers College Press, 2006); and Weinstein, *The Pathological Family*.

8. See Stephen Lassonde, "Age, Schooling, and Life Stages," in Paula Fass, ed., *The Routledge History of Childhood in the Western World* (London: Routledge, 2013), 211–26.

9. See Weinstein, *Pathological Family*, esp. chaps. 1 and 3.

10. Ritvo's son, David, has contributed a very appreciative assessment of his father's work with Evelyn, which we have included here as well.

11. Wayne Downey offers his own perspective in this volume on a second child who participated in the study for a much shorter period; see Chapter 10.

❧ I ❧

"The Child" and Family Life at Midcentury

STEPHEN LASSONDE

D uring the twentieth century, enormous changes in children's
experiences occurred across much of the world but particularly in Western Europe, East Asia, and North America. By
midcentury these changes included a decisive decline in early childhood
death, disease, and incapacitation; the conversion of most children from
economic assets to school-goers; and the extension of the minimum age
for leaving school to sixteen. Mass schooling brought together children
from widely varied social backgrounds and exposed them to roughly
similar routines, mores, and social attitudes. Schooling in areas sufficiently dense in population to sort children by age and ability greatly
increased society's sensitivity to age differences among children and to
children's sense of their own and others' physical and mental developmental progress.[1] Other changes that followed the establishment of
mass schooling for children were the creation of more leisure time for
children and, by the second half of the century, the emerging and important role of children as consumers.[2] Taken together, these developments amounted to a transformation in children's roles in their families
and in the economy. Still, we place quotation marks around "the child"

to acknowledge that the idea of the child is historically constructed and dynamic: that while children are observably different from adults physiologically and cognitively, their treatment as a category of persons needing protection, and their consequent separation from adults in many realms, are artifacts of the significant distinctions that many contemporary societies have drawn around children, particularly during the past two centuries.[3]

CHILD DEVELOPMENT MEETS HISTORY

Some years ago Glen Elder, John Modell, Ross Parke, and others urged historians to think about children developmentally and urged developmentalists to think about children historically.[4] They proposed that we examine, in a concrete way that acknowledges changes over time, the consequences of children's experiences for their psychological growth. They asserted, that is, that historians should consider how children's development at successive stages of maturation has varied qualitatively in different historical epochs as a result of large-scale social, economic, or political changes—changes that are reflected in factors such as children's mortality or their relative vulnerability to disease; the fertility rate and spacing of births; gender norms; and children's changing engagement with the institutions that sustain, nurture, or even abuse them. To consider just a few examples: compare the child in late nineteenth-century southern Italy who from the age of five or six helped on the family farm with the child in early twentieth-century Japan who attended school six days a week and whose mother devoted most of her attention through the child's adolescence to helping him master his school lessons.[5] Or a child growing up in the United States during the 1950s and 1960s in a family of five children with that of a female child in China—a society that has traditionally strongly favored males since the institution of its "One Child" policy in the late 1970s.[6]

The study of children's development in historical time contains a paradox. Because the dominant aim of the emerging field of child psychology by the twentieth century was to predict the normal progression of human cognitive capacities always and everywhere, time and place were rendered irrelevant and even antithetical to the study of the child as a subject of scientific inquiry. The application of history to children's development, however, poses a contradictory proposition—that social, cultural, and political forces at any given historical moment may affect an otherwise predictable path of physiological and cognitive growth for children. Because historical inquiry is above all concerned with what is contingent and contextual, and psychological inquiry has been, conventionally, in quest of universals, the two fields would seem to operate at cross-purposes. Whether a concern for historical change is germane for psychology (even a psychology that is serious about context) is then a potentially contentious subject.

Over the past few decades developmentalists have been working to redress this paradox by comprehending cultural differences between and within societies. They try to account for corresponding differences in the ways that humans interact with one another and perform cognitive functions, such as perception, reasoning, deliberate remembering, and language.[7] They are, increasingly, taking an inherently historical approach, assuming that questions raised and answers offered about the course of a child's development are, in Michael Cole's words, "locally contingent, not universal."[8] This approach, writes Cole, "assumes that mind emerges in the joint mediated activity of people" and "is in an important sense 'co-constructed' and distributed. . . . It assumes that individuals are active agents in their own development but do not act in settings entirely of their own choosing."[9] To this we need to add mainly the following idea, one that though now generally accepted within the discipline of anthropology was only a few generations ago unorthodox even there: models of culture that presume stasis rather than change over time distort what they seek to describe (giving us, for instance— infamously—"the primitive").[10]

If it were possible to record a life history of every child at any point in historical time, we could capture the intrusion of events into the growth and outlook of every child at particular moments in the past. We could then reconstitute, as it were, the "co-construction" of their development synchronically and then generalize about predictable patterns of their development, which make them creatures of *histori-cal* time. Psychologists and sociologists do something analogous to this when they seek to determine whether a life event, such as the divorce of a child's parents, has a future impact on that child as measured by outcomes such as educational attainment, professional achievement, or even his or her relative capacity for intimacy as an adult. They posit that certain and potentially destabilizing events in a child's life, though now relatively commonplace in American society, may be experienced as sufficiently traumatic to produce a range of predictable detrimental outcomes as child grows into adult. The more sophisticated the study, the more attuned it will be to the age of the child when the "trauma" occurred. They may also implicitly assert that these outcomes, when summed, result in social changes that reinforce the very behaviors that produced them in the first place.[11]

This, in effect, is what Glen Elder was able to approximate in his classic work *Children of the Great Depression* (1974), in which he deftly interpreted longitudinal evidence on children in Oakland and Berke-ley born during the 1920s and 1930s. Since then Elder and others have examined the dialectic of historical time and life-course events for American children before and after the mid-twentieth century.[12] Their chief contribution has been to show how chronologically distinguish-able groups of people have experienced sweeping social phenomena in the past—personal traumas induced by large-scale social-historical events—and how these coincided with developmental stages on the path to adulthood. Our data are of a different character and don't lend themselves to statistical measures, but they do offer a spectacular view into the psychic lives and development of children over a sustained pe-riod of time, at a historical moment seemingly unlike any other in the twentieth century.

COHORT AND GENERATION

Until *Children of the Great Depression*, historians studying col-lective social, political, or intellectual responses to large social forces tended to employ the term "generation" to describe any broad-gauged, time-bound experience.[13] During the late 1960s historians began to study how patterns of everyday social experience have affected the mass of human societies. They employed the methods of social and behavioral scientists to capture social experience in the past and to understand the sources of social-historical change. Periodization by political and intellectual upheavals or movements, while not altogether abandoned, was either thrown into question or regarded as irrelevant to what were considered more significant, if longer-developing, even imperceptible historical tremors caused by shifts in forms of production, transportation, and technology.[14] Social historians (and historical sociologists), who were generally critical of the imprecision of the methodologies of political and intellectual historians, discouraged the use of the concept of generation in favor of "cohort." Cohort is a narrower, less evocative term employed by demographers when considering whether similar age-related patterns (of death, or marriage, for instance) had affected those who had been born at the same time, or had lived through common historical experiences (for example, had served in a particular war, were devastated by an economic depression, or had been stricken by a pandemic).

Historical demographers found the cohort concept a useful tool for analyzing past fertility behavior, including household composition; marriage; the use of contraception before, during, and outside of marriage; and especially by the 1970s, cohabitation.[15] While demography tended to isolate the birth cohort as the unit of study in fertility patterns, by the late 1950s American demographer Norman Ryder had begun to think about how the cohort could be used more broadly to think about and comprehend contemporary social experience, as a way of anticipating the impact of demographic phenomena on the labor market, education, and standard of living in the present and future.[16]

The term cohort as used by historians, then, is simply a cluster of years in which people are born. But the identification of that cluster— that is, what makes it a cohort—is what *happens* to those people later in their lives. In other words, the collective social experience of any group over time can *only* be known in retrospect, and thus the action of "history" on this group is what constitutes it as a cohort. The phrase "Baby

Boom generation" offers an example of a pervasive social experience that requires more careful parsing. The phrase is used popularly by marketers, journalists, and even in the scholarly literature to describe a number of experiences, attitudes, and behaviors reputedly characteristic of people born between 1946 and 1964. The group it describes is often referred to as a "generation," when in fact it consists of two cohorts—those born between 1946 and 1954 and those born between 1955 and 1964.[17] Male children of the 1950s, whose childhood has often been portrayed as idyllic, were in fact vulnerable to the military draft and service in the Vietnam War if they were born between the late 1940s and early 1950s. A male born during the later years of the 1950s or early 1960s, by contrast, escaped the military draft and the horrors of war but confronted declining occupational prospects just as he left high school or college. Females of the "first" Baby Boom cohort passed through adolescence just as the "pill" was introduced as an effective means of birth control and came of age as abortion was legalized for the first time. Yet girls born in the "second" cohort of the Baby Boom generation were more likely to reap the benefits of the spreading acceptability of contraceptive techniques. Many aspired (as their grandmothers had) to careers as professionals, in contrast to the majority of their mothers who spent their adult lives raising children rather than entering the paid labor force. But because a technological innovation like birth control was variably received depending on region, religion, ethnicity, race, and socioeconomic status, its spread was also uneven, so that adolescents of the second cohort were more likely to adopt it than were their older sisters.

To assess the child at midcentury and to appreciate the qualitative difference between the experiences of discernible cohorts in historical time, then, it is helpful to look briefly to the decades just before the 1950s. What the typical American child "looked" like, experienced, and aspired to has changed markedly over the course of the twentieth century, due not only to immigration policies and reproductive practices but in good measure to the privations of the Great Depression, the mobilization for war during the 1940s, and the prosperity and political upheavals of the two-and-a-half decades after World War II.

THE GREAT DEPRESSION AND WORLD WAR II

The 1930s stamped unique, often tragic impositions on children. Elder maintains that young children, because they were entirely dependent on their parents, suffered the worst effects of family strain during the Depression years. Children born during the early 1920s, however (in their early teens during the Great Depression), were relatively better adjusted later in life because they had been semiautonomous when their parents were enduring the worst effects of the economic crisis. Their hastened sense of agency enabled them to cope with their parents' marital discord, financial privation, unstable or unsupportive family relationships, and often punitive parental behavior and anxiety, whereas their younger siblings, who were utterly dependent on parents throughout this period of profound insecurity, had comparatively greater difficulty as adults.[18]

Another factor that mitigated potentially detrimental long-term effects of family instability on socioeconomic outcomes was that the great majority of young people remained in high school rather than seeking employment during the Depression (as they might have done in a healthy economy) and so unwittingly enjoyed the dividends of higher levels of education than previous generations. While these same cohorts of males born in the early to mid-1920s suffered the brunt of death and casualties as combatants during World War II, those who survived the war were the beneficiaries of the G.I. Bill and the manifold opportunities resulting from the postwar economic expansion in the United States. By the same token, the 1930s economic collapse trapped the poorest teens in desperately low-paying jobs under the harshest of conditions and forced other young people to leave home as teenage vagabonds, "catching out" to ride the rails across the North American continent for months or even years at a time.[19] So while many young people may have had greater agency than their younger siblings, some portion of them were also saddled with staggering responsibility.

William Tuttle's description of family upheaval on the American homefront underscores the singularity of the wartime experience for children. Among the adjustments endured by young children at this time were the absence of fathers drafted into military service, frequent relocation as their families were moved from one military installation to another, and the daytime absence of mothers drawn into the work-force to support the war effort. Older children and adolescents often assumed the burden of looking after younger siblings, returned to an empty home at the end of the school day if their mothers worked, and grew estranged from fathers (or brothers) away at war. While none of these experiences were new to children—separation from one or both parents, coming home to a parentless household after school or work, living among grandparents or aunts and uncles, and frequent uproot-ing—the pervasiveness of these experiences made wartime a unique so-cial phenomenon.[20]

"FAMILY BUILDING" IN THE POSTWAR ERA

The most remarkable aspect of the Baby Boom was the surge in the birth rate that began immediately after World War II. Starting at a rate of 21.1 births per thousand in 1945, the birth rate leaped during the next five-year period (1950–1954) to a rate of 24.5 births and peaked between 1955 and 1959 at 25.2. The birth rate declined thereafter, but only until 1964, the end of the "boom," when the five-year rate settled back to 22.2 births per thousand, just above the wartime average. Other trends associated with the ideology of domesticity ushered in by the Baby Boom were not firmly established until the middle and later years of the 1950s. Historically lower ages at first marriage, an accompanying decline in the average age of entry into motherhood, an increased tendency to have a child within the first year of marriage, and the trend toward larger fami-lies took hold especially during the latter years of the decade.[21]

Home-owning was another important feature of the 1950s' dedica-tion to what John Modell has called the era's "family building" ethos: that is, the belief that the height of personal satisfaction was to be at-tained not just in marriage but also in childrearing. The single-family dwelling permitted unprecedented privacy between families, as well as for children within those households. Owner-occupied homes during the period shot up from 43.6 percent of all occupied units in 1940 to 61.9 percent in 1960. Only five years after the war had ended, 84 percent of U.S. households contained fewer than one person per room. And as Kenneth Jackson has observed, "Almost every contractor-built, post–World War II home had central heating, indoor plumbing, telephones, automatic stoves, refrigerators, and washing machines." This surge was due in large part to the Federal Housing Administration's historically generous loan policies, which effectively subsidized new single-family home construction after the war. Between 1948 and 1958, no fewer than 13 million houses were constructed, 85 percent of them in America's expanding suburbs, which absorbed almost two-thirds of the nation's prodigious population growth during these years.[22]

The expansion of consumer credit was another phenomenon associated with both postwar optimism and neo-domesticity: between 1950 and 1960, the ratio of outstanding credit to disposable income almost doubled for Americans, while the "length of installment-credit contracts increased by 40 percent for automobile loans and 18 percent for other durables." By 1956 consumer debt was owned by "two-thirds of American households in which the head was under 35," and consumer debt had increased the most among young married couples with children.[23]

Beneath the apparent placidity of family life in the two decades after World War II, it seems, American middle-class women suffered varying degrees of inner turmoil in their marital relations. Eager to live out the kind of domestic fulfillment that had eluded their own mothers during depression and war, writes Elaine Tyler May, women often felt as though they had exchanged the previous generation's deprivation and disruption for blunted ambitions, unfulfilled sex lives, and gaping emotional needs left unmet by unsympathetic or undiscerning partners. At the same time, depression and war gave an unprecedented proportion of married women experience in the workforce, which stimulated, ultimately, a desire for financial independence.[24]

A sexual revolution set in train during the 1920s quietly gathered steam with the aid of the emerging mass media during the following decades and found unanticipated outlets during World War II. After the war, "re-domesticated" women were encouraged to think of themselves as sexual creatures with natural physical longings different than men's and every bit as worthy of professional and scholarly attention.[25] Moreover, the publication of the best-selling Kinsey Reports on male and female sexual behavior in 1948 and 1949, respectively, revealed the chasm between what Americans *said* about their erotic lives and what they thought and practiced at midcentury.[26] Once women started to take their own sexual needs seriously, they began to challenge their partners' limited knowledge and the male-centered orientation to sexual gratification that had characterized American sexuality since the advent of the Victorian era.

A series of workshops conducted by marital advice experts Abraham Stone and Lena Levine in New York City in 1947 also showed the growing gap between men's and women's attitudes toward female sexual satisfaction in the postwar years. While Stone's and Levine's clientele were primarily white and middle class, the discussions they led suggested the depth of ignorance about women's sexuality that prevailed at midcentury, as well as the degree of appetite for knowledge about sexual satisfaction in marital relations. Stone and Levine, according to historian Linda Gordon, stressed the importance of the fact that sexual satisfaction was something to be achieved for both partners through learned responses and practice, rather than by instinct. They also emphasized the significance of the clitoris in women's ability to orgasm, and urged women to practice arousal on themselves even while, as physicians, they perpetuated the era's reigning Freudian insistence that vaginal orgasm was a superior, more "mature" form of sexual climax than that achieved through clitoral stimulation.[27]

Thus in the middle of the twentieth century, middle-class women received conflicting messages about their sexuality and its place in marriage. On one hand, their own sexual gratification in the context of marriage was seen as increasingly important. But on the other hand, a married woman's purpose as a sexual partner was to meet the erotic needs of her husband, even if, in the process, her individual sexual proclivities were subservient. This paradox, in part, constituted what Betty Friedan was to call "the feminine mystique." Similarly, women's emotional needs were both tamped down and hystericized by the ascendance of psychoanalysis as the instrument best suited to gaze into the human psyche. If a woman's personal and professional aspirations were frustrated, in Friedan's critique, she would be counseled by authorities of all manner to seek outlets for her stunted desires and, if necessary, psychotherapy, rather than social or political recourse.[28]

Middle-class men, by contrast, according to May, reported relative contentment with the satisfactions of home life: doting spouses; willing sex partners (or so they perceived); healthy, well-behaved children; stable, decent-paying jobs; and low-cost mortgages on newly constructed suburban homes—all exchanged for what the men described as the relatively trivial price of sacrificing self-indulgence and "hollow" independence. For increasing numbers of men, May concluded, home was a haven from the heartless world, whereas for women, there was no refuge. Home was work, since the workplace was the suburban home filled with growing numbers of children, however well-disciplined, poised, and hardy.[29]

Barbara Ehrenreich tells a complementary if somewhat contradictory tale about American men in this era. Rather than fulfillment, she argues, they experienced vague anxiety about their economic role as breadwinners and the pervasive insistence on conformity in public life, even before many American women grew restive. If "manliness" in the American past was forged in a wilderness of exploration, adventurism, and risk-taking, in the postwar mode masculinity was grounded in more prudent, sedentary, and disciplined undertakings: higher levels of educational attainment, a career as a salaried worker, devotion to one's employer, and all the benefits accruing to the company man—job security, steady pay, predictable promotion, and the capacity to plan for a comfortable retirement.[30] A well-orchestrated presentation of self was the key to being a successful "organization man." Careful grooming and a steady affect conveyed an air of reliability that enhanced credibility in one's professional relations and provided the infrastructure that undergirded private life. It is understandable why, after the tumult of depression and war, predictable employment would be so high on the list of American male aspirations. And yet, inwardly, observed Ehrenreich, men pulled against the shackles of convention in every realm.

The family-building ethos of postwar middle-class America, which framed cultural ideals such as "maturity" and "adulthood" as prerequisite to normative conceptions of individual fulfillment, had serious and negative repercussions for anyone who forsook marriage. Gays and lesbians took the brunt of this, to be sure, but anyone who chose not to marry because of career ambitions or family obligations was scrutinized warily as well. By extension, widows, widowers, and divorcees, once having "attained adulthood" through marriage, lived in the social netherworld of the uncoupled. If maturity could only be achieved and maintained through marriage, it left the unmarried in an ambiguous position at best.[31]

The status of marriage as a normative social institution served as a powerful source of pressure on women and men to form long-lasting partnerships and cast suspicions of abnormality on those who chose not to marry. Single and divorced people were by axiom considered unfulfilled and potentially mentally ill—"sick or immoral, too selfish or too neurotic to marry," according to a study conducted in 1957. As Joseph Veroff and his colleagues put it, this "sanctioning" attitude toward the unmarried (or divorced) held up across gender lines and marital status, since even single and divorced women and men had a negative view of themselves and all other single people.[32]

Historians have persuasively challenged the popular memory of the immediate postwar years as a time of calm and stability in American family life, and recast it as "the way we never were." The twin pillars of the neo-domestic regime, marital longevity and the stay-at-home-mother, were to be the first casualties of the postwar family ideal. By the end of the 1950s the divorce rate, stable from 1946 to 1955, had climbed precipitously. From its wartime trough of about 25.9 percent in 1945, the ratio of first marriages ending in divorce reached 32.2 in 1959, a 24 percent increase that alarmed contemporary observers but also pointed to the emerging acceptability of divorce in American culture. Meanwhile, workforce participation for wives with children under the age of six rose from 11.9 percent in 1950 to 18.7 percent in 1959. Again, this was the sharpened edge of a trend that would transform the shape and content of men's and women's expectations both as marriage partners and as parents. By the peak years of the Baby Boom, already about one in three married women were engaged in the paid workforce; twenty years later, 56 percent of married women held jobs.[33]

CHILDREARING ADVICE DURING THE POSTWAR YEARS

Against this demographic, economic, cultural, and ideological backdrop, there occurred a significant change of emphasis among child welfare professionals. By midcentury, as major childhood diseases came rapidly under control, concern for children's physical health yielded to efforts to understand their psychological health and development.[34] While it is always difficult to know how parents actually practiced prescriptions for contemporary childrearing, there are references to Dr. Benjamin Spock and what might be called the "child-centered" approach he advocated among all of the mothers participating in the Yale Longitudinal Study, even though their socioeconomic, religious, educational, and ethnic backgrounds varied widely. Therefore, it is instructive to be reminded of the origins of the "child-centered" approach.

Before the Baby Boom the federal government was both the primary facilitator and consumer of the most up-to-date ideas on competent childrearing. The U.S. Children's Bureau had dispensed expert advice to parents on children's health and childrearing as early as the 1910s, but in the postwar era, when the average family size expanded dramatically, the audience for childrearing expertise was seemingly boundless. Childrearing experts were only too happy to have their opinions on children's health and behavior disseminated by the U.S. Children's Bureau, and their mutual efforts at parent education reinforced each group's credibility and influence.[35]

By the early 1940s a shift in the tenor and orientation of childrearing literature had occurred according to psychologist Martha Wolfenstein, who analyzed the advice to parents dispensed by the U.S. Children's Bureau's publication *Infant Care* between 1914 and 1951. Whereas the earlier literature was concerned with helping the parent to master what Wolfenstein characterized as the infant child's "centripetal" tendencies—its impulse to get pleasure from its own body (through thumb-sucking and masturbation, for instance)—by the 1942 and 1945 editions, a more "centrifugal" image prevailed: thumb-sucking and masturbation were now regarded as natural, ready resources for the child, and worry about curbing access was dampened by child-training experts who predicted that such formerly "dangerous" impulses would in any event become more diffuse means of gratification if the baby had other objects to play with. An earlier fear that unchecked impulses in the infant would spread beyond control later in life gave way to what she called an emerging "fun morality" in American culture and the idea, eventually, that what the baby wants is probably good for it. While Wolfenstein mildly approved of the change, she also worried about the implications of this idea as the child grew into an adult. Whereas pleasure and fun in American culture were previously regarded as potentially wicked, their rising valuation, she warned, may have created a condition in which "failure to have fun occasions lowered self esteem," leading potentially to feelings of inadequacy, impotency, and being unwanted by others.[36]

Wolfenstein's essay appeared after the release in 1946 of Dr. Benjamin Spock's *Common Sense Book of Baby and Child Care*, and her detection of a sea change in childrearing advice dispensed through the government's *Infant Care* publications applied readily to Spock, whose best seller sold nearly four million copies in its first decade. The tendency of Americans to turn to expert advice on a range of issues had accelerated over the first half of the twentieth century, but this was especially true of advice about childrearing beginning during the 1920s, according to historian Peter N. Stearns. It was an inclination that only intensified in the postwar era, becoming, in Stearns's estimation, almost paralyzing for many middle-class parents by the end of the century. While the soaring birth rate accounts for some of the dramatic rise in sales of Dr. Spock's book, it is also true that there had never before been so many well-educated women entering motherhood for the first time and thus, never so many women capable of, and interested in, utilizing childrearing literature on such a vast scale.[37]

Spock's "common sense" approach, which incorporated the biology of child development pioneered by Arnold Gesell, offered a corrective to the triumph of the behaviorist childrearing methods championed by psychologist John Watson during the 1920s.[38] Spock, like Karl Menninger a decade earlier, and the U.S. Children's Bureau's experts by 1942, stressed the importance of relaxing standards that had been applied all too rigidly by Watson's disciples, in a parenting style that regarded itself as "child-centered." Child-centered parenting transformed the popular prescriptive literature on middle-class parenting from an emphasis on enforcing regimentation and maintaining emotional detachment, to an attitude that both parent and child are creatures of nature endowed with untapped and underappreciated instinctual wisdom. Child-centered training consisted of responding to a child's expressed needs and desires "instead of on a time-table of developmental stimuli." Whereas formerly a disciplined application of "culture" was prescribed to conquer the child's natural impulses, writes culture critic and historian Nicholas Sammond, child-centered parenting considered the relationship between culture and nature as a question of proportion rather than conquest.[39]

The convergence of a mass appetite for childrearing advice and an unparalleled degree of interaction among researchers and practitioner-popularizers sharply delineated the period from any that preceded it. But the extent to which social scientists connected childrearing practices to specific political predispositions, observes Sammond, made the era unique. Spock was pivotal in this respect, he says, because he served as a critical link between popular and professional figures in the field of childrearing and was the common denominator among social and behavioral scientists who sought to disseminate their findings. Spock, Margaret Mead, Erik H. Erikson, Milton Senn (director of the Yale Child Study Center), and to an even greater extent, Ernst Kris—who, as we have noted, was psychoanalyzed by Freud and initiated the Yale Longitudinal Study—were all adherents to differing degrees, but they had been able to popularize their ideas to a far greater extent than Freud had been able to during his lifetime.[40]

After World War II a consensus emerged among many American social and behavioral scientists that the inflexible childrearing practices advocated by behaviorists might have contributed to the widespread receptivity to authoritarian political regimes in Europe during the 1930s and 1940s. In response, Sammond argues, educators and social and behavioral scientists who engaged in the study of children in the United States strived to develop an approach to childrearing that could serve as "a cold-war tool for the promotion of a healthy democratic capitalism, with the power to defuse international hostilities, see past petty nationalisms, and resist psychological persuasion."[41] A number of well-respected authorities such as the anthropologist Margaret Mead, her anthropologist husband Gregory Bateson, Mead's mentor Ruth Benedict, and the child psychologists Erik Erikson, Else Frenkel-Brunswik, and Milton Senn formed associations with Spock that effectively bridged the long-standing divide between professional, research-oriented studies of children and disseminators of academic work who translated the latest literature on childrearing and broadcasted its findings.[42]

Mead's significance, observes Sammond, lay in her cross-cultural comparisons that allowed Americans to distinguish between what was endemic to biological development and what was culturally constructed, particular to their own culture, and thus subject to intervention and revision.[43] Both prominent and intent on extending the findings of her discipline to the American public, Mead effectively legitimized a movement to translate childrearing techniques into the "creation of an informed democratic society."[44] Erikson joined Mead and Spock in their efforts to champion the latest research on childrearing. A student and analysand of Anna Freud, Erikson was a key figure in assimilating Freudian psychology into the ascending vision of children's social and cultural development in the United States. His "socio-psychoanalytic theory of development," according to William Kessen, unveiled at the Mid-Century Whitehouse Conference in 1950, "epitomized the influential effect of the Conference on the future of American childhood."[45]

Frenkel-Brunswik, most famous for her contribution to Theodor Adorno's landmark study *The Authoritarian Personality*, was, like Erikson, trained as a psychoanalyst. She worked in child psychology, helped to establish personality psychology, and attempted to synthesize the findings of academic psychology, anthropology, sociology, and political science. As was characteristic of the Viennese prewar psychoanalytic community, Frenkel-Brunswik "moved easily" among psychology, politics, and ideology.[46] According to Sammond her work, in particular, represented a middle way between total permissiveness and an insistence on parental authority advocated by behaviorism, yet proponents of "permissive parenting," who were easily caricatured, never enjoyed a robust following.[47] A decade later, ironically, in the midst of one of the century's most ideologically contentious periods, Diana Baumrind took the politics out of childrearing once again while offering a synthesis of the permissive and authoritarian approaches, which she labeled "authoritative" parenting. Baumrind served up her synthesis as a happy medium between the rigid "ethnocentrism" promoted by behaviorism and the extreme permissiveness of A. S. Neill, who professed that no adult had the right to impose authority on any child.[48]

Despite the best-seller status of *Baby and Child Care*, its impact across socioeconomic, religious, racial, and ethnic lines remains more difficult to assess. Buying a "pocket size" softcover for fifty cents and applying the principles of "child-centered" discipline are distinct actions. Charles Strickland and Andrew Ambrose's review of the sociological and psychological literatures of the period shows that middle-class mothers before 1945 tended to be more demanding and severe than working-class mothers but that after the war their respective attitudes had reversed.[49] Even in the rapidly growing suburbs, where working-class and middle-class families often intermingled, these patterns seem to have prevailed. More abundance, one historian has speculated, made full-time child care by mothers possible on a wide scale, created greater "privacy, and more permissiveness in the treatment of children . . . [as] washing machines and diaper services . . . facilitated later and more relaxed toilet training." Central heating made more and restrictive clothing less necessary and so increased children's physical freedom. "In short prosperity made it possible for parents to put into practice the childrearing that Dr. Spock was preaching."[50] Still, whether they did so is an open question. Working-class African American mothers proclaimed a high regard for Spock and other authorities on childrearing, but by the early 1960s "far fewer . . . had had any direct exposure to baby-raising manuals" than did white middle-class mothers.[51] In studies conducted between World War II and the early 1960s, African American parents were found to be more "permissive than whites in the feeding and weaning of their children, but were more rigorous . . . in toilet training." They were more likely to employ corporal punishment to exact obedience from their children and were "more concerned than white, middle-class parents with nudity and preventing masturbation."[52]

Political conservatives by the late-1960s were to blame permissive childrearing for everything from the anti-patriotism they perceived in student radicalism and resistance to the military draft during the Vietnam War, to the rise in juvenile crime rates, to premarital sex, to the spreading experimentation with illicit drugs among adolescents and youths.[53] While most studies fix the turn toward more democratic childrearing at or just after World War II, a few remain skeptical and discern a shift somewhat earlier.[54] From our vantage point early in the twenty-first century, it is hard to deny Spock's influence on middle-class childrearing. Nonetheless, in retrospect, it appears to have affected the landscape of American parenting much like the vaunted prosperity of the postwar years that underwrote the prodigious birth rate and the market for childrearing expertise. That is, its impact, like the economic boom, fell unevenly on parent-consumers. Where the psychological ground had been prepared and was accepting it took hold and flourished; where it had not, which varied by race, ethnicity, religion, and socioeconomic status, an older folk style that predated behaviorism prevailed.[55]

The Yale Longitudinal Study captures the years of several children's growth and development from birth to age ten, from 1954 to 1963, at the very apex of the Baby Boom. Our focus for this volume is the twice-weekly therapeutic interactions of a girl whose family's evolution over the course of these years appears, at first glance, not to conform entirely to the mode of the times. Closer inspection, however, uncannily forecasts in microcosm some of the more significant forces of social change in American life during the coming decades. Links between the subjects' life histories to larger social trends include the increased participation of married women with children in the paid workforce, the movement of middle-class families to first- or second-ring suburbs, the emergence of the child-centered family as a cultural ideal, and the increasingly problematic nature of traditional gender roles in American society. Immediately apparent in these trends are the seeds of the postwar women's movement that would erupt by the latter years of the 1960s and pronounce the personal, "political." We can hear echoes of this phrase in the decade-long narratives that shaped one girl's middle childhood. And it is the transcript of her interactions with her therapist that constitute the object of our examination of the intersections between the field of child development and the practice of history. These ethnographic inscriptions permit us to "read over the shoulders" of a family and their clinicians, whose recorded reflections belong to an era steadily receding into the past.

NOTES

1. On global changes in children's experiences during the twentieth century, see Peter N. Stearns, *Childhood in World History* (New York: Routledge, 2006); on the establishment and extension of schooling in the United States during the early twentieth century, see Stephen Lassonde, *Learning to Forget: Schooling and Family Life in New Haven's Working Class, 1870–1940* (New Haven: Yale University Press, 2005); on children's health, see Richard A. Meckel, "Levels and Trends of Death and Disease in Childhood, 1620 to the Present," in Janet Golden, Richard Meckel, and Heather Prescott, eds., *Children and Youth in Sickness and Health: A Historical Handbook and Guide* (Westport, CT: Greenwood Press, 2004), 3–24.

2. I'm not attributing to mass schooling the rise of more leisure time and the enlarged role of children as consumers, but rather underscoring the fact that these three changes each occurred within a few decades. On children

as consumers, see Ellen Seiter, *Sold Separately: Parents and Children in Consumer Culture* (New Brunswick, NJ: Rutgers University Press, 1993); on historical changes in the expansion and use of leisure time in the United States, see Douglas A. Kleiber and Gwynn M. Powell, "Historical Change in Leisure Activities during After School Hours," in Joseph L. Mahoney, Reed W. Larson, and Jacquelynne S. Eccles, eds., *Organized Activities as Contexts of Development: Extracurricular Activities, After-School and Community Programs* (Mahway, NJ: Lawrence Erlbaum Associates, 2004).

3. Just as there is no such thing as a typical family everywhere and throughout time, or a typical woman, in any or all societies historically to speak of "the child" is misleading; see for example, Jane Collier, Michelle Z. Rosaldo, Sylvia Yanagisako, "Is There a Family?: New Anthropological Views," in Barrie Thorne with Marilyn Yalom, eds., *Rethinking the Family: Some Feminist Questions* (Boston: Northeastern University Press, 1992), 31–48. See also Bonnie Thornton Dill's classic essay on the problematic nature of an all-inclusive "sisterhood" in the women's movement during the 1980s: Dill, "Race, Class, and Gender: Prospects for an All-Inclusive Sisterhood," *Feminist Studies* 9 (March 1983): 130–49. The delineation of childhood and the division of development into discrete, sequenced stages of maturation became more highly articulated during the second half of the century in the West but also induced anxiety about individual children's progression through development and worry in instances when the boundaries between childhood, adolescence, and adulthood were blurred; see Stephen Lassonde, "Ten Is the New Fourteen: Age Compression and 'Real' Childhood," in Paula S. Fass and Michael Grossberg, eds., *Reinventing Childhood after World War II* (Philadelphia: University of Pennsylvania Press, 2011), 51–67.

4. Glen H. Elder, Jr., John Modell, and Ross D. Parke, "Studying Children in a Changing World," in Elder, Modell, and Parke, eds., *Children in Time and Place: Developmental and Historical Insights* (Cambridge, Eng.: Cambridge University Press, 1993), 3–21. While this collection of essays appeared in 1993, the impulse to unite the energies and insights of developmentalists and historians had emerged by the early 1980s (vii–ix).

5. See, for example, Leonard Covello, *The Social Background of the Italo-American School Child: A Study of the Southern Italian Family Mores and Their Effect on the School Situation in Italy and America* (Leiden, Neth.: E. J. Brill, 1967), 265–70; Mark Jones, "Narratives of Struggle and Success: Superior Students, Entrance Examinations, and the Taishō Mass Media," paper delivered at the Biennial Meeting of the Society for the History of Children and Youth, Milwaukee, WI, August 4–7, 2005.

6. See the numerous examples cited in Leslie Woodcock Tentler, *Catholics and Contraception: An American History* (Ithaca, NY: Cornell University Press, 2004), chap. 5; Susan Douglas Franzosa, ed., *Ordinary Lessons: Girlhoods of the 1950s* (New York: Peter Lang, 1999); and Susan Greenhalgh, "Fresh Winds in Beijing: Chinese Feminists Speak Out on the One-Child Policy and Women's Lives," *Signs: Journal of Women in Culture and Society* 26, no. 3 (2001): 847–86.

7. The groundbreaking work in the challenge to the developmental paradigm was of course, Esther Thelen and Linda B. Smith, *A Dynamic Systems Approach to the Development of Cognition and Action* (Cambridge, MA: MIT Press, 1994); see also Michael Cole, *Cultural Psychology: A Once and Future Discipline* (Cambridge, MA: Harvard University Press, 1996), 20; R. A. Shweder, "Cultural Psychology—What Is It?," in J. W. Stigler, R. A. Shweder, and G. Herdt, eds., *Cultural Psychology* (Cambridge, Eng.: Cambridge University Press, 1990), 1–43; D. Matsumoto and S. H. Yoo, "Toward a New Generation of Cross-Cultural Research," *Perspectives on Psychological Science* 1 (2006): 234–50; and H. R. Markus and S. Kitayama, "Culture and the Self: Implications for Cognition, Emotion, and Motivation," *Psychological Review* 98 (1991): 224–53. On the historical development of this perspective and its implication for contemporary parenting, see Stephen Lassonde, "Age, Schooling, and Life Stages in the West, 1500–Present," in Paula Fass, ed., *The Routledge History of Childhood in the Western World* (New York: Routledge, 2013), 211–26.

8. In the cultural-historical sciences, Cole points out, answers "depend upon the particular assumptions and point of view afforded by the culture in question, and both the method of arriving at an answer and what constitutes a problem or an answer are locally contingent, not universal. It is often suggested that cultural-historical understanding requires a process of empathic understanding which, while present in all people, is not the product of universally applicable rationale problem solving"; Cole, *Cultural Anthropology*, 20.

9. Ibid., 104.

10. George W. Stocking, *Victorian Anthropology* (New York: Free Press, 1987).

11. The literature in this area of research is extensive, but see Andrew J. Cherlin and Kathleen Kiernan, *Parental Divorce in Childhood and Demographic Outcomes in Young Adulthood* (Baltimore: The Center, 1995), available online at https://jscholarship.library.jhu.edu/bitstream/handle/1774.2/883/WP95-04.pdf (accessed January 5, 2014); Judith Wallerstein and Sandra Blakeslee, *Second Chances: Men, Women, and Children a Decade after Divorce* (New York: Ticknor & Fields, 1989); Nicholas Zill, Donna Ruane Morrison, and Mary Jo

Coiro, "The Long-Term Effects of Parental Divorce on Parent-Child Relationships, Adjustment, and Achievement in Young Adulthood," *Journal of Family Psychology* 7 (June 1993): 91–103; Susan M. Jekielek, "Parental Conflict, Marital Disruption and Children's Emotional Well-Being," *Social Forces* 76 (March 1998): 905–35; and E. Mavis Hetherington and John Kelly, *For Better or for Worse: Divorce Reconsidered* (New York: Norton, 2002).

12. Glen H. Elder, Jr., *Children of the Great Depression: Social Change in Life Experience* (Chicago: University of Chicago Press, 1974); Glen H. Elder, Jr., and Tamara K. Hareven, "Rising above Life's Disadvantage: From the Great Depression to War," in Elder, Modell, and Parke, eds., *Children in Time and Place*, 47–72. Elder has collaborated with many other scholars to study the impact of sociohistorical events on life course choices and other outcomes, but for a sample, see Michael J. Shanahan, Richard A. Miech, and Glen H. Elder, Jr., "Changing Pathways to Attainment in Men's Lives: Historical Patterns of School, Work, and Social Class," *Social Forces* 77, no. 1 (1998): 231–56.

13. "The social phenomenon 'generation' represents nothing more than a particular kind of identity location, embracing related 'age-groups' embedded in a historical-social process," according to Karl Mannheim in his *Essays on the Sociology of Knowledge*, ed. Paul Kecskemeti (New York: Oxford University Press, 1952), 292; and see Alan B. Spitzer's illuminating critique of the concept in his essay "The Historical Problem of Generations," *American Historical Review* 78, no. 5 (1973): 1353–85.

14. There is a wealth of historiography on this topic, but see Lawrence Stone, "History and the Social Sciences in the Twentieth Century," in Stone, *The Past and the Present* (Boston: Routledge & Kegan Paul, 1981), 3–44.

15. Andrew J. Cherlin, *Marriage, Divorce, Remarriage* (Cambridge, MA: Harvard University Press, 1981).

16. As Norman Ryder wrote, "The cohort may be defined as the aggregate of individuals (within some population definition) who experienced the same event within the same time interval. . . . Cohort data are ordinarily assembled sequentially from observations of the time of occurrence of the behavior being studied, and the interval since occurrence of the cohort-defining event. For the birth cohort this interval is age"; Ryder, "The Cohort as a Concept in the Study of Social Change," *American Sociological Review* 30 (1965): 844–45. See also Norman B. Ryder, "The Demography of Youth," in James Coleman, ed., *Youth: Transition to Adulthood* (Chicago: University of Chicago Press, 1974); Matilda White Riley, Marilyn Johnson, and Anne Foner, *Aging and Society*, vol. 3: *A Sociology of Age Stratification* (New York: Russell Sage, 1972); and

Matilda White Riley et al., "Socialization for the Middle and Later Years," in David A. Goslin, ed., *Handbook of Socialization Theory and Research* (Chicago: Rand-McNally, 1969). Social historians in the United States and Western Europe followed the example of demographers and were particularly enamored of the methods and questions posed by French historical demographers during the first half of the twentieth century. The "boom" was foreshadowed by a blip in the birthrate just as the United States entered World War II, but began in earnest in 1946. The year 1964 was the last year before the fertility rate declined once again to the level of the first year of the surge and so is considered the end of the demographic phenomenon. On the divergent economic and social experiences of "boomers," see Richard A. Easterlin, *Birth and Fortune: The Impact of Numbers on Personal Welfare* (Chicago: University of Chicago Press, 1987), appendix, table 3.2. And when political beliefs and social attitudes provoked a clash between parents (who had experienced depression and war and who subsequently married and reproduced at such prodigious rates) and their children, who experienced crowded classrooms, joined the civil rights movement, and were either drafted into, or resisted, the Vietnam War, a "Generation Gap" was born. As Arthur Marwick notes, many of the cultural and political figures who evoke the "Sixties generation" were not part of the Baby Boom at all, having been born as much as a decade earlier, such as the Beat poets or even the Beatles, who were all born before the end of World War II—see Marwick, *The Sixties: Cultural Revolution in Britain, France, Italy, and the United States, 1958–1974* (New York: Oxford University Press, 1998).

17. See Research and Development Council of the National Tour Association, "Current Assessment Report for the Baby Boomer Market," 2002, available at www.agingsociety.org/agingsociety/links/car_boomer.pdf (accessed December 9, 2013).

18. Elder, Modell, and Parke, "Studying Children in a Changing World," 7; and Glen H. Elder, Jr. and Tamara K. Hareven, "Rising Above Life's Disadvantage," in Elder, Modell, and Parke, eds., *Children in Time and Place*, 47–72.

19. Kriste Lindenmeyer, *The Greatest Generation Grows Up: American Childhood in the 1930s* (Chicago: Ivan R. Dee, 2005), chap. 4; Errol Lincoln Uys, *Riding the Rails: Teenagers on the Move during the Great Depression* (New York: Routledge, 2003).

20. William M. Tuttle, Jr., "America's Homefront Children in World War II," in Elder, Modell, and Parke, eds., *Children in Time and Place*, 32–33; Tuttle, *"Daddy's Gone to War": The Second World War in the Lives of America's Children* (New York: Oxford University Press, 1993); Stephanie Coontz, *The*

Way We Never Were: American Families and the Nostalgia Trap (New York: Basic Books, 1992); and see the work of Aimée Dechter and Glen Elder, who show that veterans were not as uniformly successful in their career paths as men who had been retained to work in essential war industries on the homefront. Contrary to the popular perception of war as a boon to individual upward mobility, among middle-class veterans only those who had served as officers had unmitigated success during their postwar working lives. Aimée R. Dechter and Glen H. Elder, Jr., "World War II Mobilization in Men's Work Lives: Continuity or Disruption for the Middle Class?," *American Journal of Sociology* 110, no. 3 (2004): 761–93.

21. Easterlin, *Birth and Fortune*, appendix, table 1.1; John Modell, *Into One's Own: From Adulthood to Youth in the United States, 1920–1975* (Berkeley: University of California Press, 1989), chap. 6; Easterlin, *Birth and Fortune*, chaps. 3–4; Steven Mintz and Susan Kellogg, *Domestic Revolutions: A Social History of American Family Life* (New York: Free Press, 1988), chap. 9; and Elaine Tyler May, *Homeward Bound: American Families in the Cold War Era* (New York: Basic Books, 1988), chap. 6.

22. On "family building," see Modell, *Into One's Own*, 253; for construction of single-family dwellings, see U.S. Bureau of the Census, *Historical Abstracts of the United States: Colonial Times to 1970*, series N 238–245 (Washington, D.C.: U.S. Department of Commerce, 1976), 646; Mintz and Kellogg, *Domestic Revolutions*, 183. Modell adds to this observation the pronounced youthfulness of this expansion, citing the fact that between 1954 and 1956, a full 76 percent of metropolitan housing occupied by families in which the husband was under thirty-five years of age was in the suburbs—Modell, *Into One's Own*, 221. For the observation by Kenneth T. Jackson, see his *Crabgrass Frontier: The Suburbanization of the United States* (New York: Oxford University Press, 1985), chap. 11, esp. 243.

23. Modell, *Into One's Own*, 220–21.

24. May, *Homeward Bound*.

25. John D'Emilio and Estelle B. Freedman, *Intimate Matters: A History of Sexuality in America* (Chicago: University of Chicago Press, 1988), chaps. 11–13; and Linda Gordon, *The Moral Property of Women: A History of Birth Control Politics in America* (Champaign: University of Illinois Press, 2002), chap. 11, esp. 268–74.

26. Alfred C. Kinsey et al., *Sexual Behavior in the Human Male* (Philadelphia: W. B. Saunders, 1948); and Kinsey et al., *Sexual Behavior in the Human Female* (Philadelphia: W. B. Saunders, 1949).

27. Stone and Levine conducted their discussion groups through the counseling services of the Clinical Research Bureau in New York City; Gordon, *Moral Property*, 265 (on the ideological influence of Freudian psychoanalysis on female orgasm during this period, see 270–72).

28. Talcott Parsons and Robert F. Bales, *Family, Socialization and Interaction Process* (New York: Routledge, 1956) best exemplifies the influence of psychoanalysis on other fields of inquiry; and of course Betty Friedan's *The Feminine Mystique* (New York, 1963) first outlines the political implications of turning the blame for women's emotional discontents back on women themselves. See also Gordon, *Moral Property*, 257; May, *Homeward Bound*, chap. 9; and Stephanie Coontz, *Marriage, a History: From Obedience to Intimacy, or How Love Conquered Marriage* (New York: Viking, 2005), 251–52.

29. May, *Homeward Bound*.

30. E. Anthony Rotundo, *American Manhood: Transformations in Masculinity from the Revolution to the Modern Era* (New York: Basic Books, 1993); and Barbara Ehrenreich, *The Hearts of Men: American Dreams and the Flight from Commitment* (New York: Random House, 2011).

31. Modell, *Into One's Own*; Joseph Veroff, Elizabeth Douvan, and Richard A. Kulka, *The Inner American: A Self Portrait from 1957 to 1976* (New York: Basic Books, 1981), 141; Ehrenreich, *Hearts of Men*.

32. Veroff, Douvan, and Kulka, *Inner American*, 147–48.

33. See Coontz, *The Way We Never Were*; May, *Homeward Bound*; and Joanne J. Meyerowitz, ed., *Women and Gender in Postwar America, 1945–1960* (Philadelphia: Temple University Press, 1994). For a summary of this literature, see Stephen Lassonde, "Family and Demography in Postwar America: A Hazard of New Fortunes?" in Jean-Christophe Agnew and Roy Rosenzweig, eds., *A Companion to Post-1945 America* (Malden, MA: Blackwell, 2002), 3–19; and Richard A. Easterlin, *Birth and Fortune*, 85, figure 5.1. See also Modell, *Into One's Own*, 61; and Andrew Cherlin, "Changing Family and Household: Contemporary Lessons from Historical Research," *Annual Review of Sociology* 9 (1983): 60.

34. On long-term trends in children's morbidity, see Meckel, "Levels and Trends," 3–24. See also my essay on the rise and fall of what I have called the "developmental paradigm" in Lassonde, "Age, Schooling, and Life Stages."

35. See Martha Wolfenstein's essay "Fun Morality," in which she examines changes in expert advice to parents published periodically in the U.S. Children's Bureau's organ *Infant Care* between 1914 and 1951, in Margaret Mead and Martha Wolfenstein, eds., *Childhood in Contemporary Cultures* (Chicago:

University of Chicago Press, 1955), 168–78; see also an assessment of the dialogue between experts and parents featured in the popular press: "Bringing Up Baby on Books . . . Revolution and Counterrevolution in Child Care," *Newsweek* 45 (May 16, 1955): 64–66, 68.

36. Wolfenstein, "Fun Morality," 174.

37. On the general and increasing reliance on expert opinion in the United States during the twentieth century, see Loren Baritz, *The Servants of Power: A History of the Use of Social Science in American History* (Middletown, CT: Wesleyan University Press, 1960); on the "immobilizing" effect of childrearing advice, see Stearns, *Childhood in World History*, 108; and Peter N. Stearns, *Anxious Parents: A History of Modern American Childrearing* (New York: NYU Press, 2003); for general treatments of childrearing expertise during the twentieth century in the United States, see Julia Grant, *Raising Baby by the Book* (New Haven: Yale University Press, 1998), chap. 7; and Ann Hulbert, *Raising America: Experts, Parents, and a Century of Advice about Children* (New York: Alfred A. Knopf, 2003). In 1940 the high-school graduation rate passed the 50 percent mark for the first time in U.S. history, and it continued to climb until the 1970s; see *Historical Statistics of the United States, Colonial Times to 1957*, Series H 233 (Washington, DC: U.S. Government Printing Office, 1960), 207.

38. Nicholas Sammond cites as Spock's "most direct antecedent" Emmett L. Holt's *The Care and Feeding of Children* (1894); see Sammond, *Babes in Tomorrowland: Walt Disney and the Making of the American Child, 1930–1960* (Durham, NC: Duke University Press, 2005), 263 (sales figures for *Baby and Child Care* can be found in chap. 5, n. 18). On Spock's precursors, see Thomas Maier, *Dr. Spock: An American Life* (New York: Harcourt Brace, 1998). Michael Zuckerman attributes a self-serving motive to Spock's approach, which he says appeared to bolster parents' trust in their own instincts only to withdraw this support with his inevitable refrain to "call the doctor" in any areas of uncertainty when dealing with children's health and discipline. The result, he concluded, was both a reinforcement of the physician's authority and a further erosion of parents' confidence in relations with their children. See Zuckerman, "Doctor Spock: The Confidence Man," in Charles Rosenberg, ed., *The Family in History* (Philadelphia: University of Pennsylvania Press, 1975), 179–208.

39. Sammond, *Babes in Tomorrowland*, 273.

40. Obviously Freud preceded them in this assertion, and before the ascendance of Adolf Hitler in Europe, an entire generation of "political Freudians" formed a movement that illuminated the cultural, political, and social

implications of psychoanalysis for civilization. Yet McCarthyism and the pall of political repression following the war chastened its European émigrés in the United States, forcing psychoanalysts to conceal their political leanings, thus eviscerating "political Freudianism." Moreover, in the United States the medicalization of psychoanalysis and continued professionalization of American medicine after the war constricted the field of potential practitioners to physicians, which further depoliticized psychoanalysis; see Russell Jacoby, *The Repression of Psychoanalysis: Otto Fenichel and the Political Freudians* (New York: Basic Books, 1983). Theodor W. Adorno's 1950 study *The Authoritarian Personality*, which sought to "detect the personality structure which was susceptible to the ethnocentric personality" by tracing the formation of an authoritarian political predisposition in adults to childrearing practices, was the most relevant work, but its influence waned; see Jans Baars and Peers Scheepers, "Theoretical and Methodological Foundations of the Authoritarian Personality," *Journal of the History of the Behavioral Sciences* 29 (October 1993): 349; see also Martin Roiser and Carla Willig, "The Strange Death of the Authoritarian Personality: 50 Years of Psychological and Political Debate," *History of the Human Sciences* 15 (Winter 2002): 71–96.

41. Sammond, *Babes in Tomorrowland*, 255.

42. "Spock and Mead studied together intermittently at the New York Psychoanalytic Institute in the mid-1930s. Spock and Erikson worked together in Pittsburgh in the 1950s," ibid., chap. 5, n. 23; see also Thomas Maier, *Dr. Spock: An American Life* (New York: Harcourt Brace, 1998).

43. See Margaret Mead and Martha Wolfenstein, eds., *Childhood in Contemporary Cultures* (Chicago: University of Chicago Press, 1955).

44. Sammond, *Babes in Tomorrowland*, 253; "Erikson also corresponded with Spock, who arranged a teaching position for him at the University of Pittsburgh [where they worked together in the 1950s] after Erikson resigned from the University of California for refusing to sign its McCarthyite loyalty oath" (265).

45. *Mid-Century White House Conference on Children and Youth, December 3–7, 1950* (Washington, D.C.: Government Printing Office, 1951); Kessen states that the "full-blown" version of his theory was published as *Childhood and Society* (New York: Norton, 1950); Kessen, "The Baby Book" (unpublished manuscript), chap. 4, n. 11; Sammond, *Babes in Tomorrowland*, 255.

46. Gardner Murphy, "Else Frenkel-Brunswik: Selected Papers," monograph 31 in Nanette Heiman and Joan Grant, eds., *Psychological Issues* 8, no. 3 (1966), 1, 3.

47. See Else Frenkel-Brunswik, "Differential Patterns of Social Outlook in Personality in Family and Children," in Mead and Wolfenstein, *Childhood in Contemporary Cultures*, 387.

48. Diana Baumrind, "Effects of Authoritative Parental Control on Child Behavior," *Child Development* 37 (December 1966): 887–907. "Ethnocentrism" is Frenkel-Brunswik's term for the political effect of "authoritarian" childrearing; see Frenkel-Brunswik, "Differential Patterns." For more, see A. S. Neill, *Summerhill: A Radical Approach to Childrearing* (New York: Hart Publishing, 1960); and Eleanor Maccoby's assessment in her article "The Role of Parents in the Socialization of Children: An Historical Overview," *Developmental Psychology* 28 (1992): 1006–17.

49. Or more likely, working-class parenting remained consistent, while new middle-class patterns were being established. See Melvin L. Kohn, *Class and Conformity: A Study in Values* (Homewood, IL: Dorsey Press, 1969). For the report mentioned, see Charles E. Strickland and Andrew M. Ambrose, "The Baby Boom, Prosperity, and the Changing Worlds of Children, 1945–53," in Joseph M. Hawes and N. Ray Hiner, eds., American Childhood: A Research and Historical Handbook (Westport, CT: Greenwood Press, 1985), 533–585.

50. Strickland and Ambrose, "Baby Boom," 544–45, quoting David Potter, *People of Plenty*.

51. Ibid., 550, n. 91, summarizing Zena Smith Blau. Blau's study of 224 mothers in three Chicago maternity wards revealed that 77 percent of white mothers had read Spock's *Baby and Child Care*, but only 32 percent of African American middle-class mothers had done so; 48 percent of white working-class women claimed to have read Spock, while just 12 percent of African American working-class women had read *Baby and Child Care* (550, citing Blau).

52. Ibid., 550–51, nn. 92 and 93, summarizing studies by Allison Davis and Robert Havighurst, Norma Radin and Constance K. Kamii, and Frank Reissman and Marie F. Peters. Leslie Woodcock Tentler demonstrates the difficulty of inferring widespread beliefs and practices about sexuality and childrearing from attributional characteristics such as religion. She discusses the attractiveness of "child-centered" parenting among middle-class, white, Anglo-Saxon Protestants and among middle-class Catholics as early as the 1930s; see Tentler, *Catholics and Contraception*.

53. See Peter N. Stearns, *American Cool: Constructing a Twentieth-Century Emotional Style* (New York: NYU Press, 1994), 131, 143–44, 170. Ironically, Spock would become one of his own best-known critics; see Benjamin M. Spock, *A Better World for Our Children: Rebuilding American Family Values*

(Washington, D.C.: National Press Books, 1994). For a more neutral assessment of the effects of "permissive" childrearing practices, however, see Robert R. Sears, Eleanor E. Maccoby, and Harry Levin, *Patterns of Child Rearing* (New York: Harper & Row, 1957).

54. Marian J. Radke, T*he Relation of Parental Authority to Children's Behavior and Attitudes* (Minneapolis: University of Minnesota Press, 1946); Duane F. Alwin, "From Obedience to Autonomy: Changes in Traits Desired in Children, 1924–1978," *Public Opinion Quarterly* 52 (1988): 33–52.

55. By "folk" style I mean childrearing methods that existed primarily in the oral tradition of households—practices and beliefs preserved and passed on from generation to generation by female household members. On socioeconomic differences in childrearing attitudes, see Kohn, *Class and Conformity.* On pre-twentieth-century religious influences on childrearing in North America, see Philip J. Greven, *The Protestant Temperament: Patterns of Child-Rearing, Religious Experience, and the Self in Early America* (New York: Knopf, 1977); and Greven, *Spare the Child: The Religious Roots of Punishment and the Impact of Physical Abuse* (New York: Knopf, 1991). Catholicism, which offered a counterpoint to the "permissive" approach, was arguably at its peak influence in the United States demographically, ideologically, and culturally during these years; see Tentler, *Catholics and Contraception,* chap. 5.

2

Thinking about Methods:
Longitudinal Research and the Reorientation
of the Postwar American Mental Sciences

> No observation and no longitudinal study has replaced or . . . will re-
> place the value of the psychoanalytic observation proper for the study
> of child development. [Yet longitudinal research is] the method to show
> how various phases of the past were interrelated; to see the life history as
> a whole, as it is organized by the personality and in turn has organized
> the personality.
>
> —ERNST KRIS, "Notes on the Development and on Some
> Current Problems of Psychoanalytic Child Psychology" (1950)

If many of the contributions to this collection represent attempts to
find meaning about postwar American society in the responses of
Yale University Child Study Center participants, this essay seeks to
do similarly for intellectual culture by looking at the types of questions
investigators asked. Why did researchers, and in the case of what follows,
those interested in the study of children, elect to use certain methods?
What counted as data, and why were these data arranged and discussed
in the ways they were? What was the relationship between researchers'

decisions to use a certain method and the underlying assumptions that organized knowledge across the fields in which they worked? Such questions are broadly interesting, historiographically salient, but above all relevant for those wishing to understand the Yale Longitudinal Study. Like much of the work carried out in the human sciences in these years, investigators involved in the Yale study gave "considerable attention . . . to methodology," even organizing a section of their archive under that heading.[1] Historians such as Jamie Cohen-Cole, Joel Isaac, and Rebecca Lemov have all recently shown that in the years around 1940 this was a fairly common stance among those who worked in the American human sciences, leading to a much greater reflexiveness about and innovation toward methods. As the quotation that introduces this chapter from Ernst Kris shows, such an orientation was equally present within the Yale Longitudinal Study. It proved crucial in shaping the study's early architecture and eventual trajectory, and, ultimately, even had a slight bearing on how the field of child psychiatry emerged and the field of psychoanalysis was reorganized.

Unlike most histories of child psychiatry, which tend to prioritize the institutional hardware that marked the formation of the field, this chapter follows a different set of coordinates. It focuses on the methods that practitioners applied to children in the years around midcentury in an attempt to consider the relationship that existed between this nascent field's epistemic ideals and the technical dimensions of its research program. The chapter therefore attempts to locate the Yale Longitudinal Study in the broader context of changes within the mental science disciplines, while illuminating specific aspects of this study, such as its methodological and epistemological attributes. It argues that child psychiatrists embraced longitudinal research because they regarded it as a means of accurately tracking and representing the psychological phenomena in which they had become interested, including ego formation, development of individuality, and mother-child interactions. Such considerations about how accurately a particular method described social phenomena were, as the historian Joel Isaac has shown, symptomatic of the "tool shock" that the American human sciences experienced more broadly in these decades. The proliferation of new tools, like longitudinal research, helped to provoke questions about investigators' root conceptual commitments, and to stimulate discussion about the relationship between tools and theories. Unlike the disciplines that Isaac and other scholars have examined from this perspective, which took up such questions in the seminar room, graduate training program, and textbook, child psychiatry had little equivalent apparatus, and relied greatly on participation in research projects to stabilize any such theoretical and technical adjustments. The longitudinal study was popular among child psychiatrists because it filled the gap between the prior lack of means of studying children and the later development of subspecialist residency programs.[2]

Children first became a serious subject of inquiry within the mental sciences only in the early years of the postwar period. Before that point, most psychiatrists associated childhood with mental deficiency, rather than mental illness, posing questions about children inspired by the recapitulation perspectives of an earlier generation of natural scientists.[3] The introduction that the pediatrician Edward Parks wrote for the first edition of Leo Kanner's landmark text *Child Psychiatry* (1935) was typical of such attitudes, referring to children as "simple," defined by "brevity of experience, the ignorance of life, the simplicity of thought."[4] Such assumptions pervaded the mental sciences in these years, underpinning practitioners' tendency to characterize the mentally defective as "childlike," as well as the American Psychiatric Association's characterization of "senile psychoses" as "childish emotional reactions."[5] This compact between age, psychological development, and mental disorders lingered through at least the mid-1940s, though such views began to be displaced thereafter, for reasons I will elaborate later. What was overwhelmingly treated with skepticism before the war then—that children had a capacity for intellect, an independence of action and thought—became the constituent parts of childhood at the dawn of the Cold War. References to children's "personalities" swiftly increased in both popular and specialist journals, and as a report by the Group for the Advancement of Psychiatry put it in 1950, "the child began to be thought of as a child and not as a miniature adult."[6]

The reasons for this shift lay in a host of factors but foremost were the rise of ego psychology and neo-Freudian precepts, developments with which Ernst Kris, the study's intellectual progenitor, was closely associated. But these changes also owed much to the growing place of epidemiological techniques in the health sciences, psychiatry's changing focus away from pathology to what Kris's wife, Marianne, called "'varieties of health'" or normality, as well as a series of more nebulous changes, including the drift of American medicine away from the notion of a universal human subject to "niche" categories such as children and adults.[7] All of these factors were at play in the Yale Longitudinal Study.

Although it might have gained a name from a book published in 1935, and had been recognized officially by the International Congress of Mental Health in 1937, it took another decade before the field of child psychiatry fully emerged in the United States.[8] Practitioners and gatekeepers writing in the early years of the postwar period regularly noted the "rather recent and very rapid" emergence of child psychiatry, while admitting the slightly longer development of child development studies, which were "concerned with problems of the mentally defective child."[9] Of course child psychiatry owed more than just its name to what the Johns Hopkins émigré psychiatrist Leo Kanner wrote in *Child Psychiatry*. But from the day of its publication sympathetic and interested commentators adopted that work as their lodestar, reflecting the field's nascent development in the interwar decades.

Anna Freud's work *The Ego and the Mechanisms of Defense* (1937), which was first published in German in 1936 and given to her father on his eightieth birthday, won a similar place among some Continental psychoanalysts with interests in these questions, especially Ernst Kris, the leading force behind the eventual Yale Longitudinal Study. Kris celebrated *The Ego and the Mechanisms of Defense* for introducing "a silent change . . . in the method of observation," and praised the work for encouraging practitioners to interpret material "in light of the patient's whole history."[10] Both of these factors would be constituent parts of the Yale study. They would also find their way more broadly into the American mental sciences through the journal *Psychoanalytic Study of the Child*, which Kris helped to establish in 1945 with Anna Freud and Heinz Hartmann.

While a growing interest in children certainly existed among mental-health officials before midcentury, before that point most who worked within the mental sciences did not take children seriously as subjects in their own right. There were a number of reasons for this outlook, including a pervasive belief that children lacked sufficient intelligence and independence of thought, and that there was an absence of individuality. The prominent New York psychiatrist Pearce Bailey wrote in 1922, for example, that it was "well known" that "distinct types of psychoses are practically unknown in childhood, the period before the intelligence is fully developed." This was hardly a revelatory view, and essentially restated what Adolf Meyer and others had contended in earlier years, it being widely believed that "well-established mental disease, aside from idiocy and imbecility, is not frequent among children." It was not just a lack of intelligence that prevented children from experiencing mental disease, though. In his earlier study on group psychology, *The Crowd: A Study of the Popular Mind* (1895; U.S. edition 1921), the French sociologist Gustave Le Bon described another strand in such conceptions. Drawing a comparison with crowd behavior, children, Le Bon argued, were also characterized by "impulsiveness, irritability, incapacity to reason, the absence of judgment and of the critical spirit." Such conceptions meant that before World War II, American mental health officials intervened in the lives of children only to treat what they thought of as mental deficiency or feeblemindedness.[11]

Only gradually did these precepts loosen their hold on psychiatric knowledge, as the mental sciences were reoriented during the war and early years of the postwar era, not least by the introduction of new modes of explanation and the arrival of hundreds of European émigrés. One index of these shifts is that in the fall of 1948 Leo Kanner finally revised his original 1935 study, rather than just republishing it. The second edition of the work was, in the words of Kanner's colleague at Johns

Hopkins, John Whitehorn, "a wholly revised edition," in fact a "wholly new work." Whitehorn welcomed the changes that Kanner had made to the study, celebrating the author's "more fully matured perspective." But like most reviewers, he did not comment on the work's most striking feature—the author's inclusion of a new chapter on "Personality." References to such a concept had been sparse in the original edition. In fact the index to the 1935 volume contained just one mention of the term, and there was no substantial discussion of it. Yet in the work's second edition, Kanner devoted over twenty pages to the discussion of children's personalities, explaining that in the intervening period "the vista [of psychiatry] has been expanded by interest in the attitudes and resulting behavior of persons as dynamic, clinically observable, and continually active molders of children's personalities."[12]

That the personalities of children began to warrant lengthy psychiatric dissection in the postwar years was indicative of the greater conceptual depth emerging in the study of children. Accepting that children had something as potentially coherent as a personality, and that these personalities could be studied, was a striking change from prior precepts, and one that resonated across a host of fields and disciplines. Such shifts in thinking were equally evident in the pages of *Child Development*, the journal of the Society for Research in Child Development. The number of articles written on children's personalities that appeared in that periodical more than trebled in the postwar decades, rising from just fifteen between 1930 and 1945 to over fifty between 1945 and 1960. The few longitudinal studies around children that spanned the inter- and postwar decades also revealed this change. The Oakland Growth Study that began in the early 1930s at the University of California, Berkeley's Institute of Human Development, performed a follow-up experiment in 1953–54 that focused, for the first time, on participants' personalities and included "personality inventories, and a psychiatric assessment" as a part of the battery of examinations it used.[13]

The Yale Longitudinal Study was a further manifestation of these trends. The study's intellectual bearings, though, were also taken from a series of prior reorientations within psychoanalytic theory and tech-

nique, not least the elevated importance of the ego, the wish to understand the effect of social and cultural factors, and the greater attention
paid to thinking about analytic inquiry. These were the chief concerns of
many émigré analysts and some of their American colleagues, especially
those affiliated with academic institutions, like Kris. It was not long before their work in these years became known by the broad title of ego
psychology. As other contributors to this volume point out, Kris was
one of the leading figures within this movement. Yet unlike a number
of his counterparts, especially Erich Fromm and Theodor Reik, Kris's
efforts to tidy up psychoanalytic theory were advanced with exemplary
caution. Typically he modified Freudian precepts by first presenting his
audience with a relevant passage from Freud's own work that seemed
to authorize the refinements he was proposing, and then framing his
thoughts as a gentle and legitimate "enlarge[ment of] the scope of psychoanalytic therapy." One of Kris's main contributions to the field was
the work he did in expanding analysts' toolboxes, an accolade he shared
with many equivalent figures in sibling disciplines, including the anthropologist Clyde Kluckhorn and the sociologists Robert K. Merton
and Talcott Parsons. Like these other scholars, Kris's interest in introducing new tools, such as "psychoanalytic observation, experimental
procedure, and systematic observation," was coupled to his ideas about
the role that theory played in the discipline. Kris believed that theory
saturated "the everyday tools of all analysts," and, citing the work of the
British physicist J. J. Thomson, suggested that theory was "not a creed
but a tool."[14] It was these tool-like properties of theory that he said allowed investigators to distinguish preconceived notions from hypotheses, to test and validate long-held precepts, and so forth. His conception
of theory as a tool clearly influenced discussions among Yale investigators, as well as within the discipline more generally.

The years around midcentury were therefore marked not only by
a change in the way the mental sciences conceived of childhood, and
the altered values given to interpretive concepts, but also by the introduction of new lines of investigation. The field of child psychiatry was
created as epistemic and methodological attitudes within the mental

sciences were recalibrated around midcentury—when earlier developments crystallized in centers of psychoanalytic importance, like New
York and Chicago, as well as London.

Longitudinal studies were hardly a new development in the postwar period. Physicians' practice of keeping and updating patients' files was one
prior, rather rudimentary example of such methods, as contemporaries
well knew. A bibliography compiled by two medical students in 1959,
and dedicated to Kris and to Milton Senn, a pediatrician and the director of Yale's Child Study Center, argued that the systematic recording
and analyzing of data over time began at least in the late 1920s, with
the various studies that Arnold Gesell conducted on human growth.[15]
Given his influence within the early child-study movement, and especially within New Haven, it would be tempting to follow this geneal-
ogy and claim a role for Gesell in shaping the later Yale study. But to
interpret events in this way is to overlook the local institutional rupture
that occurred within New Haven's psychiatric community in the years
immediately preceding the commencement of this study, as well as to
mistake the very different purposes to which longitudinal methods were
put in the medical sciences in the years following World War II.[16]

One aspect of postwar research into children that distinguished
such programs from their predecessors was their deliberate invoca-
tion of "longitudinal." Before 1945 few psychiatrists' projects used that
term in their title or literature; afterward, it was pervasive. The effect
was contagious, with studies begun in earlier decades that had taken
time as a variable gradually adopting the rubric of "longitudinal." The
acclaimed Fels Study carried out by researchers at Antioch College in
Yellow Springs, Ohio, and begun in the late 1920s, formally located its
research within this bracket in the postwar years. Only in 1958 did the
Fels Study publish a report with the word in its title. It was a symptom
of the moment. Between the early 1950s and mid-1970s, longitudinal
studies proliferated across the human and medical sciences. In North
America, new longitudinal studies were begun to investigate a variety of
conditions, diseases, and statuses, the best known being the Framing-

ham Heart Study (begun in 1947), the Twin Cities Business and Pro-
fessional Men Study (1947), the Stirling County Study in Nova Scotia,
Canada (1948), the Midtown Manhattan Study in New York (1952), the
Duke Longitudinal Studies of Normal Aging (1955), the National Insti-
tute of Mental Health Human Aging Study (1955), and the Baltimore
Longitudinal Study of Aging (1958).[17]

But we should not be misled by the profligacy with which the term
was used in these years. After all, longitudinal studies differed greatly
in size, shape, and sort. The common usage of "longitudinal" in the
title of such studies tends to conceal the variations that existed between
them. One striking point of difference was the scale at which longitudinal studies were organized. Such studies tended either to be very large
or quite small. The Framingham Study into cardiovascular disease that
started in Massachusetts in 1947 is a good example of one of the period's
largest programs, with 5,200 participants.[18] In the mental sciences, Alexander Leighton's Stirling County Study and Thomas Rennie's Midtown
Manhattan Study, which enrolled approximately 1,000 and 1,700 participants respectively, should be cast in a similar light. The longitudinal
child study at Yale should not. As other contributors to this volume
note, the Yale study initially enrolled sixteen families, though this figure
fell to ten, and then to six when some lost interest and when others were
no longer needed. Accordingly it was one of the smaller longitudinal
studies undertaken in these years, similar in this respect to a parallel
study begun at the Child Health Center of the University of Washington in Seattle that enrolled twenty families, but qualitatively different
from Stella Chess's medium-sized New York study, which began in 1956
and enrolled 110 children from "middle-class urban and suburban"
families.[19]

The small number of participants enrolled in studies like those at
Yale and the University of Washington allowed practitioners to obtain
their data with, as Senn later wrote, "intensive and personalized concentration on each family." Where Chess's staff for the larger New York
study examined participants every three months using a predetermined
interview, practitioners at Yale saw their subjects twice a week for a

number of hours at a time. The Yale study thus showed that longitudinal methods were not just used for "quantitative stud[ies], involving large numbers of people," though it was such studies that would later define popular understandings of the term.[20] (Other points in the taxonomical placement of longitudinal research that would later become crucial—between cohort and panel studies, for example—mattered less when the Yale study began, and therefore to the present discussion.)

In other ways too, the manner in which practitioners at Yale and elsewhere approached children departed from how an earlier generation of investigators had done so. Prenatal registration was a major point of distinction between the two. A planning memo from April 1951 confirmed that such goals were present in the Yale study from the beginning. "Gathering of data starts at the earliest possible stage, i.e. the prenatal interview," the memo read. "These data and their connection with the later behavior of the child can be used to increase the predictive powers in future cases," it continued.[21] Such priorities had been absent from earlier investigations. The Oakland Growth Study carried out in Berkeley in the 1930s had drawn most of its samples from the city's fifth- and sixth-grade elementary schools. By contrast, it was de rigueur for postwar researchers in this field to observe their subjects from before birth. This change in practice stemmed largely from what historian Carl Degler has called the "triumph of culture" in the human sciences—a shift that led to the general thought that, as one committee pointed out in 1960, cultural conditioning "commenced in the womb and continues through the intimate relationship of mother and child." The second edition of Kanner's *Child Psychiatry* had conveyed this shift in opinion by lessening the first edition's heavy reliance on physiological explanations. "The advance of psychiatry has brought an increasing appreciation of what happens *to* children in the process of development, over and above that what goes on *within* them instinctively," Kanner wrote in 1948.[22]

On occasions in the early 1950s, those affiliated with the Yale study framed their work in similar terms, that is, as an intervention in debates over the roles that nature and nurture played in shaping human devel-

opment. In late 1952 those who sat on the study's research team characterized their work as being concerned with "the development of personality as an interaction between the child's equipment and the effects of
the environment." The study's psychoanalysts placed these claims into
their own register, describing their research as attempting "to distinguish as early as possible between those sectors of the ego which develop
autonomously and those sectors of the ego which develop as defenses."[23]
When Anna Freud visited New Haven in October 1952, she urged those
involved in the Yale study to think of "ego development [as] both inward and outward."[24] This newfound emphasis on sociocultural factors
was, as Deborah Weinstein has shown, a common feature of much work
in the postwar human sciences, but it was more elevated among American psychoanalysts than their British counterparts.[25]

The decision to begin the Yale study prenatally was also inspired
by researchers' attempts to supplement psychoanalysis's reliance on
the "reconstructive method" with other types of information, including contemporaneous observation and prediction.[26] Such practices were
more broadly evident within the mental sciences in these years. A number of Yale psychiatrists began experimenting with electronic recording
equipment in the mid-1940s, for example. Their efforts won the endorsement of the analyst Lawrence Kubie at an American Orthopsychiatric
Association meeting at which Kris also spoke, in February 1946. It was
at that meeting that Kris proposed other ways of expanding analysts'
toolboxes. These included the idea that the psychoanalytic interview
be supplemented by and compared to "other types of observation and
better checks on the interview procedure."[27] Elizabeth Lunbeck's recent
work on another Austrian analyst, the émigré Heinz Kohut, reminds us
that Kris was not alone in attempting to bring observational techniques
to psychoanalysis at this time. But the point I wish to emphasize here
is the manner in which the Yale study attempted to interweave these
various types of data, imagining longitudinal research as a neat way of
making "observational and reconstructive data . . . comparable." As Kris
told a meeting of analysts in Detroit in 1950, "Only the systematic longitudinal study of life histories, combined with attempts to predict at each

point all that can be predicted about future developments, seem to meet the requirements of the moment."[28]

There were other reasons why child psychiatrists in these years started to embrace prenatal registration and contemporaneous observation. For instance, inaccuracies would develop when patients either deliberately or mistakenly remembered past experiences. Writing in 1959, one analyst criticized the practice of taking information from parents on the basis that "mothers' accounts are neither complete nor entirely reliable."[29] Stella Chess made a similar claim in the *American Journal of Psychiatry* the following year. "The inaccuracies of recall by patients in psychiatric treatment has been repeatedly observed," she complained.[30] But this shift was also given greater force by a prior conceptual shift. "Retrospective data are insufficiently powerful for the delineation of the processes involved in the development of individuality," Chess added in her article. By the late 1970s, some within the mental sciences were describing retrospective methods as "much maligned."[31]

Longitudinal research was also regarded in these years as providing a framework for coordinating different types of data. In the mid-1960s, the prominent American analyst Roy Schafer would conceptualize longitudinal studies as making it possible for researchers "to compare propositions based on different fields of observation," while prompting them to clarify how propositions formulated in the course of such research "are related to specific areas of theory formation."[32] Anna Freud had made a broadly related point during her visit to Yale, commenting, "One must get the interaction of a multiplicity of factors to be able to trace the development of a personality." There was, therefore, a clear symmetry in the value that child psychiatrists attached to composite methods, like longitudinal studies, and the subject of the Yale study, that is the personalities of children, which they also understood to be "interdependent," interacting entities. Both the ego and the longitudinal study drew information from a number of sources and organized it through what were imagined to be analogous processes of integration. Part of this field's attraction to such research methods, then, lay in the way these tools were imagined to mirror the social phenomena they were purportedly representing.[33]

In addition to their use of observation, researchers with the Yale Longitudinal Study also recorded the testimonies of children. This was a remarkable departure from how research on children had previously been conducted. As the historian Alice Boardman Smuts observes, "Before the 1930s reports on patients in children's hospitals contained comments by parents, other relatives, and social workers, but never by the children themselves."[34] Indeed, where the Yale study's use of observation distinguished it from previous psychoanalytic practices, an interest in children's testimonies similarly set it apart within the field of child developmental studies. Children were now speaking subjects within the mental sciences, and the weight of attention of the Yale study in the mid-1950s fell on the discursive interactions between investigators and subjects. The shift was evident in a number of similar studies at this time, notably the University of Washington's investigation of the "mother-child relationship." It received equal encouragement at Yale Medical School, as some of the records published in this volume show, with their attempts to capture the children's voices, and to report conversations between subjects and investigators.[35]

In addition to the hundreds of observational reports that the study's social workers filed, the physical examination forms that pediatricians completed, and the psychoanalytic case notes written about the children's parents, by the mid-1950s Yale researchers were also gathering data from instruments developed in psychology. In fact the proliferation of new tools within the American human sciences in these years was certainly captured in studies like this one, which made extensive use of the Wechsler Adult Intelligence Scale (WAIS), the Thematic Apperception Test (TAT), and the ubiquitous Rorschach Test. That they did so was a further symptom of what Rebecca Lemov has rightly called the human sciences' "overweening love of data." Some of the issues raised by this habit—for both investigators and later archivists—are addressed in Chapter 6.[36]

Although in their most basic form longitudinal studies were concerned with the lives of specific people, part of the method's function was to compare potentially great numbers of individual records, plotting and illustrating broader trends in the process. As one technical guide put it, the method allowed researchers to accumulate reams of data from which general patterns might be discerned, such that "the curves for individuals [could be plotted] on log paper for comparison with a model curve appearing on transparent paper." Two members of the Yale Longitudinal Study, Katherine Wolf and Jennie Mohr, attempted to do likewise using bar charts, and their efforts prompted Kris to note how such a representation "may teach us something on one child, but better, it can enable us to compare this child with another child." In this view, longitudinal surveys mirrored American social scientists' general enthusiasm for what the historian Sarah Igo has termed "aggregating technologies," those mass surveys and polls that pervaded Western science and society around midcentury.[37]

Yet while the use of the longitudinal method fitted neatly with these broader trends, we should not miss the fact that it also potentially stood in opposition to psychiatry's traditional unit of examination, the individual patient. Accordingly critiques accompanied the emergence of all manner of epidemiological methods, and the profession's old guard grumbled that such surveying techniques "violate[d] the concept of the complete individuality of man."[38] It was, in part, for this reason that well into the late 1960s the principal officers of the Yale study would insist that their research be seen "in terms other than quantity, averages or predictive values." "Interviews, conversations, and observation techniques over an extended period do reveal more pertinent information than questionnaires," Senn claimed in the retrospective report he co-wrote in 1968 with Claire Hartford, a staff member at the Child Study Center.[39] Yet this public wish mistook the surreptitious ways in which quantification entered and structured such arenas. Frequently, qualitative research simply became enfolded in the increasingly powerful language of statistics.[40] In the case of Stella Chess's parallel longitudinal study in New York, for example, qualitative observations were made to fit quantitative methods. Upon receiving a case report in which it was said a child had "'cried because he was hungry,'" researchers would process such remarks only "with regard to the fact of crying."[41] Adapting subjective remarks about children's behavior to fit binary categories—in this case, whether the child cried or not—was one of the ways in which the boundaries between previously held discrete types of research dissolved.

Psychoanalysts' views about disease and development fitted more comfortably with longitudinal modes of research. Writing in 1952, one of the country's best-known psychoanalysts, Karl Menninger, declared that mental diseases "always have a developmental history." Indeed neo-Freudians like Kris, as well as psychotherapists more generally, found much that they could appreciate in the longitudinal method's historicization of individual lives. When Kris wrote in the pages of the *Psychoanalytic Study of the Child* that longitudinal "studies would supply data to some extent similar to those to which we are used [to] in psychoanalysis," this is what he meant.[42] Longitudinal research could therefore be made to align with some existing psychoanalytic techniques, as well as be made to answer a number of the other administrative, epistemological, and experimental ideals that those interested in the study of children aspired to meet in these years; it is to these latter considerations that we shall now turn.

Explanations for why the longitudinal method suited the needs of the fledgling discipline of child psychiatry frequently rested on shifting modes and valuations of scientific practice. Scholars outside the mental sciences shared such opinions. Nathan Goldfarb, a professor of business and marketing at Hofstra University, praised the method because "in terms of statistical reliability, the longitudinal design is preferable to the use of independent samples." Similarly, researchers in other countries celebrated longitudinal research not just for what such programs could reveal, but for how they might reveal it. A British child psychiatrist writing shortly after World War II was drawn to the longitudinal study's potential to "produc[e] a more objective attitude in the study of behaviour, particularly in the earliest years of life." These were all qualities coveted by the postwar human sciences, and their presence in such research programs allowed practitioners to parry charges about the field's supposed lack of rigor. Child psychiatrists took up longitudinal studies then as much for what they could reveal about children, as for the garb of scientific credibility that they could drape around their field.[43]

The first thing that emerges from reading the work of those affiliated with the Yale study is the way they thought of themselves as pioneers. Some adopted this term explicitly, excitedly discussing their involvement in a "pioneer study," and later referring to the research program as a "giant step" for psychoanalysis.[44] The Yale study, which was part of the first wave of sustained research within the American mental sciences, did in fact mark a new era in psychoanalytic, indeed psychiatric, science. Kris's study began at a moment when, as one contemporary report noted, "psychiatry [did] not have a strong research tradition oriented to systematic, empirical investigation of important problems," though the creation of the National Institute of Mental Health in 1949, and formation of the *Journal of Psychiatric Research* some years later, gradually adjusted those conditions.[45] To encourage the introduction of research within the mental sciences, many professional bodies held conferences and roundtables throughout the 1940s at which research principles were debated. The historian Harry Marks has demonstrated that these trends were broadly evident in American medicine at this time, and has explained how medical experimentation became synonymous with certain scientific ideals, including the randomization of variables, detachment between subject and investigator, and separation of research and therapy.[46]

While these ideals found their way into the discipline of psychiatry too, some scholars, like Kris, opposed such notions, arguing that they were inappropriate for the mental sciences. He told his colleagues that they should design studies that would allow for "constant interrelation between theory and clinical observation." The Yale Longitudinal Study was in fact designed to make this point. Described by Kris as an instance of "action-research," or an investigation "in which the observer takes part," it was imagined to have almost as many therapeutic functions as experimental ones. Such studies were by no means uncommon in academic psychiatry in the 1950s, or indeed the 1960s, though they diminished thereafter. In contrast to many medical studies, these projects refused to arrange staff and subjects so that they remained distant from one another, and instead emphasized the need for researchers to develop relationships with their subjects. Staff at Yale "learned to investigate as part of the therapeutic procedure," Kris said, and were "trained to take our own actions into account."[47]

During the study's planning and active phases, these casual interactions between staff and patients were presented as a necessary facet of such investigations. Yet when Senn, the study's main public chronicler after Kris's death, described the relationships between researchers and subjects in the late 1960s, he placed the emphasis differently. Although he admitted such close relationships were inescapable ("it could not be avoided"), he nevertheless felt obliged to reassure his colleagues that "their influence was recognized and reckoned with." This shift in how Kris perceived and Senn presented researcher-subject relationships was not just due to personal differences between the two men. But it did reveal a change in how objectivity was conceived: now it was organized around detachment and the supposed impersonality of methods, rather than involvement and intuition.[48]

A number of essays in this volume note that those involved in the Yale Child Study were drawn from a variety of disciplinary backgrounds. Their common participation in the study was symptomatic of the period's general enthusiasm for interdisciplinary and collaborative modes of research, and a swarm of factors, general and specific, helped to create such conditions. It helped that many of those interested in child psychiatry understood the need for their field to remain "plastic and adaptable," as Karl Bowman, president of the American Psychiatric Association told his colleagues in 1944—"ready to try out new methods that offered some chance of adding to our knowledge."[49] Twenty years later, the analyst Roy Schafer would still be adamant that "the study of certain structural and maturational aspects of the early ego requires assistance from other disciplines and other methods."[50] Such support for interdisciplinarity had long been evident at Yale, and Chapter 3 of this volume elaborates on the issue. A study that involved pediatricians, psychologists, psychoanalysts, social workers, and eventually nursery school teachers therefore had some precedent at Yale.[51] As with the Institute of Human Relations, though, the Yale Longitudinal Study was also encouraged along these lines by those bodies that financially supported its work. When the Foundations' Fund for Research in Psychiatry and the Commonwealth Fund gave almost $90,000 in grants to those working on the study, they singled out such interdisciplinarity as noteworthy.[52]

Kris was particularly enthusiastic about what he termed "intra-scientific communication," having long called for "an intense study of the child by a team of participant observers of many skills." His understanding of interdisciplinarity crucially paralleled his more general ideas about how "to integrate observational data into the general flow of psychoanalytic thought." Kris had long recognized that it was not enough to bring together a diverse group of investigators, and that any such expansion "must necessarily be based on a more systematic foundation."[53] Operationalizing such ideals proved less than straightforward, though. During the study's first eighteen months, some investigators were left feeling that their work resembled "a number of isolated sub-studies," and called on Kris and Senn to reorganize the project so they could "work in a united fashion toward a common end." The doodle that one member of the Yale team drew during this period captures both their understanding of the study's future focus—that is, the development of subjects' personalities—as well as his own frustrations with the study's lack of coordination. The introduction of weekly research meetings, frequent staff consultations in which a "systematic pooling of . . . data" took place, and an "organized method of working together" helped to alleviate these tensions by building interdisciplinarity into the structure of the study.[54]

Like many in the human sciences in these years, Yale investigators also took an approach to their research that valorized methods and theories over the rote pursuit of empiricism. This was quite different from those earlier programs of research on children, like the Berkeley Growth Study that Nancy Bailey had headed in the late 1920s, where facts were generally preferred to theories.[55] "The first goal of the pres-

Figure 1: Doodle by a member of the investigative team

ent collaboration should be to *work out methods* and *not* to consider getting at any *results*," Katherine Wolf wrote in 1951. One virtue of such research, she added, was that "there is no . . . pressure of time [because] the study is one that will run over a *long period of time*."[56] The opinion revealed a confidence that such programs would not be hurried along by funding concerns: as Rebecca Lemov has argued, "new funding, new prestige, and new research alliances [in the mental sciences had] pushed open a window once closed."[57] Indeed the Yale study would receive generous grants from a number of sources, most notably the Commonwealth Fund and the Foundations' Fund for Research in Psychiatry.[58] Still, Wolf's comment was mainly epistemological, and foreshadowed Kris's own view that the study's chief purpose was to "pose problems and develop hypotheses."[59]

The comments of Wolf and Kris thus bear some similarity to what Joel Isaac has described as the postwar human sciences' preoccupation with "epistemic design," that is, with devising theoretical frameworks and, secondarily, arranging empirical data to fit those schemes.[60] Although Kris resisted the view that "psychoanalytic theory represent[ed] a structure of thought superimposed upon 'the empirical material' that would have precedence," he still regarded the study as a means of "organiz[ing] hypotheses according to their actual importance," and championed longitudinal frameworks because they allowed for the "structural interconnection of hypotheses."[61] To achieve these ends thought was given to the writing, organization, and cataloguing of meeting minutes and other records. At a general meeting in early 1951, staff decided that they should record all future minutes "in a way that Case Discussions can easily be separated from General (Method, techniques, etc.) and [an] outline of categories for indexing."[62] It was one mundane, but nevertheless revealing, way in which information produced by the study was subtly arranged so that different species of data could be easily distinguished.

Those who were asked publicly to comment on the Yale study were similarly drawn to reflect on the way that longitudinal studies served as "a tool for organizing a mass of information which otherwise remains unmanageable."[63] Across the human and mental sciences, longitudinal studies were therefore imagined as one way of achieving this desired coordination of theory and data, permitting some investigators to pose "unanticipated questions," and others to find "answers . . . quickly in data collected many years before."[64] Lester Sontag, a physician involved in the Fels Study, commented in the late 1950s that "longitudinal research . . . sometimes must begin with broad goals in mind, collecting data which may be analyzed when specific problems are formulated at a later date."[65] For those in the nascent field of child psychiatry, these were valuable considerations, and researchers' embrace of this view aligned them with the human sciences' broader proclivity for a heightened self-awareness about the mechanics of knowledge production.

Writing about the projective testing movement, the historian Rebecca Lemov has noticed how researchers in this period possessed a

clear "self-consciousness about method," a stance she found so pronounced "as to be nearly meta-methodological."[66] Staff involved in the
Yale Longitudinal Study also revealed such attitudes toward their work.
For instance, they took an interest not just in the data they were able to
harvest from the study, but also in the opportunity it presented them to
experiment with their methods. A psychiatric social worker involved in
the early phases of the Yale study said that the "longitudinal study was
of considerable value . . . since she gained increasing skill" in interviewing families. At research meetings in the early 1950s, Kris had expressed
such views to others working on the project, describing how longitudinal studies allowed investigators "to *develop and to improve [their]*
methods," and particularly to determine in "the long run . . . which type
of observation yields the best material." Senn similarly called the study a
"unique learning experience" for practitioners.[67] Evidently, programs of
research like that undertaken at Yale encouraged investigators to think
about methods in two ways: as a means of considering the effectiveness of certain techniques in tackling certain problems, and as a way
of gauging their own skill in using those methods. Such an orientation
was a crucial feature of research in the human sciences during these
decades.

To locate the origins of child psychiatry in the early years of the postwar period, rather than in any previous era, is not simply about getting
one's dates right. Rather, it is to associate the foundations of the field
with a general reorientation in psychiatric concepts and the outlook of
mental health professionals. Child psychiatry in the postwar decades
was not defined simply by the greater attention practitioners paid to
children; it was also characterized by the view that childhood marked
a stage in a person's life with a mental currency of its own. In their
determination to uncouple the study of children from the axioms attached to adults, psychiatrists worked hard to fashion a field with distinct intellectual precepts. Accepting that children had the capacities
to be individuals—a view often expressed via references to their ability
to develop personalities—was a crucial moment, and one that rippled

beyond just the psychiatric profession, as the pages of the journal *Child Development* testify.

Between roughly 1950 and the mid-1970s the method of choice for many child psychiatrists was the longitudinal study, a technique that was by no means exclusive to that particular arena. To some degree, the method's popularity reflected a research community awash with federal and philanthropic largesse.[68] But the longitudinal study also reflected contemporaries' interest in epidemiological techniques, preventative forms of intervention, and new ideas about disease etiology. Finally, with their statistical models, and mechanisms for tracking temporal change, longitudinal methods squared neatly with psychiatrists' wish to be taken seriously as scientists of the psyche. As I have tried to emphasize, the longitudinal method became pervasive among those who called themselves child psychiatrists because of the particular priorities of the mental sciences at this moment. The greater reflexiveness that these scholars showed toward their research was, it has been argued, a widespread feature of research in the American human sciences during the postwar decades. Such reflexiveness even extended to the purpose to which some imagined the material they had assembled would be put, with Senn wondering out loud if they might entice "future historians interested in knowing how a few Americans lived through a critical period in their lives."[69] This volume indicates that Senn's prediction would eventually be proved correct.

NOTES

1. Audrey T. McCollum, "A Clinical Caseworker in Interdisciplinary Research," *Social Work* 1 (January 1956): 88–102, quotation at 89. On the organization of the study's archive, see folder 163: "Methodology, 1958," box 16, series 1, Yale Child Study Center, School of Medicine, Yale University, Longitudinal Study, MS 1967, Yale Archives and Manuscripts, Sterling Memorial Library, New Haven, Connecticut (hereafter cited as LngYC/YAMS).

2. Joel Isaac, "Tool Shock: Technique and Epistemology in the Postwar Social Sciences," in *The Unsocial Social Science? Economics and Neighboring*

Disciplines since 1945, eds. Roger Backhouse and Philippe Fontaine (Durham, NC: Duke University Press, 2010), 133–64.

3. See David Hoogland Noon, "The Evolution of Beasts and Babies: Recapitulation, Instinct, and the Early Discourse on Child Development," *Journal of the History of the Behavioral Sciences* 41 (Fall 2005): 367–86.

4. Edward Parks, "Preface," in Leo Kanner, *Child Psychiatry* (1935; Springfield, IL: Charles C. Thomas, 1937), viii.

5. Clemens E. Benda, Malcolm J. Farrell, and Catherine Chipman, "The Inadequacy of Present-Day Concepts of Mental Deficiency and Mental Illness in Child Psychiatry," *American Journal of Psychiatry* 107 (April 1951): 722. See also "001–79x. Senile Psychoses," in Committee on Statistics of the American Psychiatric Association, *Statistical Manual for the Use of Hospitals for Mental Diseases* (Utica, NY: Utica State Hospitals Press, 1934), 32.

6. Committee on Child Psychiatry of the Group for the Advancement of Psychiatry, *Basic Concepts in Child Psychiatry*, report 12 (Topeka, KS: Group for the Advancement of Psychiatry, 1950).

7. On the unduly neglected place of longitudinal research in these years, see Tiago Moreira and Paolo Palladino, "'Population Laboratories' or 'Laboratory Populations'? Making Sense of the Baltimore Longitudinal Study of Aging, 1965–1987," *Studies in History and Philosophy of Biological and Biomedical Sciences* 42 (2011): 317–27; Marianne Kris, "The Use of Prediction in a Longitudinal Study," *Psychoanalytic Study of the Child* 12 (1957): 175–89, quotation at 176. Psychiatry's growing interest in the normal is charted in Elizabeth Lunbeck, *The Psychiatric Persuasion: Knowledge, Gender and Power* (Princeton, NJ: Princeton University Press, 1994); the shift from a universal human subject to "niche" groups is explained in Steven Epstein, *Inclusion: the Politics of Difference in Medical Research* (Chicago: University of Chicago Press, 2007).

8. On the existence of prior groups of mental health professionals interested in children, see Alice Boardman Smuts, with the assistance of Robert Smuts, R. Malcolm Smuts, Barbara Smuts, and P. Lindsay Chase-Lansdale, *Science in the Service of Children, 1893–1935* (New Haven: Yale University Press, 2006).

9. Beatrix Hamburg, "Current Literature on Child Psychiatry," *Psychiatry* 16 (November 1953): 404–13, quotation at 404.

10. Ernst Kris, "Review of *The Ego and the Mechanisms of Defense*, by Anna Freud" (1938), in Lottie Newman, ed., *Selected Papers of Ernst Kris* (New Haven, CT: Yale University Press, 1975), 343–56, quotation at 351. Useful accounts of Kris's life and influence can be found in Samuel Ritvo and Lucille B. Ritvo,

"Ernst Kris, 1900–1957: Twentieth-Century Uomo Universale," in Franz Alexander, Samuel Eisenstein, and Martin Grotjahn, eds., *Psychoanalytic Pioneers* (New Brunswick, NJ: Transaction Publishers, 1966), 484–500; Bernard Fine, "Ernst Kris, Teacher—'How Much There Is to Learn,'" in Edward Joseph, ed., *Beating Fantasies: Regressive Ego Phenomena in Psychoanalysis* (New York: International Universities Press, 1965), 3–10.

11. Pearce Bailey, "A Contribution to the Mental Pathology of Races in the United States," *Mental Hygiene* 6 (April 1922): 379–80; Adolf Meyer, "Schedule for the Study of Mental Abnormalities in Children" (1895), reprinted in Alfred Lief, ed., *The Commonsense Psychiatry of Dr. Adolf Meyer: Fifty-Two Selected Papers, edited with Biographical Narrative* (New York: McGraw-Hill, 1948), 71; Gustave Le Bon, *The Crowd: A Study of the Popular Mind* (1895; New York: Penguin Books, 1981), 35–36.

12. John Whitehorn, "Preface," in Leo Kanner, *Child Psychiatry*, 2d ed. (1935; Springfield, IL: Charles C. Thomas, 1948), vii; Kanner, *Child Psychiatry*, 110.

13. Glen H. Elder, Jr., *Children of the Great Depression: Social Change in Life Experience* (New York: Westview Press, 1999), 17.

14. On ego psychology in general, see Nathan G. Hale Jr., *The Rise and Crisis of Psychoanalysis in the United States: Freud and the Americans, 1917–1985* (New York: Oxford University Press, 1995), 232–37; Edward Gitre, "Importing Freud: First-Wave Psychoanalysis, Interwar Social Sciences, and the Interdisciplinary Foundations of an American Social Theory," *Journal of the History of the Behavioral Sciences* 46 (Summer 2010): 239–62; Ernst Kris, "Notes on the Development and on Some Current Problems of Psychoanalytic Child Psychology" (1950) in Newman, *Selected Papers of Ernst Kris*, 54–79, quotation at 55. An example of Hartmann doing similarly can be found in "Comments on the Psychoanalytic Theory of the Ego," in Heinz Hartmann, ed., *Essays on Ego Psychology: Selected Problems in Psychoanalytic Theory* (London: Hogarth Press and the Institute of Psycho-analysis, 1964), 113–41. On the role these other figures played in introducing new "tools" to their respective disciplines, see Willow Roberts Powers, "The Harvard Study of Values: Mirror for Postwar Anthropology," *Journal of the History of the Behavioral Sciences* 36 (Winter 2000): 15–29; Rebecca Lemov, "X-Rays of Inner Worlds: The Mid-Twentieth-Century American Projective Test Movement," *Journal of the History of the Behavioral Sciences* 47 (Summer 2011): 251–78; and Isaac, "Tool Shock." See also Ernst Kris, "The Nature of Psychoanalytic Propositions and Their Validation" (1947) in Newman, *Selected Papers of Ernst Kris*, 3–23, quotation at 22. The J. J.

Thomson quotation is from Heinz Hartmann, Ernst Kris, and Rudolph Loewenstein, "The Function of Theory in Psychoanalysis," in Rudolph Loewenstein, ed., *Drives, Affects, Behavior* (New York: International Universities Press, 1953), 13–37, quotation at 14.

15. See Alan Stone and Gloria Cochrane, *Longitudinal Studies of Child Psychiatry: Abstracts with Index* (Cambridge, MA: Commonwealth Fund, 1959). The volume's foreword was written by Milton J. E. Senn. Other contemporary reviews of longitudinal methods within child studies can be found in Jerome Kagan, "American Longitudinal Research on Psychological Development," *Child Development* 35 (March 1964): 1–32. Studies that presented themselves as "longitudinal" in the interwar decades tended to concentrate on children's physical growth; see William W. Greulich et al., *A Handbook of Methods for the Study of Adolescent Children*, serial no. 15 (Washington, DC: Society for Research in Child Development, 1938). John Wolfe's chapter in that collection, entitled "Some Psychological Aspects [of Growth]," made no mention of personality.

16. Kris distinguished between Gesell's focus on human "maturation" and his own interest in "personality development"; see Kris, "On Psychoanalysis and Education" (1948) in Newman, *Selected Papers of Ernst Kris*, 36–53, quotation at 51.

17. Lester Sontag, Charles Baker, and Virginia Nelson, *Mental Growth and Personality Development: A Longitudinal Study* (Washington, DC: Society for Research in Child Development, 1958). In general see Moreira and Palladino, "'Population Laboratories' or 'Laboratory Populations.'"

18. The Framingham Study is described in Thomas Dawber, William B. Kannell, and Lorna P. Lyell, "An Approach to Longitudinal Studies in a Community: The Framingham Study," *Annals of the New York Academy of the Sciences* 107 (1963): 540–41. For a general assessment of the emergence of epidemiological methods see Harry Marks, *The Progress of Experiment: Science and Therapeutic Reform in the United States, 1900–1990* (Cambridge, Eng.: Cambridge University Press, 1997).

19. The social profiles of the families enrolled in the Yale study are described in Milton J. E. Senn and Claire Hartford, *The Firstborn: Experiences of Eight American Families* (Cambridge, MA: Harvard University Press, 1968). Stella Chess et al., "Implications of a Longitudinal Study of Child Development for Child Psychiatry, *American Journal of Psychiatry* 117 (November 1960): 434–41, quotation at 436. See Nikolas Rose, *Governing the Soul: The Shaping of the Private Self*, 2d ed. (1989; London: Free Association Books, 1999), 186–90.

20. Senn and Hartford, *Firstborn*, both quotations at 16.

21. Research Meeting: "The Aim of the Study and Its Methods," April 10, 1951, folder 2, box 23, series 2, LngYC/YAMS.

22. See Elder, *Children of the Great Depression*, 5; Smuts, *Science in the Service of Children*, 323. The Fels Study showed an interest in registering subjects prenatally, but it seems that in practice researchers did not end up registering anyone before the age of six. See Sontag, Baker, and Nelson, *Mental Growth and Personality Development*, compare 13 and 91; Carl N. Degler, *In Search of Human Nature: The Decline and Revival of Darwinism in American Social Thought* (New York: Oxford University Press, 1991); Richard J. Plunkett and John E. Gordon, *Epidemiology and Mental Illness: A Report to the Staff Director, Jack R. Ewalt* (New York: Basic Books, 1960), 30–31; and Kanner, *Child Psychiatry*, 109 (emphasis in original).

23. Collaboration Meeting, November 29, 1952; Memorandum, May 29, 1953, both in folder 9, box 23, series 2, LngYC/YAMS.

24. Anna Freud in "General Research Meeting," October 13, 1952, folder 4, box 23, series 2, LngYC/YAMS.

25. Deborah Weinstein, "Culture at Work: Family Therapy and the Culture Concept in Post–World War II America," *Journal of the History of the Behavioral Sciences* 40 (Winter 2004): 23–46. See especially Heinz Hartmann, Ernst Kris, and Rudolph Loewenstein, "Some Psychoanalytic Comments on 'Culture and Personality,'" in George Wilbur and Warner Muensterberger, eds., *Psychoanalysis and Culture: Essays in Honor of Géza Róheim* (New York: International Universities Press, 1951), 3–31.

26. Ernst Kris, "Opening Remarks on Psychoanalytic Child Psychology," *Psychoanalytic Study of the Child* 6 (1951): 9–17, quotation at 17. On the formalization of observation in American psychoanalysis see Elizabeth Lunbeck, "Empathy as a Psychoanalytic Mode of Observation: Between Sentiment and Science," in Lorraine Daston and Elizabeth Lunbeck, eds., *Histories of Scientific Observation* (Chicago: University of Chicago Press, 2011), 255–75, esp. 266–70.

27. Ernst Kris, "Problems in Clinical Research" (1947) in *Selected Papers of Ernst Kris*, 24–30, quotation at 30.

28. Kris, "Notes on the Development and on Some Current Problems," 55.

29. Richard Meili, "A Longitudinal Study of Personality Development," in Lucie Jessner and Eleanor Pavenstedt, eds., *Dynamic Psychopathology in Childhood* (New York: Grune & Stratton, 1959), 109.

30. Stella Chess et al., "Implications of a Longitudinal Study of Child Development for Child Psychiatry," *American Journal of Psychiatry* 117 (November 1960): 434–41, quotation at 434.

31. Ibid., 434; John S. Strauss and Haroutun M. Babigian, *The Origins and Course of Psychopathology: Methods of Longitudinal Research* (New York: Plenum Press, 1977), 216.

32. Roy Schafer, "Contributions of Longitudinal Studies to Psychoanalytic Theory," *Journal of American Psychoanalytic Association* 13 (1965): 605–18, quotation at 605.

33. Anna Freud in "General Research Meeting," October 13, 1952, folder 4, box 23, series 2, LngYC/YAMS.

34. Smuts, *Science in the Service of Children*, 225.

35. See Ann Stewart, "Excessive Crying in Infants—A Family Disease," in Milton J. E. Senn, *Problems of Infancy and Childhood: Transactions of the Sixth Conference, March 17 and 18, 1952, New York* (New York: Josiah Macy Foundation, 1953), 138–59. Historian Elizabeth Lunbeck and therapist Bennett Simon provide a sterling example of how such case material might be read as historical records; see Lunbeck and Simon, *Family Romance, Family Secrets: Case Notes from an American Psychoanalysis, 1912* (New Haven, CT: Yale University Press, 2003).

36. On the use of these other instruments see Ethelyn Klatskin, "Psychological Examination," February 25, 1959, volume 1, box 8, series 1, LngYC/YAMS; Lemov, "X-Rays of Inner Worlds," 276. The pervasiveness of the Rorschach test is discussed in Peter Galison, "Image of Self," in Lorraine Daston, ed., *Things That Talk: Object Lessons from Art and Science* (New York: Zone Books, 2004), 257–96.

37. Nathan Goldfarb, *An Introduction to Longitudinal Statistical Analysis: The Method of Repeated Observations from a Fixed Sample* (Glencoe, IL: Free Press of Glencoe, 1960), 171. Wolf and Mohr were the leading proponents of organizing the study's data using "quantitative summaries"; see Research Meeting, December 4, 1951, folder 2, box 23, series 2, LngYC/YAMS; Sarah E. Igo, *The Averaged American: Surveys, Citizens, and the Making of a Mass Public* (Cambridge, MA: Harvard University Press, 2007).

38. A survey of this opposition is found in Paul V. Lemkau, "The Epidemiological Study of Mental Illnesses and Mental Health," *American Journal of Psychiatry* 111 (May 1955): 801–809, quotation at 808.

39. Senn and Hartford, *The Firstborn*, quotations at 16 and 523.

40. On the growing power of statistics in this period see Theodore M. Porter, "Statistics and Statistical Methods," in *The Cambridge History of Science*, vol. 7: *The Modern Social Sciences*, eds., Theodore M. Porter and Dorothy Ross (Cambridge, Eng.: Cambridge University Press, 2003), 238–50.

41. Alexander Thomas et al., "A Longitudinal Study of Primary Reaction Patterns in Children," *Comprehensive Psychiatry* 1 (April 1960): 103–12, quotation at 107.

42. Karl Menninger, *A Manual for Psychiatric Case Study* (New York: Grune & Stratton, 1952), 18; Kris, "Opening Remarks," 17. See also Albert Solnit, "Introduction," *Journal of Clinical Psychoanalysis* 5 (1996): 102–6.

43. Goldfarb, *Introduction to Longitudinal Statistical Analysis*, 124; Emanuel Miller, "Child Psychiatry," *British Medical Bulletin* 6, nos. 1–2 (1949): 49.

44. McCollum, "A Clinical Caseworker in Interdisciplinary Research," 90; Ritvo and Ritvo, "Ernst Kris, 1900–1957," 492.

45. Group for the Advancement of Psychiatry, *Some Observations on Controls in Psychiatric Research* (New York: Group for the Advancement of Psychiatry Publications Office, May 1959), 538. In general see Bert E. Boothe, Anne H. Rosenfeld, and Edward L. Walker, eds., *Toward a Science of Psychiatry: Impact of the Research Development Program of the National Institute of Mental Health* (Monterey, CA: Cole Publishing, 1974).

46. Marks, *Progress of Experiment.*

47. Ernst Kris, "Problems in Clinical Research" (1947) in *Selected Papers of Ernst Kris*, 24–30, quotation at 24; Kris, "Opening Remarks," 11–12. For further evidence of how these questions were posed within the study, see "Research Meeting," March 11, 1952, folder 2, box 23, series 2, LngYC/YAMS.

48. Senn and Hartford, *The Firstborn*, quotations at 25 and 28. By way of introduction to this subject in the sciences more generally, see Lorraine Daston and Peter Galison, *Objectivity* (New York: Zone Books, 2007).

49. Karl Bowman, "The Psychiatrist Looks at the Child Psychiatrist," *American Journal of Psychiatry* 101 (July 1944): 23–9, quotation at 28.

50. Roy Schafer, "Contributions of Longitudinal Studies to Psychoanalytic Theory," *Journal of the American Psychoanalytic Association* 13 (1965): 605–18, quotation at 605.

51. See also Jill Morawski, "Organizing Knowledge and Behavior at Yale's Institute of Human Relations," *Isis* 77 (1986): 219–42. On the importance of interdisciplinarity in America's postwar human sciences, see Joel Isaac, *Working Knowledge: Making the Human Sciences from Parsons to Kuhn* (Cambridge, MA: Harvard University Press, 2012).

52. *Report of Grant Activities for the Year Ending June 30, 1957* (New Haven, CT: Foundations' Fund, 1957), copy in folder 4, box 8, series 2, Foundations' Fund for Research in Psychiatry, Yale record group 37, record unit 484, Archives and Manuscripts, Yale University, New Haven, Connecticut (hereafter

FFRP/ YAMS). On the role that funding bodies played in encouraging patrons' interests in interdisciplinarity see Jamie Cohen-Cole, "Instituting the Science of Mind: Intellectual Economies and Disciplinary Exchange at Harvard's Center for Cognitive Studies," *British Journal of the History of Science* 40 (December 2007): 567–97, esp. 573–76.

53. Kris, "Opening Remarks," 11; Kris, "The Nature of Psychoanalytic Propositions," 21; Kris, "Notes on the Development and on Some Current Problems," 72; and Kris, "On Psychoanalysis and Education," 50.

54. All quotations are from Memorandum to Milton Senn [Copy to Ernst Kris], December 19, 1952, folder 9, box 23, series 2, LngYC/YAMS; McCollum, "A Clinical Caseworker in Interdisciplinary Research," 91. On the operational difficulties of interdisciplinary research see Cohen-Cole, "Instituting the Science of Mind."

55. See Elisabeth Lomax, "The Laura Spelman Rockefeller Memorial: Some of Its Contributions to Early Research in Child Development," *Journal of the History of the Behavioral Sciences* 13 (July 1977): 283–93, quotation at 287.

56. "Aim of the Study and Its Methods," April 10, 1951 (emphasis in original). On Wolf's career and general contribution, see "Katherine M. Wolf: In Memoriam," *Child Study* 35 (Winter 1957–58).

57. Rebecca Lemov, "'Hypothetical Machines': The Science Fiction Dreams of Cold War Social Science," *Isis* 101 (2010): 401–11, quotation at 411.

58. The Commonwealth Fund was the Yale study's original source of funding. Later the study received a three-year grant of almost $65,000 from the Foundations' Fund for Research in Psychiatry. This was greater per annum funding than the foundation typically awarded, and rare in that it related to child psychiatry. See Foundations' Fund for Research in Psychiatry to Katherine M. Wolf, February 12, 1957, folder FFRP, box 39, series IV, LngYC/YAMS. The funding profile of the fund is described in *Foundations' Fund for Research in Psychiatry: Tenth Annual Report for the Years 1953–1963* (New Haven, CT: Foundations' Fund for Research in Psychiatry, 1963), folder 10, box 9, series 2, FFRP/ YAMS.

59. Ernst Kris and Sally Provence, "The Study of Variations of Early Parental Attitudes—A Preliminary Report," *Psychoanalytic Study of the Child* 8 (1953): 20–47, quotation at 28.

60. Joel Isaac, "Epistemic Design: Theory and Data in Harvard's Department of Social Relations," in Mark Solovey and Hamilton Cravens, eds., *Cold War Social Science: Knowledge Production, Liberal Democracy, and Human Nature* (New York: Palgrave-Macmillan, 2012), 79–95, esp. 80–81.

61. Kris, "Problems in Clinical Research," 26.

62. "Instruction for Taking Meeting Notes," n.d. (ca. January 1951), folder 1, box 23, series 2, LngYC/YAMS. Further examples of this concern for the organization of information can be found in Sally Provenance to all Secretaries, n.d. (ca. July 1957); and "Research Meeting," December 4, 1951, both in folder 23, box 23, series 1, LngYC/YAMS.

63. David French quoted in McCollum, "Clinical Caseworker in Interdisciplinary Research," 102.

64. Strauss and Babigian, *Origins and Course of Psychopathology*, 209–10.

65. Sontag, Baker, and Nelson, *Mental Growth and Personality Development*, quotation at 13.

66. Lemov, "Hypothetical Machines," 408.

67. McCollum, "A Clinical Caseworker in Interdisciplinary Research," 101; "Research Meeting," February 19, 1952, folder 2, box 23, series 2, LngYC/YAMS (emphasis in original); Memorandum from Milton Senn to "Staff of Longitudinal Research Study," n.d. (ca. May 1957), folder 23, box 23, series 2, LngYC/YAMS.

68. The role of funding bodies in encouraging longitudinal research is found in Jerome Frank, "Postwar Psychiatry: Personal Observations," in Roy Menninger and John Nemiah, eds., *American Psychiatry after World War II, 1944–1994* (Washington, DC: American Psychiatric Press, 2000), 197.

69. Senn and Hartford, *The Firstborn*, 525.

ༀ 3 ༁

The Longitudinal Study and Its Setting

DAVID A. CARLSON

The 1950s in America, so often described as a conservative, conformist time, was also an era of radical change in psychiatry, psychoanalysis, and the study of child development. In New Haven, Yale's Child Development Clinic was transformed into the Child Study Center with a heavy psychoanalytic interest, the Yale Psychiatry Department became a leading center for the application of psychoanalytic thinking, and a local psychoanalytic society and institute were formed. In Andrew Fearnley's apt phrase, it was a time of "institutional rupture," and the longitudinal study emerged in that time of rupture.

The radical changes of the 1950s had been foreshadowed twenty years earlier and a few yards away from the Child Study Center, where Yale had brought analysts and other researchers together in an interdisciplinary center. The Institute of Human Relations, heavily underwritten by the Rockefeller Foundation, opened in 1931 and represented the interests and ambitions of Yale's dean of medicine, Milton C. Winternitz, a pathologist, and its president, James Angell, a psychologist. Winternitz, memorably characterized as "a steamroller in pants," thought social medicine required the input of law, psychology, psychoanalysis, anthropology, economics, psychiatry, child development, and perhaps religious studies. He proposed that Yale move its law and divinity schools to adjoin the medical school and that their major departments share the new institute building. The law and divinity faculties fought off what they saw as Winternitz's power grab, and though the Institute of Human Relations continued through the 1930s as a place of broad interdisciplinary study, Arnold Gesell early on foreshadowed the institute's fate when he literally closed off the space of his Child Development Clinic.

Similarly, one of the institute's psychoanalytic researchers encountered problems like those that Mayes and Lassonde have described facing the study's investigators: more data than one knows what to do with. The researcher was Earl Zinn, a psychologist who from 1920 had pioneered psychologists' study of sexuality. In 1925 he had been sent to Europe by the Committee for the Study of Sex to investigate the applicability of psychoanalysis to their studies, and he took some analytic training before being drawn back to the Institute of Human Relations, where psychologist and learning theorist Clark Hull was attempting to test analytic formulations in behavioral terms.[1] In New Haven, Zinn took part in the ambitious interdisciplinary discussions of the institute and analyzed some of its faculty. He had earlier made a pioneering electrical recording of his four-year treatment of a schizophrenic patient and found that there were more data than he could analyze with the tools available to him. He recruited Geoffrey Gorer, later a very well known social anthropologist, to search the material for what might have been distinctive about the patient's early life. Gorer decided he needed to know more about what normal childhood was like, and one much later result was his book *The American People: A Study in National Character*. Gorer and Zinn wrote but finally did not publish a book based on the recorded material.[2]

Another analytically trained faculty member at the institute was the psychologist John Dollard, who became well known for his writings on psychoanalysis and learning theory. A program developed in which either Zinn or Dollard would analyze a staff member whom the other would supervise in a required one-year analysis of a patient—a rudimentary analytic training to prepare young social scientists to apply analytic insights to their work. Dollard, who remained in New Haven for the rest of his life, was involved in the earliest formation of local psychoanalytic organizations, though his views of aggression as something developed entirely in relation to frustration put him at theoretical odds with many analysts.[3]

In 1935 Yale extended an invitation to Erik Erikson, a Viennese-trained child analyst then struggling to support himself and his family in Boston, to consult at the Institute of Human Relations, in pediatrics and in psychiatry, and at the Child Development Clinic. He accepted the invitation with the encouragement of a three-year grant from the Macy Foundation. Erikson was the first psychoanalyst at what became the Child Study Center, but his career there was cut short. The Child Study Center's director, Arnold Gesell, had begun the systematic study of preschool children in 1918 and had accumulated a mass of normative observations with photographs and film. At a conference one year after Erikson's arrival, Gesell ordered that a photograph of a three-year-old boy with an erection and masturbating be omitted from the record. Erikson challenged the decision and soon afterward Gesell cut off Erikson's access to Yale Child Study materials, citing confidentiality concerns.[4] Erikson and his group later published their own findings on the basis of incomplete data they had managed to accumulate.[5]

Erikson decided to devote more time to the Institute of Human Relations, where John Dollard was spelling out a view relating psychoanalytic drive-based development to social and economic factors, both through childhood and beyond—an outlook that clearly contributed to Erikson's later eight-stage plan of the life cycle. Both Dollard and Erikson stressed the importance to development of historical and economic considerations, but they apparently had no influence on the later Child Study Center work.

Marian Putnam joined the Yale Pediatrics Department in 1921 and then took several years away to study psychiatry with Adolf Meyer in Baltimore and for other clinical work in Boston. In 1933 she went to

Vienna for psychoanalytic training, and returned to Yale with an appointment in psychiatry and mental hygiene. She became convinced that eating disorders in children often reflected the mother's ignorance about the infant's emotional development and she developed an educational program that encouraged maternal interest. She also studied early differences in temperament as predictive of later pathology.[6] The then-chair of psychiatry, Eugen Kahn, was known for his antipathy to psychoanalysis, and it is likely that her position in his department was made possible by her family's social standing as Boston Cabots and Putnams. Her father, James Jackson Putnam, had been the founding professor of neuropathology at Harvard, had met Freud and hosted his Adirondack trip after the Worcester lectures in 1909, and had been a leading defender of psychoanalysis in the United States.[7]

Marian Putnam returned to Boston in 1938, where she later founded the James Jackson Putnam Center and taught early courses on child analysis, but while still in New Haven she took part in the Institute of Human Relations discussions and served as psychiatric consultant to pediatrics. She and Erikson both knew Putnam's Hopkins classmate Edith Jackson from their Vienna days, and they urged Jackson to come to New Haven, where she took Putnam's place as psychiatric consultant to pediatrics.

Edith Jackson was from a wealthy, troubled Colorado family. Her mother had committed suicide when Edith was three, as did an older brother when she was a young adult. She had come to Yale as a junior faculty member in pediatrics but interrupted her New Haven years in 1927 to pursue analysis in Washington with Lucille Dooley, whom she had known in medical student days at Hopkins. In 1931, she decided to go to Vienna for analysis with Freud; she soon began analytic training there, met for two hours a week with Anna Freud to discuss child analysis, and had a practice of five analytic patients.[8] During her Vienna years she contributed funds to several analytic causes and financed a preschool nursery at 13 Bergasse that was known as the Jackson Nursery from its founding in 1936 until the Nazis closed it in 1938. The Jackson Nursery was the forerunner of the wartime nursery project of Dorothy Burlingham and Anna Freud.

Soon after Jackson's return, Joan Erikson was to deliver her third child. She pressed to be able to have the child with her immediately after delivery, which New Haven Hospital refused to do until Mrs. Erikson came down with mumps, whereupon, with Jackson's urging, she was allowed to keep the baby with her in an isolation unit. Edith Jackson cited this experience of a "contented" mother and baby in her later campaign for the establishment of an experimental rooming-in project. Her vision was of a warm obstetrical service where experienced nurses cared for mothers and babies, where both mothers and pediatric residents could observe and learn about babies, and where pediatric and obstetrical residents might learn to listen more attentively to new mothers. While the project in its six-year experimental phase attracted international attention and some grant support, the initial construction expense for a four-bed unit was guaranteed by Edith Jackson herself, at a cost of half her Yale salary. The experiment ended in 1952, by which time the rooming-in concept was well established and enthusiastically embraced by many in Yale obstetrics and pediatrics.[9] Edith Jackson continued as clinical professor of pediatrics and psychiatry at Yale until she moved to Denver in 1960; and she served as a member of the editorial board of *Psychoanalytic Study of the Child* from its first appearance in 1945 until her death. Ernst Kris used her observations on infants from the rooming-in project at an early stage of the Yale Longitudinal Study.[10] Soon after the eventful birth of that third child, Erik Erikson accepted a five-year Rockefeller grant to participate in a new longitudinal study in Berkeley. He went on to a career at Berkeley, only to return to our story in 1951.[11]

Through much of the 1930s, on the other side of New Haven, Dollard and others had been instrumental in encouraging Harold Lasswell, the author of *Psychopathology and Politics*, to visit and teach at the Yale Law School, where after 1946 he became the Edward J. Phelps Professor of Law and Political Science.[12] In his early adulthood Lasswell had some analysis with Theodor Reik in Vienna and some form of analytic training.[13] In Chicago in 1930 he conducted what he called psychoanalytic interviews on a couch, recording both the interviews and associated pulse, blood pressure, and body movements, thereby becoming apparently the first person to call for the collection of such data.[14] Lasswell became a "non therapeutic" member of the early Chicago Psychoanalytic Society in 1933.[15] His early study of rationalization led to extensive work on the propaganda of World War I, and to work in Washington, D.C., in World War II; in addition, with Harry Stack Sullivan and the anthropologist-linguist Edward Sapir, he formed a research team that strove for "the fusion of psychiatry and social science."[16] He was a prolific and influential political scientist who continues to be republished.

Most of the psychoanalysts engaged in the longitudinal study came from the New York Psychoanalytic Institute. Milton Senn and Ernst and Marianne Kris had their professional homes in New York, the Krises having left Vienna at the time of the Anschluss. Samuel Ritvo had pursued analytic training there, graduating in 1948 and moving to New Haven in 1950; and Albert Solnit would finish his analytic training as the longitudinal study got under way. Sally Provence, the pediatrician who was a central figure in both the research and clinical aspects of the study, had trained under Senn at Cornell. Seymour Lustman, who began a Yale psychiatry residency as the study began, was an exception to the New York rule: he came from Chicago, where he had obtained a Ph.D. in psychology and an M.D. He became an early graduate of the Western New England Institute for Psychoanalysis.

The longitudinal study had three overlapping psychoanalytic environments beyond the Yale Child Study Center: the New York Institute, mentioned earlier; the newly forming regional Western New England Psychoanalytic Society and Western New England Institute for Psychoanalysis; and the Yale community, especially its medical school and departments of psychiatry and of pediatrics. All three of the groups were at least partially disposed to favor the study because of the central role of infantile neurosis in the growth of psychoanalytic thought.

Two major figures in launching area psychoanalysis were Robert Knight and Fritz Redlich. Of the two, Knight was the more experienced clinician, teacher, and administrator. As a young midwesterner visiting Europe, Knight obtained a letter of introduction to Freud, and upon being granted a brief visit asked Freud to autograph not one but several photos. Freud refused, then gave in with some grumbling about American mass production. The incident captures something of Knight's confident effectiveness. Like most of the first analysts at the Menninger Clinic, he had trained at the Chicago Institute for Psychoanalysis and had been involved in the establishment of the Topeka Psychoanalytic Society and Institute in 1936, immediately becoming involved in national psychoanalysis as the new society's councilor. Knight had long been regarded as the outstanding clinician at the Menninger Clinic and in 1947 he became director of the Topeka Psychoanalytic Institute. He grew restless, however, and after a few months accepted an offer to lead the Austen Riggs Center in Stockbridge, Massachusetts. Riggs had used a kind of reeducative therapy developed by its eponymous founder, and Knight quickly developed it as "a center for inpatient psychotherapy of all types, but mostly dynamically oriented, for voluntary patients who can live in an open building under minimal supervision."[17]

Knight assembled a remarkable group in Stockbridge: Roy Schafer, already an experienced researcher but still short of his doctorate, became chief psychologist, with the understanding that everything possible would be done to make possible his training in analysis; and within a year funding was found to bring David Rapaport as a full-time researcher and teacher, with the assurance that he could devote all his time to the continuation of his study of thought processes. The young Margaret Brenman and Merton Gill accompanied Rapaport from Topeka. Both Brenman and Gill were recent analysands of Knight's and were much involved in joint research, to which half their time was apportioned. Brenman once described the resulting organization as "incestuous."

As early as April of 1950 Knight organized a meeting in Stockbridge that anticipated some of the developments of the next few years in New Haven. Anna Freud discussed Ernst Kris's paper "Psychoanalytic Views on Child-Psychology." She addressed the question of whether the direct observation of children could break new ground for psychoanalytic knowledge, or whether it was useful to confirm or refute findings made during treatment. Some of the results of this work had already been published in collaboration with Dorothy Burlingham in *Young Children in War-Time in a Residential War Nursery* and *Infants without Families.*[18] She felt that the direct observation of children had a legitimate place in the psychoanalytic study of childhood because the sources of psychoanalytic knowledge of children had always been mixed, though she said that the most important findings were derived from reconstruction during adult analysis.[19]

In 1951 Erik Erikson reappeared on the local stage when he accepted Knight's standing offer of a position at Riggs. While at Berkeley, Erikson, despite his lack of formal degrees, had become a professor of psychology and lecturer in psychiatry, as well as a training and supervising analyst in the San Francisco Institute and president of its society and institute. But when in 1950 the California legislature enacted a law requiring all state employees to sign a loyalty oath, Erikson led a protest and conducted a national campaign to urge analysts not to accept appointments in the California system. Erikson thought Knight would be sympathetic to his liberal perspective; he knew, for instance, that Knight and his wife had opened their Topeka home to Paul Robeson a few years earlier when no Topeka hotel would register an African American, an action that had led to Mrs. Knight being snubbed by many of her Kansas friends. Even as Knight assembled his Stockbridge team and reorganized the Riggs Center, he served as second chair of the American Psychoanalytic Association's newly organized Board on Professional Standards and then as president of the local association when the society and the institute were founded in 1952. This was also when he was engaged in founding the *Journal of the American Psychoanalytic Association.*[20]

Fritz Redlich was a Viennese who had begun his analytic training before leaving at the time of the Anschluss. He came to Yale in 1942, and was about to finish his analytic training at the New York Institute when he was tapped to take over chairmanship of the Psychiatry Department from Eugen Kahn in 1949. Upon assuming the chairmanship, Redlich made known his dream of a psychoanalytic society and institute in New Haven. Although at the outset Redlich was a less experienced administrator than Knight, he quickly assembled a group of talented analysts and created a remarkable psychiatry department. Redlich brought in

Lawrence Kubie from New York and Robert Knight from Stockbridge as visiting clinical professors, and recruited an outstanding full-time faculty that came to include Theodore Lidz, Norman Cameron, Jules Coleman, and others.

In 1949 Alfred Gross, who had trained in Berlin and who had successively been a training and supervising analyst in the British Society and at Topeka, left the Menninger Clinic for New Haven. He soon encouraged Henry Wexler and William L. Pious, another Topeka training analyst, to follow him. Eventually these three shared a secretary and a waiting room with the new institute. For several years that waiting room was the institute's only space. In effect, then, a Topeka group functioned across town from the Child Study Center's mostly New York group, while the Yale Psychiatry Department next door combined both neo-Sullivanian and New York influences.

In 1951, just as Erik Erikson accepted the position in Stockbridge, the New York Institute adopted a policy requiring all its trainees to practice in New York. With Erikson's arrival the area had four experienced training and supervising analysts, the number then thought advisable for the organization of a new institute, and indeed, the New York policy and the presence of so many experienced analysts sped the local institute's development. When in 1951 a psychoanalytic society formed, it was mentioned in the *Bulletin of the American Psychoanalytic Association* as the "New Haven–Stockbridge Group."[21] The institute was founded on a revolution or at least on a coup d'état in January 1952.[22] Two hours before the society held its first scientific meeting in Litchfield, Erikson, Gross, Knight, and Pious met and constituted themselves as an education committee (ignoring their tentative earlier appointment as such by the society). They then declared their intention to apply in their own name for recognition as a new training facility and adopted procedures for application, for screening and enrollment, and for drawing up a curriculum. The institute's unusually thoughtful procedures evolved over years of deliberations, some of which have been preserved in committee minutes and others in detailed memoranda circulated among the group for written comment. Some of the most extended discussions that survive are typescripts dictated to their common secretary by Pious or by Wexler to forward to the other, who then responded in a similar way, all across that small waiting room. Helen Ross wrote in 1958 that the Western New England's remarkable written materials constituted "a Doctor Spock on how to conceive and bring up an institute."

It is still the case that most institutes are offspring of societies and that societies and institutes are to varying degrees less independent of each other than is the case at the Western New England. The decision of the education committee to seek its own recognition resulted in an institute that grew out of an education committee, rather than an institute that appointed an education committee. The founders succeeded in minimizing the educational impact of the political and guild issues that are inescapable in a professional organization like a psychoanalytic society: the education committee controls all educational issues and is a self-perpetuating group, like the governing bodies of some universities. This organization helped reassure the founders that education wouldn't be compromised by political pressures as was then happening not only in California but even at Harvard, where appointments of some faculty members with left-wing affiliations were not being renewed.

But the institute's founders felt that a much more real and immediate threat to educational autonomy was Fritz Redlich, who had proclaimed his wish to have a complete department of psychiatry, including a psychoanalytic institute. The Yale Child Study Center was an interdisciplinary organization that was closely involved with the medical school and its psychiatry department and was the site for Yale's child psychiatry training, but in the days of the study it maintained an independence that, among other things, ensured that child psychiatry was not subsumed, as was usual elsewhere, under a department dominated by adult psychiatry. The Yale Child Study Center, like the institute, was mindful of its independence.

Within a year of his arrival in Stockbridge, Erik Erikson gave a talk on "The Irma Dream—50 Years Hence."[23] This psychoanalytic classic incorporates material from the newly published Fliess letters about Freud's life at the time of the dream, with a new perspective on the manifest, particularly visual, parts of the dream. The paper strained Erikson's relations with Anna Freud, who is thought to have been displeased with his presumption in adding to her father's published self-analysis.[24]

While the Child Study Center and the Yale Department of Psychiatry were in New Haven, the new institute was split between New Haven and Stockbridge, with a part-time secretary maintaining a full set of records, correspondence, and so on, in each place. Meetings of the education committee, like classes for candidates, might be scheduled in either place; and some society meetings were held in Stockbridge. The work done by the secretaries was enormous, when one reflects on the volume of correspondence, drafts of policy statements, curriculum and organizational plans, and bibliographies in a pre-word-processor, pre-photocopier, pre-answering-machine, and pre-fax age. Some articles available only in German at that time were translated by early faculty members.

The first institute class of seven, which began its studies in 1954, was selected from thirty-five applicants, and the second class, one year later, included Seymour Lustman, who managed to take part in the longitudinal study and to study psychoanalysis simultaneously. Most applicants for training were from New Haven but half the training analysts were in Stockbridge. Some candidates made the long commute for their analyses and many more, in each direction, for classes and supervision. Despite the logistical problems, many Yale faculty members undertook training, and through the 1950s there were almost no ward chiefs or service chiefs in Yale psychiatry who were not analysts or candidates or, in a few cases, dropped candidates; and many of the next generation of child psychiatrists from the Child Study Center pursued psychoanalytic training.

It is common to speak of those days as a golden age for psychoanalysis, and perhaps it was for the practitioner. For those concerned with psychoanalytic education, however, the success of psychoanalysis in the university threatened a future in which analysis and the analytic procedure might be co-opted by the much greater resources and academic opportunities available for psychotherapy or some other modification or application. Indeed, Gerald Klerman, who transferred to the Western New England Institute from the Boston Institute as a candidate in the 1960s, when he assumed a Yale professorship, presented his initial proposal for a manualized Interpersonal Psychotherapy as a way of making a case for psychoanalytic treatment by demonstrating the efficacy of even a stripped-down procedure, one teachable to modestly educated assistants and designed to be so simple as to be testable. Within a few years the psychiatric literature abounded with claims that interpersonal psychotherapy had been demonstrated to be effective, unlike psychoanalysis, which of course is much less easily tested.[25] The Klerman phenomenon captures a tension that ran through those years between the Yale Psychiatry Department, where Klerman had been recruited to direct a new mental health center, and the psychoanalytic institute.

In 1954, as classes first began, the institute had accepted the psychologists George Mahl and Roy Schafer as candidates. This occasioned intense questioning from the American Psychoanalytic Association, as did David Rapaport's teaching, since in 1953 the association had adopted a motion stipulating that faculty members must be eligible for membership (at the time, membership was open only to physicians). There was a thoughtful but intensely argumentative correspondence between Pious and successive chairs of the Board on Professional Standards that extended over several years. When the association insisted that Schafer not be given any control cases, Pious pointed out that he had already started one, so it was insisted he not start another. Board and committee debates continued for three years. Interestingly, the issue of nonmedical training did not divide the Psychiatry Department, the institute, and the Child Study Center but rather united them in a common cause, though there was smoldering discontent in the forming psychoanalytic society, which was composed mostly of psychiatrist-psychoanalysts.

Another kind of fame came to the psychologist Margaret Brenman, whom the institute appointed in 1954 as a training and supervising analyst. Then, as now, such appointments are reviewed by the Board on Professional Standards, and this one caused a floor fight at the December meetings. Brenman had trained at the Menninger Clinic under one of the early research waivers, and one condition of the waiver as it had been understood by most members was that it was for research training only; waivered graduates would agree not to practice. In Pious's words at the board meeting on December 7, "Prior to the actual vote there was a long and, at times, very rancorous discussion and argument." Several motions that would in effect have deferred approval of the appointment were debated heatedly and at length. Again in the words of Pious, "At that point our application came up for consideration and the fur really flew! Every effort was made by a few individuals to put off bringing this matter to a vote. These efforts even included threats of resignation, etc." The appointment was finally accepted by a 4 to 1 majority. Next day at the Executive Council, Joan Fleming mentioned the Brenman appointment at the end of her description of the board meeting. Roy Grinker said the American Psychoanalytic Association was establishing a precedent that would gravely affect its relations with American medicine and called for a vote of no confidence in the Board on Professional Standards.[26] Ives Hendrick, who was by then president, denounced at length the action by the board and by the Western New England Psychoanalytic Society and Institute, ending with, "How are we going to hold up our heads if we continue these practices? How can we represent ourselves to American medicine?"; and Robert Knight spoke with open scorn of what he called the hypocrisy of Hendrick's statement. After a long debate, the council voted to reject Hendrick's motion. This set a local pattern of welcoming and appointing highly qualified candidates from several disciplines and of opposing on the national level what Henry Wexler called the attempt "to make the world safe for medicalocracy."[27]

In 1951 Merton Gill left Riggs for New Haven, where he was soon appointed a training analyst, the first addition to the original group of four. Gill, however, left New Haven after only two years, and Erikson left Stockbridge in 1960. Roy Schafer moved to New Haven in 1953, where he wrote, taught, published extensively, and became a training and supervising analyst until he, in turn, left in 1975 for a Freud Professorship in London and then for New York City. In the new institute, much thought was given to education for research and there was a research course at the beginning. Pious, in fact, organized the faculty into three departments: psychoanalytic theory, psychoanalytic practice, and psychoanalytic research.

David Rapaport helped launch an unspoken but powerful tradition of scholarship and intense application to teaching. He had been discovered by Karl Menninger on a trip to the Osawotomie State Hospital in Kansas, where the psychologist had administered the Rorschach and Szondi tests to Menninger and astonished him with a lengthy and sophisticated report on the results. Rapaport had learned of psychoanalysis as a boy in Hungary from a relative of his father, a psychoanalyst who professed a reluctance to write. The young Rapaport wrote two psychoanalytic books for that relative, both published before his twenty-first birthday. After two years in Palestine he returned to Hungary at the behest of his Zionist organization to promote youth recruitment. While in Hungary he completed degrees in mathematics and experimental physics, a doctorate in psychology and philosophy, as well as a Montessori teaching certificate, and had two or three years of personal analysis. He is said to have learned testing "almost entirely on his own." He hoped that a unified theory of thinking and learning would lead to a demonstration of the validity of Kant's view of knowledge as codetermined by experience and inherent mental tendencies. "He was intense and restless, worked endless hours, and expected others to do the same. His badly damaged, rheumatic heart led him to feel that his days were numbered, and he carried on as if life were a race against time. An insomniac, he read half the night and taught himself to take notes in the dark while tossing in bed." Robert Knight claimed that in his first years in America, Rapaport had sat up most of each night reading the entire back issues of all the English language psychoanalytic literature, having already covered all that had been published in German and Hungarian. At Topeka, Rapaport audited every institute class but declined to seek graduation. He worked incessantly and had almost no social life. Margaret Brenman noted that when he made a major point he "pronounced it in a loud, evangelical, and absolutely authoritarian tone that hardly promoted discussion." He criticized loose thinking and even in casual conversation required all assertions to be supported by precise and abundant references; he expected his associates and later his students to recall not only exact passages but also their page numbers. Transcripts of his famous series of Western New England metapsychology courses bear out the picture of an extremely intelligent, endlessly demanding, and severely formal seminar leader. One early candidate, a junior faculty member at Yale, took off a whole day a week to prepare for each Rapaport seminar; nights and weekends seemed insufficient. By 1955 Rapaport's special place was formally acknowledged when he was appointed chair of the Department of Psychoanalytic Theory and faculty consultant. The preserved correspondence between Pious and Rapaport indicates that Rapaport made himself something like a dean of faculty, raising questions about scheduling, course sequence and content, facilities, and so on. Pious assured him at one point that the commuting demands on students would be lessened because courses would be held from now on in Torrington, halfway between New Haven and Stockbridge, at the Yankee Drover Inn, though the plan fell through. Rapaport was a leading systematizer of psychoanalytic thought and his work aligned with that of Hartmann, Kris, and Loewenstein. In that sense, his work was naturally sympathetic to the theoretical leanings of the Yale Child Study group, though his lack of a clinical orientation made for some tension. Kris and Hartmann for their part supported Erikson against charges of excessive environmentalism brought by Anna Freud and some other analysts.

With Hans Loewald's arrival from Baltimore in 1955, New Haven gained one of the most thoughtful and quietly revolutionary voices in psychoanalysis. Loewald was not a child analyst, though his wife, Elizabeth, trained in child psychiatry and worked at the Yale Child Study Center. His formulations on the development of psychic structure stressed the internalization of infant interactions with the caretaker as constitutive of the psyche, including the drives. His writings were not always easily accepted by analysts, who were then finding their way toward increasingly clear formulations based on the structural theory, but civility permitted a very fruitful tension among Loewald's views, those of the New York-Child Study cadre, and those of the Topeka-Stockbridge group.

Events that boded ill for the study and for the nascent analytic community happened in early 1957, when Ernst Kris, fifty-six years old, died unexpectedly on February 27 and Alfred Gross, 64, passed away two days later. Much more happily, in March, Sam Ritvo began his long career as a training and supervising analyst and member of the Education Committee. Ritvo's appointment, the first of a New York–trained analyst, brought a new point of view into the institute's educational arm and heralded the development of a close interweaving of the study's analysts with the new institute. In 1960 the first students trained at the Western New England Institute graduated, and Jack Plunkett and Roy Schafer were elected to society membership.

On December 14, 1961, David Rapaport died at the age of forty-nine. Erikson had left the Austen Riggs Center the year before Rapaport's death, and Robert Knight soon fell ill with the cancer that was to take his life in 1965. The psychoanalytic powerhouse that had been Riggs, and that had been a vital center of the intellectual and educational lives of those in the institute, rapidly wound down. Analysts remained there and one was briefly a training and supervising analyst before he left for California. Some institute courses continued to be held there for a few more years. By the end of the 1960s Wexler wrote to the Committee on Institutes, "We no longer receive requests for training in psychoanalysis from residents of the Austen Riggs Center, nor do any members of the Austen Riggs staff teach at our Institute." Rapaport's death cleared the way for Seymour Lustman to lead the institute's research teaching.

In the institute's first bulletin Erik Erikson had outlined a plan for the study of the infant, child, and adolescent, but the implementation of this plan only came about in 1962 in New Haven, with Seymour Lustman, Sally Provence, Sam Ritvo, and Albert Solnit as faculty members and Marianne Kris as a consultant. Infant and preschool observation for all candidates was introduced. The Yale Child Study Center was and remained the source of child analytic faculty and of most child analytic students. The child program flourished for many years under the joint and alternating chairmanships of Samuel Ritvo and Albert Solnit, and more recently under Wayne Downey and Kirsten Dahl. The longitudinal study and its staff probably influenced the analytic community more than the community affected the study. This was in large part due to the caliber and energy of the child analysts, who taught in the basic medical school curriculum, led courses in adult psychiatry residency, consulted on pediatric cases, and educated others in every part of the institute curriculum, in addition to being very active in the society and in outreach programs. Ritvo, Solnit, and Lustman became training and supervising analysts and played leading roles locally and nationally.

A second revolution of sorts now took place and is succinctly described by one of its principals. In a 1966 report, Albert Solnit, clearly building on the experience that he had gained from serving on a subcommittee with Roy Schafer and Henry Wexler as part of the institute's first review of curriculum, wrote:

> 1962 is also a dividing line in time in terms of other revisions of the curriculum and in terms of the marked decrease of the influence of David Rapaport. . . . Additions to the faculty and to the Education Committee from 1962 until the present, and the great void created by the death of Robert Knight in the past year have gradually changed the Institute and its curriculum from one mainly influenced by the Topeka group to one influenced by graduates of other institutes, especially the New York Psychoanalytic Institute, and most importantly by graduates of our own Institute who have become faculty members. . . . This changing influence has tended to decrease the gulf between metapsychological and clinical theory which David Rapaport and his students emphasized.[28]

Anna Freud, whose 1950 appearance at Stockbridge we have noted, made month-long visits to New Haven from 1964 through 1971. While there, in addition to teaching with Jay Katz and Joseph Goldstein at the Law School, she took part in meetings at the Yale Child Study Center, led two clinical seminars for analytic candidates, was a guest at a meeting of the Education Committee and of its new Clinic Screening Committee, and presented a paper at one society meeting. Her visits related to collaborations on family law that eventually were published in *Beyond the Best Interests of the Child*, *Before the Best Interests of the Child*, and *In the Best Interests of the Child*, all with Joseph Goldstein and Albert Solnit.[29]

Meanwhile, research in the Yale Psychiatry Department led in many directions. Redlich promoted interdisciplinary work, and in this respect both the Psychiatry Department and the Child Study Center could be described as natural successors to the Institute of Human Relations. His work in the 1950s included a major collaboration with the sociologist August B. Hollingshead on *Social Class and Mental Illness*, which provides an extensive description of New Haven at the time of the longitudinal study, and a characterization of psychiatry as it was then practiced in the community and the university. The book has inspired an extensive literature on social psychiatry and is still cited.[30] Another early fruit of the Redlich chairmanship was a remarkable symposium on the psychotherapy of schizophrenia, timed to celebrate the beginning of the Lidz era at the Yale Psychiatric Institute.[31] In collaboration with Merton Gill and Richard Newman, Redlich also published the best discussion of its time on psychiatric interviewing.[32]

The orientation of the major study of schizophrenic patients under Theodore Lidz and Stephen Fleck was influenced by the typically adolescent onset of the symptoms and by Lidz's earlier exposure to Sullivanian thought and his formative years as a resident and chief resident under Adolf Meyer at the Phipps Clinic in Baltimore. He and his group were analysts but thought that the ego psychologists, and by implication the Yale Child Study group, paid too little attention to the social surround; some of their best work described the family setting of schizophrenia.[33] Like Dollard and Erikson, they questioned the existence of aggressive drives and stressed that aggressive behavior and psychological conflict could most usefully be studied in the social, especially family, context. Lidz and Fleck were members of the local psychoanalytic society, but unlike the Child Study Center analysts, were not deeply involved. Lidz for some years led a yearlong medical student course on the life cycle, in which Child Study analysts taught, and one of his most ambitious books was a study of the life cycle, which relies on his own thought and also on Erikson's formulations, particularly those outlined in *Childhood and Society*.[34] Interestingly, although his disagreements with the points of view of the Yale Longitudinal Study's analysts were clear, it was Lidz who provided one of the most perceptive outside appreciations of the longitudinal study:

> Planned, scientific study of the infant's development has been carried out only during the past three or four decades. It has not always been obvious that the infant's personality development is a topic for scientific study. Direct observation of infants and children over the course of time probably started with Gesell's careful studies of maturation that established landmarks for comparison, and with Piaget's studies of the cognitive development of his own children in the service of epistemology. Currently, a variety of direct studies are expanding our knowledge of the period. Longitudinal studies through infancy and childhood are difficult to carry out, and many of them tend to focus on some specific facet of the problem to avoid a complexity that cannot be handled with scientific rigor. Only an occasional study is conducted in the infant's natural habitat, the home. The longitudinal studies of the infant and his family being carried out at the Yale Child Study Center are unique in their efforts to combine direct observation with psychoanalytic study, and to consider the essential data despite its inordinate complexity because simplification is possible only at the price of considerable error. These studies seek to consider the child's make-up at birth, his or her particular abilities, the mother's personality and problems, child-rearing patterns, and the influence of other family members, etc. They seek to relate the interplay of such factors during infancy to later personality development and characteristics.[35]

Another major figure in the Psychiatry Department was Norman Cameron, who completed a Ph.D. in psychology before attending medical school and who had preceded Lidz as a student of Adolf Meyer at the Phipps Clinic. He had initially been dismissive of analysis but during a two-year period of forced bed rest for tuberculosis he read philosophical and psychoanalytic books and became fascinated.[36] He trained in analysis in his fifties, which was remarkable at the time. In 1953 Redlich convinced him to leave a chairmanship of psychiatry at the University of Wisconsin with the promise of time to write, and Cameron finished his analytic training at the Western New England Institute. Cameron's *Personality Development and Psychopathology: A Dynamic Approach* is one of the most successful general descriptions of psychopathology from a psychoanalytic point of view, and his paper "Introjection, Reprojection, and Hallucination in the Interaction between Schizophrenic Patient and Therapist" is considered a classic.[37] Cameron's wife, Eugenia, was a child psychiatrist who had coordinated mental health outreach programs for children in Wisconsin and who had a Yale appointment. In his writings Cameron drew heavily not only on studies in developmental psychology but also on Sally Provence's work on maternal deprivation and on some of the early publications from the longitudinal study, especially Ritvo and Solnit's "Influences of Early Mother-Child Interaction on Identification Processes," which is based on the case of Evelyn, reported elsewhere in this volume.[38]

On the clinical front, psychiatry residents were deeply affected by the teaching of another of Redlich's recruits: Jules Coleman, who had left a professorship in Denver to head up outpatient teaching at Yale. Coleman had received his medical education in Vienna and had been influenced by the work of Wilhelm Stekel, whose intuitive genius and ability to divine the unconscious of others resembled Coleman's own. Coleman was a New Yorker but had obtained his analytic education in Chicago, commuting there from Denver by train, and like Lidz, Fleck, and Redlich he remained peripherally involved in local psychoanalytic organizations. Every psychiatry resident passed through Coleman's service, learning a form of brief but intense therapy that quickly highlighted character resistances, formulated them in a good-humored way, and left them alone. A student who later became one of the most thoughtful observers of modern psychoanalysis and psychotherapy wrote that he thought Coleman "the most creative teacher I have known, and, to my mind, the most sophisticated psychotherapist of our day."[39]

Coleman's and Redlich's interests in social psychiatry were timely in another way. In 1953 Richard C. Lee was elected mayor of New Haven, and remained mayor through the years of the longitudinal study. The Lee administration effectively oversaw a far-reaching redevelopment program, which involved relocation and property redevelopment and some ambitious attempts at social development. For years New Haven received more funding per capita for social and construction projects than any other American city and was the focus of national attention. So the longitudinal study proceeded in a city of dramatic, hopeful physical and social changes and in a rapidly developing university and psychoanalytic community characterized by social and political optimism.

NOTES

1. Ernest Jones to Sigmund Freud, November 30, 1925, and December 18, 1925, both in R. Andrew Paskauskas, ed., *The Complete Correspondence of Sigmund Freud and Ernest Jones, 1908–1939* (Cambridge, MA: Belknap Press of Harvard University Press, 1993), 583, 587–88.

2. Geoffrey Gorer, *The American People: A Study in National Character* (New York: W.W. Norton, 1948); Geoffrey Gorer and Howard Zinn, unpublished manuscript in the author's possession.

3. John Dollard et al., *Frustration and Aggression* (New Haven: Yale University Press, 1939).

4. Lawrence J. Friedman, *Identity's Architect: A Biography of Erik H. Erikson* (New York: Scribner, 1999), 128.

5. Erik H. Erikson, *Studies in the Interpretation of Play: Clinical Observation of Play Disruption in Young Children*, Genetic Psychology Monographs 22, no. 4 (New Haven: Yale University Press, 1939), 557–671.

6. Eleanor Pavenstedt, "Marian Cabot Putnam," *Psychoanalytic Study of the Child* 28 (1973): 17–20.

7. George Prochnik, *Putnam Camp: Sigmund Freud, James Jackson Putnam, and the Purpose of American Psychology* (New York: Other Press, 2006). Freud later asked Putnam to assume the presidency of the International Psychoanalytic Association; see "James J. Putnam," in Sigmund Freud, *The Standard Edition of the Complete Psychological Works of Sigmund Freud*, trans. from the German under the general editorship of James Strachey, in collaboration with Anna Freud, and assisted by Alix Strachey and Alan Tyson (London: Hogarth Press, 1957–74); and "An Infantile Neurosis and Other Works," in *Standard Edition of the Complete Psychological Works of Sigmund Freud*, vol. 17 (1917–1919), 271–72.

8. D. J. Lynn, "Freud's Psychoanalysis of Edith Banfield Jackson, 1930–1936," *Journal of the American Academy of Psychoanalysis* 31 (2003): 609–25.

9. S. L. Silberman, "Pioneering in Family-Centered Maternity and Infant Care: Edith B. Jackson and the Yale Rooming-in Research Project," *Bulletin of the History of Medicine* 64 (1990): 262–87.

10. Ernst Kris, "Notes on the Development and on Some Current Problems of Psychoanalytic Child Psychology," *Psychoanalytic Study of the Child* 5 (1950): 24–46.

11. Friedman, *Identity's Architect.*

12. Harold D. Laswell, *Psychopathology and Politics* (Chicago: University of Chicago Press, 1930).

13. Roy R. Grinker, Sr., "The History of Psychoanalysis in Chicago, 1911–1975," *Annual of Psychoanalysis* 23 (1995): 155–95.

14. A. W. Fraser, review of Arnold A. Rogow, ed., *Politics, Personality, and Social Science in the Twentieth Century: Essays in Honor of Harold D. Lasswell* (Chicago: University of Chicago, 1969), *Psychoanalytic Quarterly* 40 (1971): 701–3.

15. "Chicago Psycho-Analytical Society," *Bulletin of the International Psycho-Analytical Association* 15 (1934): 365–66.

16. P. Cushman, "Confronting Sullivan's Spider—Hermeneutics and the Politics of Therapy," *Contemporary Psychoanalysis* 30 (1994): 800–44.

17. "Events in the Psychoanalytic World," *Bulletin of the American Psychoanalytic Association* 4 (1948): 28–31.

18. Dorothy Burlingham and Anna Freud, *Young Children in War-Time in a Residential War Nursery* (London: Allen & Unwin, 1942); Dorothy Burlingham and Anna Freud, *Infants without Families* (London: Allen & Unwin, 1944).

19. Dorothy Burlingham, "The Anna Freud Lectures in America—1950," *Bulletin of the American Psychoanalytic Association* 7 (1951): 126.

20. "Robert Knight," *Journal of the American Psychoanalytic Association* 1 (1953): 5–6.

21. "Events in the Psychoanalytic World," *Bulletin of the American Psychoanalytic Association* 8 (1953): 66.

22. Much of what follows and is otherwise without citation is based on David A. Carlson, "Western New England: The First Fifty Years; An Anniversary Speech," September 14, 2003, New Haven, CT, unpublished paper in the archives of the Western New England Institute for Psychoanalysis, New Haven.

23. Erik H. Erikson, "The Dream Specimen of Psychoanalysis," *Journal of the American Psychoanalytic Association* 2 (1954): 5–56; Erikson, "Events in the Psychoanalytic World," *Bulletin of the American Psychoanalytic Association* 8 (1952): 66–73.

24. Friedman, *Identity's Architect*, 284–91.

25. Gerald L. Klerman et al., *Interpersonal Psychotherapy of Depression* (New York: Basic Books, 1984).

26. Grinker was a Chicago neurologist and analyst who was analyzed by Freud and established a major psychiatry program at the Michael Reese Hospital after World War II. His writings on the treatment of combat neuroses had done a lot to popularize psychotherapy and psychoanalysis at the end of the war.

27. Henry Wexler, Memorandum to the Education Committee, December 9, 1954, in the archives of the Western New England Institute for Psychoanalysis.

28. Carlson, "Western New England," n.p.

29. Albert J. Solnit, "Biography," *Journal of the American Psychoanalytic Association* 44 (1996): 13–25; Joseph Goldstein et al., *The Family and the Law* (NewYork: Free Press, 1965); Jay Katz, Joseph Goldstein, and Allan M. Dershowitz, *Psychoanalysis, Psychiatry and the Law* (New York: Free Press, 1967); Joseph Goldstein, Anna Freud, and Albert J. Solnit, *Beyond the Best Interests of the Child* (New York: Macmillan/Free Press, 1979).

30. August B. Hollingshead and Frederick C. Redlich, *Social Class and Mental Illness: A Community Study* (New York: John Wiley & Sons, 1958).

31. Eugene B. Brody and Frederick C. Redlich, *Psychotherapy with Schizophrenics: A Symposium* (New York: International Universities Press, 1952).

32. Merton M. Gill, Richard Newman, and Frederick C. Redlich, *The Initial Interview in Psychiatric Practice* (New York: International Universities Press, 1954).

33. Theodore Lidz, Stephen Fleck, and Alice R. Cornelison, *Schizophrenia and the Family* (New York: International Universities Press, 1965); Theodore

Lidz, *The Person: His Development Through the Life Cycle* (New York: Basic Books, 1968); Erik H. Erikson, *Childhood and Society* (New York: W. W. Norton, 1950).

34. Lidz, *The Person*; Erikson, *Childhood and Society*.

35. Lidz, *The Person*, n. 118.

36. R. M. Crowley, "Psychiatry, Psychiatrists, and Psychoanalysts: Reminiscences of Madison, Chicago and Washington-Baltimore in the 1930s," *Journal of the American Academy of Psychoanalysis* 6 (1978): 557–67.

37. Norman Cameron, *Personality Development and Psychopathology: A Dynamic Approach* (New York: Houghton Mifflin, 1963); Norman Cameron, "Introjection, Reprojection, and Hallucination in the Interaction between Schizophrenic Patient and Therapist," *International Journal of Psychoanalysis* 42 (1961): 86–96; Hans W. Loewald, "Norman A. Cameron, M.D—1896–1975," *Psychoanalytic Quarterly* 45 (1976): 614–17.

38. Samuel Ritvo and Albert J. Solnit, "Influences of Early Mother-Child Interaction on Identification Processes," *Psychoanalytic Study of the Child* 13 (1958): 86–91.

39. Lawrence J. Friedman, *The Anatomy of Psychotherapy* (Hillsdale, N.J.: The Analytic Press, 1988), xiv.

❧ 4 ❧

The Right Place (and Persons)
at the Right Time

LINDA C. MAYES

Children's developmental maturation is a biological and psychological narrative written partly in their endowment, partly in their experiences, and partly in their parents' own developmental backgrounds. Clinicians working with children implicitly try to predict the future by understanding a child's developmental past—that is, they are engaged in a fundamentally historical endeavor. Hence developmentalists and historians share a naturally collaborative perspective and understand the value of personal narrative for explicating developmental processes. Curiously, however, historians have made little use of developmental narratives gathered in the course of clinical studies and, vice versa, developmentalists have only rarely stepped back from their close study of specific developmental phenomena, capacities, or diagnoses to wonder about the cultural and social contexts of their observations. The Yale Longitudinal Study offers the opportunity to study up close the social context of a remarkably creative piece of clinical scholarship, both from the vantage point of historical narratives and from archives of clinical insight into the lives of a small group of children and families growing up in a small New

England college town during a time of sweeping, dramatic change in the United States.

INTELLECTUAL BACKGROUND AND ORIGINS
OF THE LONGITUDINAL STUDY

Even in science, some initiatives are possible only when an unusual collection of persons comes together at an unusual time. The history of child development as a scientific field of study is primarily a story of the twentieth century and of events in New Haven that set a fertile ground for the scholars of the longitudinal study to come together. We begin in 1911 with the founding of the Yale Child Study Center, which more than forty years later offered a synergistic academic setting for the Yale Longitudinal Study.

In 1911, the Yale School of Medicine provided Arnold Gesell a small room in the New Haven Dispensary to serve as the starting space for his new Yale Psycho-Clinic for children. Devoted to the study and care of children with intellectual and mental disabilities, this clinic was the first of its kind in a medical school in the United States and was the beginning of what is now the Child Study Center. Gesell was one of the first American scholars to focus on the science of child development. Indeed, at the beginning of the twentieth century, there were no major American centers applying the rigorous criteria of scientific research to the issues of growth and development in children.[1] Even as late as 1938 but well into the most productive phase of his career, in a lecture at a conference on growth convened by the Department of Agriculture, Gesell was still imploring scientists to consider the science of child development to be as lawful and ordered as the study of plant biology: "The mind is not amorphous; it is not some shapeless essence or force that comes from the outside and works upon the body. The mind itself has a pattern."[2]

Like many of the physicians, psychologists, and social workers who joined Gesell in his clinic, Gesell was broadly trained. Born and educated in Wisconsin, he spent much of his early career as a classroom teacher and school principal before he went to Clark University to study under G. Stanley Hall (at the time one of the leading psychologists interested in the mental life of children), where he received a Ph.D. in psychology in 1906, three years before Freud's visit to Clark at Hall's invitation. After some time with Terman at Stanford, Gesell decided he needed to understand more about "the physical basis and the physiological processes of life and growth" and entered medical school at Yale on a part-time basis so that he might also work as an assistant professor of education in a new Department of Education at Yale.[3]

Upon his graduation from medical school in 1915, Gesell began a "systematic survey of the developmental patterning of behavior at ten levels in the first five years of life . . . to define normative criteria which could be used in the diagnostic appraisal of normal, deviant and effective infants."[4] This led to the publication of *The Mental Growth of the Pre-School Child: A Psychological Outline of Normal Development from Birth to the Sixth Year, Including a System of Developmental Diagnosis. Illustrated with Two Hundred Action Photographs.* This book, essentially an atlas of early child development, was listed as one of the most notable books published in 1925. The book brought attention to Gesell's use of the new technology of photography, which he applied to such studies for the first time, and to his emphasis on the value of observation. In this study and all his subsequent ones, he made extensive use of both still and motion pictures to provide a permanent and ongoing record of the basic observational data from which his conclusions were derived. He coined the term "cinemanalysis" for the frame-by-frame study of various behaviors that made it possible for this cadre of researchers to view and describe the behaviors independently. Through this innovation, radical for its day, Gesell introduced careful behavioral observation as a standard method for studying the notion of developmental trajectories in childhood. The tradition of careful behavioral observation became the guiding principle of Gesell's clinic, which was named the Clinic of Child Development (CCD). He emphasized that behavioral observation gave direct clues to the lawful, ordered unfolding of the mind and self: "We have used the cinema systematically at Yale because we believe that the outward, patterned manifestations of this inward organism that we call the mind are so lawful, so sequential, and so real that they can be photographed."[5]

In the late 1920s, Yale University developed the concept for an Institute of Human Relations to facilitate cooperative research in the study of man. Included in it were the Clinic of Child Development; an adult psychobiology unit; the graduate divisions of psychology and the social sciences; and a research and clinical group in mental hygiene and psychiatry. Although the multidepartmental collaboration envisioned by the creators of the Institute of Human Relations proved difficult to achieve, the concept interested talented young investigators—and the new facilities housing the institute made possible a wide variety of studies and attracted an increasing number of children and families for evaluation. These developments, along with the founding of a normal nursery school, set the reputation of the clinic in the New Haven community as a place where families might receive guidance and help with their children, a reputation that endured for many decades and surely facilitated the longitudinal study. The normal nursery school also provided a large number of normally developing children for observation; and Gesell issued a steady stream of publications over the next fifteen years. Chief among these were *The First Five Years of Life* (1940); *Infant and Child in the Culture of Today* (1943); and *The Child from Five to Ten* (1946).

As Gesell was approaching retirement age, a university search committee was successful in recruiting a very distinguished academic—Milton J. E. Senn, M.D. Another midwesterner, Senn was born and grew up in Minnesota and was educated there through medical school. Although his early work and publications were largely devoted to issues of chemical imbalance in disease, Senn brought psychoanalysis to what had been the Clinic of Child Development but was now, upon his recruitment, called the Child Study Center. He himself summed up his interest in psychoanalysis:

I looked upon psychoanalytic theory as the way out of the cramped confines of pediatrics as I felt it was generally taught and practiced when I began my medical career. As a resident and instructor in pediatrics at Washington University in St. Louis, where I went in 1929, I became aware of the many behavior problems which practicing pediatricians faced and was appalled by their—and my own—incompetence in dealing with them. Such matters had not been part of my academic exposure and were regarded by a large part of the pediatric establishment as irrelevant to the profession. . . . I became increasingly critical of the pediatricians who studied chemistry and physiology in order to deal with the problems of digestion but shied away from anything dealing in depth with human behavior. It bothered me that so many of my colleagues were antagonistic to psychiatry. . . . At the St. Louis Children's Hospital interest in child development was confined to physical growth, and the strict scheduling of John Watson was the pediatric contribution to parental guidance. When I went to the New York Hospital-Cornell Medical Center in 1933 as an associate in pediatrics, I continued to feel impeded in my own progress toward becoming a contributing pediatrician by the same narrow pediatric viewpoint, and so I determined to equip myself with knowledge of child psychology. My years of formal training in psychiatry were spent at the New York Hospital-Westchester Division and the Child Guidance Clinic in Philadelphia, after which I returned to Cornell with a joint appointment in pediatrics and psychiatry. A personal psychoanalysis and courses at the New York Psychoanalytic Institute provided training in psychoanalytic theory and practice.[6]

Upon returning to Cornell and his teaching role, Senn converted from using the behaviorist ideas of John Watson as a guide and instead began to inform his thinking and research with the ideas of both Sigmund and Anna Freud. Among other topics, he focused on issues around the treatment of children in hospitals, believing that current practices were psychologically traumatic. In 1948, Senn came to Yale and to a center that was already attracting a number of young and creative developmentalists using both experimental and observational methods in an extension and elaboration of Gesell's approaches. Senn brought with him three younger colleagues with whom he had been working in New York. Two were pediatricians—Drs. Sally Provence and Rose Coleman (Lipton)—and one was a child psychiatrist and psychoanalyst, Dr. Samuel Ritvo, one of the first to be trained in that field. He also recruited Dr. Seymour Lustman, a psychologist-psychiatrist-psychoanalyst and brilliant theoretician. These professionals, along with Dr. Albert Solnit who came in 1950 to become the first trainee in child psychiatry in the center and quickly became a core member of the faculty as well, formed the nucleus of a remarkably synergistic team that would soon change the center's agenda.

Whereas the center under Gesell had been largely concerned with normative development, the new faculty, experienced in clinical practice and care, were committed to understanding the roots of developmental problems and in creating innovative approaches for helping children and families in greatest need. They brought a clinical focus to Gesell's normative concentration but they were also very interested in honing their skills in understanding the individual differences in normative development. If not self-identified as such, they were nonetheless "Gesellians" with the notable difference that they chose to use the tools of psychoanalysis to guide their observations and understanding of normative trajectories. But whatever their lens, their method was close behavioral observation followed by detailed discussions regarding the meaning of each behavior. They were focused on developing "methods of evaluating what might be referred to as 'varieties of health' rather than . . . focus[ed] on pathology."[7] Ritvo, Provence, Solnit, and Lustman, each talented clinicians, were an intellectually powerful quartet—assembled and conducted by Dr. Senn—whose curiosity, creativity, and commitments to teaching, caring, and studying were key to setting the tone for the longitudinal study.

Whereas the highly structured developmental testing and observation of children's behavior had been the heart of Gesell's Clinic of Child Development, used to demonstrate and codify the progressive stages of children's early lives, Senn and his colleagues added an increasing interest in the inner life and feelings of the child and in the dynamic relationships between children and their external world—especially in relation to their parents. Indeed, Gesell had also recognized that "in every household, in every nursery, there is a web of life, an interdependence of persons which becomes registered in the growing personality."[8] To that end, Senn had a special appreciation for working with children and families over time and supported a number of longitudinal studies including the work of Provence and Coleman on infants in an orphanage just a few blocks from the center. Their work, published in 1961 in the now-classic book *Infants in Institutions*, demonstrated how depersonalized, episodic care of young children led to depression in the infants and limited their physical, cognitive, and emotional growth.

During Senn's leadership, he encouraged all junior faculty to consider psychoanalysis as one of the basic sciences for research and clinical care. The center was internationally recognized as the base of cutting-edge child psychoanalytic research and thinking and included a number of the major figures in the field as full or visiting faculty. Almost all the faculty members of the Child Study Center received training in psychoanalysis and became leaders in the field of child psychoanalysis. To this day, there are very close relations between the center and the Western New England Institute for Psychoanalysis, and almost all of the supervision and training of child psychoanalysts in the institute is conducted by members of the Child Study Center faculty.[9]

An important consequence of the Child Study Center's interest in psychoanalysis was its close relationship with the Hampstead Child Therapy Clinic (now the Anna Freud Centre) in London. After her father's death, Anna Freud began her work with children in wartime London and established a center in Hampstead that became the world's foremost clinic specializing in child psychoanalysis. It was natural that the two institutions should be attracted to each other. Anna Freud visited Yale a number of times beginning in the 1960s and spent considerable time in both the Child Study Center and the Yale Law School helping to establish linkages that led to the remarkable series of books by Freud, Solnit, and their close friend and colleague Professor Joseph Goldstein of the Yale Law School on the subjects of child placement, custody, and adoption. These books, beginning with the seminal *Beyond the Best Interests of the Child*, developed and defined the concept of psychological parentage as differentiated from biological parentage and had a profound effect not only in the mental health fields but in the juvenile and family legal system as well. Later another distinguished attorney, Sonja Goldstein, joined the research team. The intellectual work behind these books was completed during trips to Yale by Freud and to London by Solnit and Goldstein. Psychoanalysis was in the air at Senn's center and that was given further credence by the link to Anna Freud.

While still in New York before assuming leadership at Yale, Senn's deepening commitment to psychoanalysis had brought him together with another couple, Ernst and Marianne Kris, who would also follow him to New Haven and who would serve as the catalysts for harnessing the enthusiasm and talents of Senn's young quartet and his commitment to psychoanalysis. Recently arrived from Vienna by way of London, Ernst and Marianne Kris were part of the wave of European psychoanalysts fleeing Nazi occupation, a forced immigration that greatly energized the fledgling American psychoanalytic movement.[10] These exiles brought their close contact to the European psychoanalytic community and their keen interest in psychoanalytic metapsychology. Ernst Kris was an art historian who had studied in the Department of Art History at the University of Vienna. One of his professors, Emanuel Loewy, was a close friend of Sigmund Freud and introduced his talented student to Freud. In 1927, Kris married Marianne Rie, the daughter of another of Freud's close friends, Oscar Rie, a pediatrician with whom Freud had published *Klinische Studie über die halbseitige Cerebrallähmung der Kinder* (Clinical study of cerebral hemiplegia in children; 1891). Marianne Kris was already a physician at the time of their marriage and had completed psychoanalytic training in Berlin from 1925 to 1927 as well as an analysis with Freud. A year later, in 1928, both Ernst and Marianne joined the Vienna Psychoanalytic Society. He lectured at the Vienna Psychoanalytic Institute while working as an art historian. Marianne worked closely with Anna Freud with whom she remained lifelong friends. In 1933, Freud asked Kris to become editor of *Imago*, a journal dedicated to the application of psychoanalysis to nonmedical fields.[11]

The Kris family fled Vienna in 1938, the same year the Freuds also were forced to leave, and they joined the Freud family in London. While there, Kris became a training and supervising analyst at the London Institute of Psychoanalysis and Marianne joined the British Psychoanalytic Society. The Kris family stayed in London for two years before they came to New York in 1940. In New York, Ernst Kris was a professor at the New School for Social Research and a lecturer at the New York Psychoanalytic Institute and the College of the City of New York. Marianne Kris started a practice and became an active member of the New York Psychoanalytic Society. In 1945, Ernst Kris cofounded with Anna Freud and Marie Bonaparte the journal *The Psychoanalytic Study of the Child*, where many of the papers and discussions from the longitudinal study would be published and for which Marianne Kris would be chief editor for many years. Ernst Kris met Milton Senn through their mutual psychoanalytic colleagues in New York and after Senn left for New Haven, Kris maintained his New York ties while continuing his friendship with Senn by consulting to Senn's dream team of young clinicians and psychoanalysts. Both Ernst and Marianne Kris became active contributors to the psychoanalytic community in New Haven through their teaching in the medical school as well as their membership in the Western New England Psychoanalytic Society.

Kris brought his art historian's eye for detail to his practice of analysis and became interested in how detailed, close observation of children's behavior under the psychoanalytic lens informed predictions of their later adjustment and development.[12] Ernst Kris was not only well matched with Senn, given Senn's commitment to psychoanalysis; he also was well placed to continue and amplify Gesell's faith in the predictive power of careful behavioral observation. Indeed, it may well be that the longitudinal study would not have had such a substantial commitment had there not already been an institutional commitment to and familiarity with careful observation already instantiated through Gesell.

THE LONGITUDINAL STUDY

Through Ernst and Marianne Kris's interest in observation and prediction, Milton Senn's directorial support, and the collegial analytic climate, the group, including Albert Solnit, Samuel Ritvo, Sally Provence, and Seymour Lustman working with Ernst and Marianne Kris, decided to embark upon a normative longitudinal study to demonstrate the value of the psychoanalytic observational method applied to a family.[13] Using close psychoanalytic study of both parents and children, the group hoped to test some basic principles of psychoanalytic developmental theories and especially to understand the roots of individual variation in normative development:

> It is evident that all clinicians employ prediction implicitly or explicitly in their work with patients. It is inherent in diagnosis and prognosis and employed so routinely that it is taken for granted. This is, of course, equally true for the analyst who, in making an interpretation, has a prediction in mind, though it may be more often preconscious than conscious. Perhaps the major difference between the use of prediction in such a study as ours and in individual practice lies in our effort to systematize the procedure: to re-examine the correctness of the predictions in terms of the relevance of data and assumptions on which they are based.[14]

Through the Krises' connections in London and specifically to Anna Freud, the study was deeply informed by the close process methods of the Anna Freud Centre and by Anna Freud's ideas about "lines of development."[15] The clinical investigators were particularly interested in the developmental vicissitudes of aggression—in part because the issue of how to think about normative aggression in young children was not well worked out in developmental psychoanalytic theory, and in part because the effects of societal aggression on young children's development was a concern of both the Krises and Anna Freud, given their war experiences.[16]

The new longitudinal study, referred to only by that phrase, was ambitious and profoundly optimistic. The study began in 1949 as part of larger one in which newborn infants and their mothers were seen shortly after delivery. During their first pregnancy, mothers were regularly interviewed by social workers who continued their contact with the family, usually in home visits. A pediatrician (Sally Provence) saw both mother and child at well-baby clinics, administered infant developmental tests at regular intervals, and visited the home when the children were sick. All members of the study team observed in the well-baby clinics but the psychoanalysts began their contact with the children when they were just over two. A smaller number of children and their parents were taken into psychoanalytic treatment when the children were three. Thus, the psychoanalytic phase of the study began between 1953 and 1954 with some of the earlier papers from the study reflecting observations from the well-baby clinics and discussions among the group.

The study was ambitious in the scope of what it offered—analytic treatment without cost for every member of the family, both parents and children; free pediatric care provided by Provence; free nursery school at the Child Study Center's preschool program; and what today might be called ongoing family support services through a very astute clinical social worker on the team. Each of these services afforded a different observational lens and every encounter with a family was recorded through detailed, typewritten notes. Between 1953 and 1963, five families were seen for, on average, five to seven years with periodic follow-up after the various family members ended therapy. For at least three of the families, members of the study team continued to have periodic contact with the parents and/or children. Samuel Ritvo saw two of his child patients periodically well into their middle age. The team's remarkable ability to recruit and retain families in such an intensive study speaks both to their sensitivity and skills as clinicians and scholars and perhaps to the general public's more trusting view then for the power and efficacy of science and research to help individuals struggling with life's burdens.

The study was optimistic in its confidence that through this very detailed observational approach, the team would demonstrate the predictive power of the psychoanalytic method. Their faith in observation was a part of the Child Study Center's Gesell tradition. Their optimism was a reflection of the time. Postwar America was an optimistic country, relieved by the war's end and proud of the national accomplishment. Peace had been achieved and the just cause had triumphed. The clinicians who conceived and carried out the longitudinal study had been themselves influenced by the war and the postwar enthusiasm. Further, in postwar America psychoanalysis was immensely popular. Analysts had been practical and therapeutic on the front in their role as psychiatrists for exhausted and traumatized soldiers.[17] At least among some segments of American culture, there was enormous faith in the possibility that analysis could cure all that ailed the soul and mind. In retrospect this view was oversold and overpracticed, but the 1950s were nonetheless a golden time for psychoanalysis in general and for child analysis specifically. Children raised by psychoanalytic insight would not suffer the conflicts and disappointments of their parents—or so the optimism belied. It was also a tremendously buoyant time at the Child Study Center under the first decade of Senn's energetic leadership—a leadership that had forged links to Anna Freud and was propelled by the enthusiasm and optimism of the new faculty who had followed him to New Haven.

The study was also overly ambitious from the perspective of contemporary developmental science. Its investigators were master clinicians but they were not trained investigators, and they felt that their hypotheses would take shape as they gathered their observations. This would have been a fair enough assumption for some investigations, but in this case, the investigators' keen observational skills provided them with far more records and details than they could possibly synthesize and assimilate without a prior plan for how to handle their findings.[18] Ultimately they became overwhelmed by their own data, a problem compounded by the untimely death of Ernst Kris in the middle of the study. Kris was the study team member most skilled with data synthesis, and the group had depended on him to pull the study to its many possible conclusions. Without his talents for organizing, integrating, and synthesizing the material, they continued to collect data but were not able to bring the study to a grand conclusion. Fortunately, they maintained and preserved their meticulous records.

Fifteen papers that built on the ideas of the longitudinal study or explicitly referenced data from it were published between 1950 and 1962, with at least five additional papers by Ritvo reporting in later years on the follow-up of two of the children as adults or theoretically building on observations from clinical material gathered during the study.[19] But each of the clinical scholars would speak for the rest of their lives about the impact of the study on their own thinking. And although we can only surmise from the handful of follow-up letters in the files about the influence on the participants themselves, Ritvo saw one of his patients just a few weeks before his own death and she gave permission for a letter she had mailed him after their last meeting to be read at his memorial service. In that letter, reprinted in Chapter 9, she wrote of the lasting effects on her life of his work with her.

THE YEARS AFTER THE LONGITUDINAL STUDY

After Ernst Kris's death in 1957, the study continued for another six years until the last participant completed analysis. Lasting nearly a decade and a half (1949–1963), the study left a strong imprint on the Child Study Center. The value of making close process psychoanalytically informed observations, working with families over time, and combining clinical care and research (a hybrid that Solnit and others termed "action research") remained central to the Child Study Center for many decades hence.

The Yale Longitudinal Study was among the first in America to engage members of a family in sustained child psychoanalysis and adult analysis. The participating clinicians went on to become leaders in the field and to influence the next several generations of psychoanalysts and child mental health clinicians. While Senn's impact on the center extended beyond the longitudinal study, the work from the study influenced many of his other efforts. He continued to focus primarily on pediatrics and pediatricians. In 1951, Dr. Grover Powers, longtime chairman of pediatrics, retired and Dr. Senn was appointed his successor while maintaining his appointment at the Child Study Center. And through the work of Dr. Edith Jackson—a pediatrician in the Yale Department of Pediatrics whose work centered especially on establishing rooming-in for parturient mothers and their newborn infants, and a psychoanalyst who had spent time with Freud in Vienna—the Department of Pediatrics had generated more interest in psychological issues than had many other pediatric departments around the country.

Senn augmented the faculty of the Yale Department of Pediatrics, and established a free flow of faculty between it and the Child Study Center. One of his additions to the department was Albert Solnit, who, with the aid of social worker Mary Stark, established a strong teaching component in the outpatient department so that medical residents would learn about the developmental and psychological aspects of child health care as he and his colleagues had come to understand them through the longitudinal study. An example was Solnit's work with Dr. Morris Green in developing the concept of the "vulnerable child": that is, the long-term effects on parents and children of neonatal or very early serious illness or threatened illness. Many parents saw such infants as permanently weak or weakened even when they were completely recovered and robust. Both parents and child continued to have an image of vulnerability that was an undercurrent at all times but erupted at the time of real or possible illness. This concept and others of great relevance to the practice of pediatrics were directly linked to the efforts of clinicians in the longitudinal study to understand the enduring impact of early parental perceptions and experiences on their children, and how children in turn might internalize those perceptions.[20]

Solnit succeeded Senn as chairman of the Child Study Center and in that time led the center through another expansion and faculty recruitment. He maintained the close collaboration with Anna Freud that had been so much a part of what Ernst and Marianne Kris brought to the center and served on the board of the Anna Freud Centre. A leader in psychoanalysis, he served as president of the American Psychoanalytic Association and devoted much energy to facilitating the development of child psychoanalysis both through his efforts on the editorial board of the *Psychoanalytic Study of the Child* and as president of the Association for Child Psychoanalysis, originally founded by Marianne Kris along with other child psychoanalytic colleagues.

Long concerned for the needs of poor and underprivileged children, Solnit had been working as a consultant to various school districts and many child-serving social agencies in the New Haven community and the state during the same time he was involved in the longitudinal study. He had demonstrated his interest in the family needs of such children by developing and working with a group of fathers in an inner-city housing project. In the late 1960s, too, he worked with the state government of Connecticut to develop a new department of juvenile delinquency, the Department of Children and Youth Services. Now, as chairman of the Child Study Center, he encouraged other faculty members to do the same. Sally Provence, the consulting pediatrician to families in the longitudinal study, became a supportive consultant to the daycare centers in the inner city and their directors and teachers. She assumed a national leadership role in the area of training young clinicians to work with infants and toddlers, and for over three decades coordinated the center's child development unit. In the tradition of Arnold Gesell but heavily influenced by her psychoanalytic colleagues and experience in the longitudinal study, she developed an assessment instrument for infants and toddlers. She was recognized as an outstanding teacher of the clinical art of understanding something about children's feelings and thoughts through careful behavioral observation. One of the founders of the National Center for Clinical Infant Programs, she summed up much of her experience during and after the longitudinal study in her 1983 book *Working with Disadvantaged Parents and Their Children.*[21]

Lustman continued a distinguished career in psychoanalysis until his untimely death in 1971. He had completed his psychoanalytic training at the Western New England Institute for Psychoanalysis in New

Haven in 1962, toward the end of the longitudinal study. He had then immersed himself in a psychoanalytic career and become a training and supervising psychoanalyst at the Western New England Institute. Just before his death, he had served as chairman of the Task Force on Research and Manpower of the Joint Commission on Mental Health of Children and a councilor-at-large of the American Psychoanalytic Association. Prominently involved in the professional and scientific activities of the American and International Psychoanalytic Associations, he was also actively involved in the training of child psychiatrists through the American Academy of Child Psychiatry.

Ritvo immersed himself in child and adult psychoanalysis, and of the members of the original quartet became the one most committed to the original tenets of the longitudinal study. Devoted to psychoanalysis, he too served as president of the American Psychoanalytic Association and gained a national and international reputation as a master psychoanalytic theoretician and clinician. He was a training and supervising analyst at the New York Psychoanalytic Institute and the Western New England Institute of Psychoanalysis in New Haven, and was a founding member of the latter. He also served as president of the Association for Child Psychoanalysis and was a founding member of the American Academy of Child and Adolescent Psychiatry. Ritvo was most at home with his patients and he maintained relationships with families long after their treatments had ended as evidenced by his sustained contact with the children he had seen in the longitudinal study. Ritvo was a Connecticut native who had grown up in both Hartford and New Haven. He had attended Yale for medical school and was thus familiar in a very personal way with the community that his young patients were growing up in. He maintained through his professional life a keen interest in the clinical issues that he had encountered in the longitudinal study—aggression, eating disorders, the turbulence of adolescence, life-crippling anxiety—and he remained committed to the basic premise of the longitudinal study that it was possible to understand the unfolding of normal development through the lens of psychoanalysis. An engaging storyteller, Ritvo had the most well-honed ability among his colleagues for seeing and synthesizing threads of continuity across the stories of his young patients and their families. He returned time and time again to the material he had heard from his patients in those nine years of the study and used their stories as a prism through which to view much of their current lives. He was also the one member of the group who continued to publish about the clinical material and ideas from the longitudinal study years after the last patient was seen.

The body of papers published from the longitudinal study contributed to the canon of child psychoanalytic theory and practice by underscoring both the strengths and frailties of clinical prediction. As Ernst Kris emphasized, for the clinical team understanding normative individual variations proved more difficult than spotting pending difficulties:

> As time and experience have accumulated it has become apparent to us that in general we have been more accurate in predicting areas of conflict, difficulty and pathology than we have been in predicting conflict-free functioning and the use of normal defenses. This may be due to a general tendency in many of us to look for the "defect." But then also, most members of our team come from clinical fields, and are, by training and motivation, oriented to pathology and to the diagnosis and treatment of disease. Therefore we readily recognize the familiar signs and configurations of pathological phenomena. Knowing that neurotic behavior is repetitive and relatively immune to outside events, we tend to select as having predictive value those characteristics of the mother's personality which reflect the greatest inflexibility. We assume that her behavior with the child is then dominated by her own inner conflicts which make her less aware of the child's needs and therefore less responsive to clues from the child—in other words, that she will, with her pathology, disturb the natural rhythm of the child's evolving endowment and narrow its potentialities.[22]

The lead investigators made explicit their theoretical approach to prediction and were among the first child psychoanalysts to make clear statements regarding the interaction between endowment or biology

with experience. They also put forth the beginnings of a relatively sophisticated notion of developmental psychopathology: that for all individuals certain experiences may, temporarily at least, disrupt a normal
developmental trajectory. While it is sometimes possible to anticipate
any individual response to the unpredictable experience, sometimes
adversity becomes an opportunity for growth and personal transformation that would have not been possible otherwise in the absence of an
unpredicted challenge:

> The more complex and long-term predictions result from our
> evaluation of the mutual interaction of the child's equipment
> with his environment. . . . They were based on (1) what we
> knew about the mother's conscious attitudes and what we in-
> ferred about her unconscious tendencies, and (2) on what we
> knew about the child's innate capacities. There are some fac-
> tors, however, which we cannot foresee. We know very little
> about the nature and intensity of a particular child's drives. In
> addition, we do not know what new facets of the equipment
> the maturational impact will bring to the fore. Another factor
> which we cannot foresee are the real incidents that life brings
> along: for instance, the birth of siblings; a friendly or unfriendly
> teacher when entering school; the role of classmates; grandpar-
> ents moving in or out of the house; the prolonged absence, or
> death of a parent. Though we cannot predict the occurrence of
> such reality events, we nevertheless could make a systematic at-
> tempt at prediction, as if we knew the future, by assuming such
> typical and accidental situations and picturing how the child
> would react to them at different stages of development. When
> such incidents then actually occur, we would be able to learn
> from these "as if" predictions. Unfortunately we did not use
> this type of systematic prediction ourselves, but only realized its
> possibility in the course of the study.[23]

Their understanding of how challenge and adversity may positively
shape development emerged only in the course of the study; it was not

an explicit goal or hypothesis of their original work. With their close attention to parents as well as children, they also brought into clearer focus how early interactions, in concert with the infant's core temperament, formed lasting memories or representations of experiences of being in distress and being soothed. These moments, repeated time and time again, became the core of the infant's self-identity:

> The earliest frustration-gratification experiences leave the imprint of their characteristics on the process by which psychic representations of the object are formed, and on their content. The firm establishment of these object representations plays an essential part in the process of identification. These early experiences consequently leave their imprint on later identifications, including superego identifications.[24]

While others including Donald Winnicott were calling attention at the same time to the centrality of the parent's care of the infant for the child's own personality differentiation, the longitudinal study clinicians brought observed material from work with non-clinically-referred families. The themes of the last sets of papers to emerge from the study in the late 1950s and early 1960s were especially focused on the impact of early parenting relationships on infant self-differentiation and the development of cognitive and emotional regulatory skills.

CONCLUSION

In addition to the contributions of the longitudinal study to psychoanalytic theory and practice, there remains the very important resource of the carefully collected and maintained study materials. Extant records of clinical encounters are particularly common from the late nineteenth and twentieth centuries. Physicians like Oliver Sacks have surely written firsthand accounts of their work with complicated patients and have left detailed narratives of their treatments (as with the case reports of Freud). Medical historians have used medical charts and individual physician records to study changes in the treatment of a disease or changes in the application of a particular procedure.[25] In the professional journals, more case summaries and discussions are available than is true in the popular literature.

Clinical records of psychological/psychotherapeutic interventions have some special features. While there may be a more technical summary at the end of the clinical record, the details of a psychotherapeutic hour are more often written as a narrative describing what the patient said, how he behaved, and how the clinician responded—so-called process notes. These records, then, may be similar to letters in that they provide a window on a person's day-to-day life and the social context in which they live. Yet all process notes are created by the clinician—they are the clinician's summary from memory of a given hour or even set of hours. However hard the clinician may strive for a faithful rendering of the hour's events before applying his own summary, the notes will still be a distilled accounting of what he experienced as most salient—and hence, most memorable. Similarly, however much a clinician may strive to report "just the facts" apart from any theoretical or diagnostic bias, it is impossible to achieve such in any clinical accounting. The internist certain that she is on the track of diabetes will be sure to report the increased appetite and thirst but pay less attention perhaps to the individual's recent job loss or divorce. This is the inevitable nature of the synthetic, integrative, clinically trained mind. Hence, from the historical perspective, process notes of a clinical hour reflect the explicit voice of the patient and the implicit selection and exclusion of the clinician based on his theoretical perspective, working diagnosis, or formulation. Process notes are not a verbatim account of the hour at hand. The notes from the longitudinal study offer both the processed observations of the clinicians and, as much as possible, their efforts to detail the narrative accounts from their participants. These notes are also quite different from diaries and letters in the sense that they are the records of an intimate relationship between two persons who have come together so that one can help another reach greater self-understanding. They are then in one sense highly subjective reports on the lives of families, reports crafted by viewing them through a therapeutic lens that has a particular theoretical concavity.

Often the authors of what years later become "historical documents" wrote their letters and recorded their observations with little appreciation or anticipation of their value to the next generations. The records of the longitudinal study are in some ways exactly those kinds of archives. They were created by a remarkably collaborative and synergistic group of scholars, some looking for opportunities for creative growth in response to their losses from the world war, others young and optimistically just embarking on their careers though still impacted by the recent world upheavals, and still others captivated by the promise of psychoanalysis. They came together with the shared idea that by careful observation and listening, they might learn more about what they could not directly observe, that is, the emerging minds and personalities of their patients. They also believed that from those carefully processed observations, they could not only predict their patients' developmental paths but also might be able to head off future difficulties. It was a hope born of both clinical caring and abiding faith in the power of the psychoanalytic lens. Whatever the longitudinal study yielded in terms of immediate scholarly output, its impact was nonetheless felt deeply by the clinicians whose careers it informed and by the families whose lives became so intimately a part of those careers and clinical stories. The impact of the study may be even more powerfully realized in the carefully maintained clinical records and meticulous notes from all aspects of contact with the participating families. These records, now preserved, are the unforeseen time capsule whose contents illuminate a dynamic time in American family life.

NOTES

1. On the rise of developmental science in the United States, see Emily D. Cahan, "Toward a Socially Relevant Science: Notes on the History of Child Development Research," in Barbara Beatty, Emily D. Cahan, and Julia Grant, eds., *When Science Encounters the Child: Education, Parenting, and Child-Welfare in Twentieth-Century America* (New York: Teachers College Press, 2006); Willem Koops and Michael Zuckerman, eds., *Beyond the Century of the Child: Cultural History and Developmental Psychology* (Philadelphia: University of

Pennsylvania Press, 2003); Davis Pillemer and Sheldon H. White, eds., *Developmental Psychology and Social Change* (Cambridge, Eng.: Cambridge University Press, 2005); Robert R. Sears, *Your Ancients Revisited: A History of Child Development* (Chicago: University of Chicago Press, 1975); Robert Cairns, "The Emergence of Developmental Psychology," in Paul Mussen, ed., *Handbook of Child Psychology*, 4th ed. (New York: Wiley, 1983), 41–102.

2. Arnold Gesell, "Child Development and Individuality," in *Understanding Ourselves: A Survey of Psychology Today* (Washington, D.C.: Graduate School of the United States Department of Agriculture, 1938), 13.

3. Arnold Gesell, *History of Psychology in Autobiography*, ed. E. G. Boring et al., vol. 4 (Worcester, MA: Clark University Press, 1952), quotation on 126.

4. Ibid., 130.

5. Arnold Gesell, *The Mental Growth of the Pre-School Child* (New York: Macmillan, 1925); ibid., 12.

6. Milton Senn, *Insights on the Child Development Movement in the United States* (Chicago: University of Chicago Press for the Society for Research in Child Development, 1975), 45–46.

7. Marianne Kris, "The Use of Prediction in a Longitudinal Study," *Psychoanalytic Study of the Child* 12 (1957): 175–89.

8. Gesell, "Child Development and Individuality," 19.

9. See Chapter 3 on the historical relationship between these two institutions.

10. For example, individuals such as Heinz Hartmann were influential in introducing ideas about adaptation into the classical drive-defense model of psychoanalysis. See Heinz Hartmann and Ernst Kris, "The Genetic Approach in Psychoanalysis," *Psychoanalytic Study of the Child* 1 (1945): 11–30; Heinz Hartmann, Ernst Kris, and Rudolph Loewenstein, "Comments on the Formation of Psychic Structure," *Psychoanalytic Study of the Child* 2 (1946): 11–38; Heinz Hartmann, "Psychoanalysis and Developmental Psychology," *Psychoanalytic Study of the Child* 5 (1950): 7–17; and Hartmann, "The Application of Psychoanalytic Concepts to Social Science," *Psychoanalytic Quarterly* 19 (1950): 385–92.

11. In 1938, when *Imago* was suppressed in Europe, Hanns Sachs established *American Imago*; it was first published in Boston in November 1939.

12. Kris was an internationally recognized authority on cameos; see, for example, Ernst Kris, *Catalogue of Postclassical Cameos in the Milton Weil Collection* (Vienna: A. Schroll & Co., 1932).

13. M. Kris, "The Use of Prediction."

14. Ibid., 176–77.

15. "Lines of development" described Anna Freud's conceptual strategy for indicating the interaction—or harmony, disharmony as she coined the phrase—for different areas of development; see Anna Freud, "The Concept of Developmental Lines," *Psychoanalytic Study of the Child* 18 (1963): 245–65. For example, children's ability to manage their aggression is greatly enhanced by language. Developmental lines also provided overarching organizational constructs to illustrate the various behavioral/functional requirements for achieving autonomy or for moving toward separation/independence. While Anna Freud worked in relative isolation from developmental psychology, she was not alone in her efforts to define overarching phases that integrated physical and psychological developmental functions; see Linda Mayes and Donald Cohen, "Anna Freud and Developmental Psychoanalytic Psychology," *Psychoanalytic Study of the Child* 51 (1996): 117–41.

16. Anna Freud, in particular, wrote about the problem of aggression's playing a role in normative development. See Anna Freud, "Aggression and Emotional Development: Normal and Pathological," *Psychoanalytic Study of the Child* 3 (1949): 37–42; Anna Freud, "Notes on Aggression," *Writings* 4 (1949): 60–74; and Anna Freud, "Relation Aggression, Emotional Development: Normal, Pathological," *Writings* 4 (1949): 489–97. For a description of the Hampstead war nurseries, see Ilse Hellman, "Work in the Hampstead War Nurseries," *International Journal of Psychoanalysis* 64 (1983): 435–40.

17. Daniel Blain and Robert G. Heath, "Nature and Treatment of Traumatic War Neuroses in Merchant Seamen," *International Journal of Psychoanalysis* 25 (1944): 142–46; S. Davidson, "Notes on a Group of Ex-Prisoners of War," *Bulletin of the Menninger Clinic* 10 (1946): 90–100; Felix Deutsch, "Civilian War Neuroses and Their Treatment," *Psychoanalysis Quarterly* 13 (1944): 300–12; Daniel K. Dreyfuss, "Delayed Epileptiform Effects of Traumatic War Neuroses," *International Journal of Psychoanalysis* 30 (1949): 75–91; C. Fisher, "Amnesic States in War Neuroses: The Psychogenesis of Fugues," *Psychoanalytic Quarterly* 14 (1945): 437–67; Ralph R. Greenson, "Practical Approach to the War Neuroses," *Bulletin of the Menninger Clinic* 9 (1945): 192–205; Robert P. Knight, "Treatment of Chronic 'War Neurosis' by the Psychoanalytic Method," *Bulletin of the Menninger Clinic* 6 (1942): 153–63; Robert P. Knight, "The Treatment of the Psychoneuroses of War," *Bulletin of the Menninger Clinic* 7 (1943): 148–55; Margaret Mead, "Anthropological Techniques in War Psychology," *Bulletin of the Menninger Clinic* 7 (1943): 137–40.

18. Ritvo's process notes of his therapy sessions with one patient surpass a thousand pages of typescript.

19. Ernst Kris, "Notes on the Development and so Some Current Problems of Psychoanalytic Child Psychology," *Psychoanalytic Study of the Child* 5 (1950): 24–46; E. Kris, "Ego Psychology and Interpretation in Psychoanalytic Therapy," *Psychoanalytical Quarterly* 20 (1951): 15–30; E. Kris, "Opening Remarks on Psychoanalytic Child Psychology," *Psychoanalytic Study of the Child* 6 (1951): 9–17; E. Kris, "Some Comments and Observations on Early Autoerotic Activities," *Psychoanalytic Study of the Child* 6 (1951): 95–116; Rose Coleman, Ernst Kris, and Sally Provence, "The Study of Variations of Early Parental Attitudes—A Preliminary Report," *Psycholanalytic Study of the Child* 8 (1951): 20–47; E. Kris, "Neutralization and Sublimation—Observations on Young Children, *Psycholanalytic Study of the Child* 10 (1955): 30–46; E. Kris, "The Recovery of Childhood Memories in Psychoanalysis," *Psycholanalytic Study of the Child* (1956): 54–88; M. Kris, "The Use of Prediction"; Samuel Ritvo and Albert J. Solnit, "Influences of Early Mother-Child Interaction on Identification Processes," *Psycholanalytic Study of the Child* 13 (1958): 64–85, 86–91; Anna Freud, "Child Observation and Prediction of Development—A Memorial Lecture in Honor of Ernst Kris," *Psycholanalytic Study of the Child* 13 (1958): 92–116; Samuel Ritvo and Albert J. Solnit, "The Relationship of Early Ego Identification to Superego Formation," *International Journal of Psychoanalysis* 41 (1960): 295–300; Sally Provence and Samuel Ritvo, "Effects of Deprivation on Institutionalized Infants—Disturbances in Development of Relationship to Inanimate Objects," *Psycholanalytic Study of the Child* 16 (1961): 189–205; E. Kris, "Decline and Recovery in the Life of a Three-Year-Old or Data in Psychoanalytic Perspective on the Mother-Child Relationship," *Psycholanalytic Study of the Child* 17 (1962): 175–215 (published posthumously); Samuel Ritvo, "Late Adolescence—Developmental and Clinical Considerations," *Psycholanalytic Study of the Child* 26 (1971): 241–63; Ritvo, "The Psychoanalytic Process in Childhood," *Psycholanalytic Study of the Child* 33 (1978): 295–305; Ritvo, "The Image and Uses of the Body in Psychic Conflict—With Special Reference to Eating Disorders in Adolescence," *Psycholanalytic Study of the Child* 39 (1984): 449–69; Ritvo, "Plan and Illusion," in Albert J. Solnit et al., eds., *The Many Meanings of Play: A Psychoanalytic Perspective* (New Haven: Yale University Press, 1993), 234–51; and Ritvo, "Observations on the Long-Term Effects of Child Analysis: Implications for Technique," *Psycholanalytic Study of the Child* 51 (1996): 365–85.

20. See, e.g., Ritvo and Solnit, "Relationship of Early Ego Identification."

21. Sally Provence and Audrey Provence Naylor, *Working with Disadvantaged Parents and Their Children: Scientific and Practice Issues* (New Haven: Yale University Press, 1983).

22. M. Kris, "Use of Prediction," 186.

23. Ibid., 187–88.

24. Ritvo and Solnit, "Influences of Early Mother-Child Interaction," 80.

25. See, e.g., Gina Kolata, *Flu: The Story of the Great Influenza Pandemic of 1918 and the Search for the Virus That Caused It* (New York: Farrar, Strauss & Giroux, 1999).

❧ 5 ❧

Notes on Notes: Results of the
Yale Longitudinal Study, as Evidence for
History and Psychology

VIRGINIA DEMOS AND JOHN DEMOS

T he remarkable materials produced decades ago by the Yale Longitudinal Study invite many forms of response—substantive,
methodological, epistemological, heuristic—not to mention
straightforward appreciation. There are few similar collections to match
it for depth, density, or duration. Lives come sharply into view; so does
an entire era of American history. What political historians call the "Age
of Eisenhower" reappears in human, and cultural, flesh. Our task in
the current chapter is to evaluate the study's evidence—the so-called
process notes—from both historical and psychological viewpoints. We
discuss the historical first.

The record of the past—any past—is invariably complex and frag-
mented. One basic line of distinction is that which separates verbal and
material evidence—in simpler terms, words and things. In practice, the
former element is usually uppermost; indeed most historians fashion
their work entirely from words.

Verbal evidence divides, in turn, between two broad categories: one
that comprises official records of (for the most part) activities in the

public sphere, and another that embraces personal documents reflecting various aspects of private life. The latter include autobiography, diaries and journals, personal correspondence, even (in certain cases) fictional writing. Clearly, it is with this second category that the process notes from the Yale Longitudinal Study should be grouped. Clearly, too, the notes eclipse most other forms of personal evidence for the close-up, interior views they provide. Historians rarely, if ever, can access such a dense array of privately held thoughts, feelings, and attitudes. Moreover, the notes document childhood experience—always a difficult area for study of the past. At first glance, then, historians might well see the Yale study as a veritable treasure trove.

To be sure, it has some intrinsic limitations. For the most part, it involves observation of, and interaction with, the family members (the Olsens) at the Yale Child Study Center; few parts can be considered truly "first-person." It should be said, though, that it was (and is still) standard practice for a therapist to write detailed "process" notes about encounters with their subjects. Process notes are intended as records of the session and the therapist is trained to write these to reflect as closely as possible the events and interactions with the subject as they actually happened. Some writers are better than others, of course, and this adds yet another dimension to the nature of this kind of record. Thus a scholar who seeks to work with the notes stands at two removes from actual experience: the child (or other family member) is observed by the researcher, who translates this observation into a description that is then read by the scholar.

We might acknowledge, if only in passing, a different type of historical inquiry—one that would explore the development of child psychiatry and psychoanalysis as a discipline (and profession). The process notes express quite fully a theoretical stance and a treatment approach that were central to child psychoanalytic practice at midcentury; thus a historian concerned with such matters will find rich material to investigate. In the present discussion, however, we retain the focus of the Yale Longitudinal Study itself—in short, the behavioral and inner-life experience of a designated "subject" population. Bear in mind, as Mayes details elsewhere in this volume, that the focus of the study was prediction and it was premised on the idea that the more one could know or learn about a child's inner life, the more accurate would be later predictions about successful adaptation.

The stance informing the Yale Longitudinal Study was that of Freudian psychoanalysis and was, moreover, deeply influenced by Anna Freud's work with children, since all of the therapists in the study had close ties to Anna Freud. It is important to remember that by the 1950s there were already several established variants of psychoanalysis—from Melanie Klein to ego psychology. The Freudian approach, with its emphasis on drives, the oedipus complex, and psychosexual development, has shaped the notes and process they inscribe, from first to last. An additional shaping factor of great importance was the study's offer of therapy to each of its subjects. Most of the principal investigators were actually clinicians. Yet the project was not meant to assess treatment outcomes per se, but rather to observe developmental outcomes. The notion was that the psychoanalytic therapeutic setting was an instrument or "lens" for observation. The result is a sort of hybrid: the empirical alongside the clinical, the observation linked to the therapy.

In order to identify additional characteristics here, it may be helpful to compare the process notes with material generated by other longitudinal studies not so directly tied to psychoanalysis. (One of us was herself a participant in such a project, during the 1980s.) The following points of contrast seem pertinent:

1. Many, if not most, longitudinal studies strive to maximize the element of sheer observation, with researchers standing well apart from their subjects; the goal is to be as open-ended as possible. The Yale study was quite otherwise. There, for example, interaction between the child (Evelyn) and the clinician-researcher ("SR," Samuel Ritvo) was continuous and powerful. Over time Evelyn developed a many-sided transference relationship (in psychoanalytic terms), which itself shaped

behavior. From a certain perspective, its effects seem contaminating. Much of the material in the process notes reflects the interventions (indeed the entire underlying viewpoint) of the researcher; open-ended they certainly are not. But as historical evidence such "contamination" need not be disqualifying; indeed some version of the same appears in all records of the past. Historians "correct" for this in many ways—by checking different sources against one another, by carefully evaluating context, by using their own expertise about period and place— and so on. Which is to say that the notes remain—and will always remain—a striking and valuable window into one child's interior world.

2. A common feature of other longitudinal studies is filming—the camera in the service, one might say, of open-endedness, with an attendant presumption of objectivity. (Of course, in such cases much depends on the camera-holder.) Perhaps one might regard the process notes as themselves a kind of film equivalent. But, in any case, they hardly constitute an unfiltered record. Rather, they involve several distinct kinds, or levels, of filtering: the observer's own eye, the theories that shaped his perceptions, his own predilections in note-taking and verbal expression, and so on. There is the further point that film permits all sorts of microanalytic "dissection," that if sequences are broken—and individual frames isolated—a detailed inspection is possible. Such opportunities were not present in the Yale study.

3. Like other longitudinal projects, the Yale study involved multiple observers. Every family had several clinicians attached to them: one for each child; one for each parent; a pediatrician; a teacher, and a social worker. Thus there were many observations of children and parents from a variety of perspectives. These were brought together in the clinicians' group rounds, when every case was discussed. The therapist's interactions with each child occurred one-on-one, however, so in those instances

the therapist was the sole arbiter of both description and interpretation. Had two or more researchers been present, there would have been an opportunity for cross-checking—always a useful strategy—but this entire enterprise was a "hybrid" of research and therapy, a fact reflected in every aspect of the collection and interpretation of the data.[1]

4. The observational context is also—and invariably—a matter of much importance. Whereas many studies of family interaction are conducted within the home—which is, after all, its "natural" environment—the Yale project engaged its subjects in a variety of settings: the home, the nursery school, and the pediatrician's office, as well as the therapist's office. While the bulk of the process notes between the therapists and the children they studied occurred at the Yale Child Study Center—an artificial environment to be sure—there were as many settings for the observations of these children as there were observers.[2] Visits occurred a few times a week with the therapist on a set schedule and on a regular schedule with the nursery school. All of the children in the study were seen routinely by pediatrician Katie Wolf, whose sequenced observations were featured regularly in the discussions of the research team.

5. Like other fully systematized longitudinal studies, the Yale Longitudinal Study followed a carefully sequenced program of observations, starting prenatally and continuing at consistent intervals for the duration of the project. Detailed family histories are a part of every family's record and were elicited by the team's social worker. These "external"/historical data were known to all the team and these sequential observations were discussed on a regular basis.

6. Most longitudinal studies develop elaborate coding systems in order to guide the process of evaluation and interpretation; these, in turn, are meant to ensure consistency across different record sets (and among an array of individual investigators). The Yale study employed a coding system developed

by Marianne Kris (spouse of the study's "lead investigator," Ernst Kris). Marianne Kris was the record-keeper of the Yale Longitudinal Study and she was the one who reviewed the process notes and assigned codes. Her codes were "backed up" by a second coder for reliability. Unfortunately, these weren't preserved and are no longer a part of the record, but the team's clinicians understood the need for coding their work.

7. The Yale study included no systematic sampling procedure that can be evaluated.[3] Subjects were recruited from Wolf's "birth cohort"—families delivering at the Yale–New Haven Hospital whom Wolf had been following in a study on infant development. Because the archival record does not include the total number of infants in her study, how she sampled, how many of these infants were subsequently included in the Yale study, how many declined, as well as differences of class, race, educational level, and so forth, the study's generalizability is obviously limited. This means—for historians in particular— that the material cannot easily be correlated with predominant social, cultural, and demographic patterns in the period it purports to represent.

Each of these points should be taken into account in assessing the representativeness of this sample for New Haven's population at large, for they suggest some inherent limitations of the process notes. Still, much of value remains here. Again, in terms of sheer depth and density, the notes easily surpass results from many other projects of far more "systematic" design.

We move now from essentially methodological issues to more substantive ones. The focus of the process notes (those we have reviewed) is the young subject, Evelyn, and the investigator-cum-therapist Ritvo. In addition, Evelyn's siblings and parents are frequently in view.

Evelyn was the oldest child in her family. Even at the age of four or five, she seemed to operate as a kind of manager of family relations; her

mother, indeed, regarded her maneuvers in this role as "sly." Evelyn believed, apparently for good reason, that the middle child—a somewhat
tempestuous girl named "Wendy"—was her father's favorite, and the
youngest, named, "Tammy," her mother's. (One of the clearest points
in the process notes—at least to our eyes—is Evelyn's outsider status
within this affectional system.) Evelyn expressed her attitudes and feelings freely in her sessions with Ritvo. She offered detailed accounts of her
life at home, reported numerous dreams and fantasies, engaged in vivid
play, and interspersed her behavior with many articulate comments.

Ritvo, for his part, readily took on the role of transference object—
and thus drew his young counterpart into many kinds of meaningful
interaction. His expectations about her behavior were (as noted earlier)
heavily conditioned by his psychoanalytic viewpoint. Thus the process
notes are filled with comments about triangular situations (oedipal and
otherwise), rivalrous concerns, covert and overt evocations of sexual
and aggressive impulses, thinly veiled references to oral and anal preoccupation, and other time-honored Freudian themes. Indeed transference along these lines was not simply noted, but also actively encouraged and elicited by Ritvo's quite pointed interventions. For example,
on one occasion, when Ritvo had evoked some speculations about his
wife, he noted: "I said . . . she and my wife could remain friends and
they wouldn't have to be jealous of one another because I was out of the
way." (Interestingly, "she [Evelyn] didn't think much of this idea"—
with its patently oedipal implication.) At another point, when Evelyn
had been using predominantly brown colors in painting a picture,
Ritvo "said making brown is like making messy stuff, and . . . it is the
same color as bam [feces] which is a messy stuff." (Of this obvious nod
toward anal influence, Evelyn was even more dismissive: "she thought
[it] . . . ridiculous.")

All this—to repeat—seems broadly representative of the emerging
field of child pyschoanalytic techniques in its mid-twentieth-century
incarnation. But during the years and decades since, a different range
of theoretical and clinical viewpoints has emerged, many of them en-
capsulated by the term "object relations." (Another variant is "self psy-

chology.") Were the Yale study undertaken today, the process notes—
and the process itself—would look very different. And even within the
original material, there is ample room for reconsideration. Consider a
few more examples. In one of the sessions described in the notes, Evelyn
elaborated a fantasy—complete with painted pictures—of an excursion
with Ritvo and his wife. First, the three of them entered a restaurant, with
"Evelyn . . . between my wife and me and . . . holding each of us with a
hand." Then they went to a movie; the picture she painted showed "the
three of us in the audience [with] . . . again . . . Evelyn in the middle."
Ritvo understood this to be an oedipal wish: she sought to divide them
by being "in the middle," and (presumably) to replace his wife as Ritvo's
most proximate partner. An alternative explanation might, however,
implicate Evelyn's concurrent (and actual) family situation. The fantasy
could then be seen as an expression of her yearning for an ideal family,
one in which she was no longer an outsider. (Indeed it depicted her as
fully, and happily, "inside"—not to say, surrounded.)

In another session, Evelyn had Ritvo draw her outline on an office carpet, then reversed the procedure by drawing his outline nearby.
She compared the size of the two, and asked Ritvo to draw her outline
again, but this time placing it inside his own. Minutes later she reversed
this as well. Outlines mingled with outlines, until "we had worn out
the chalk" (!). Evelyn's comment was simply: "it was like she was inside
me." Ritvo went from this to another apparently oedipal interpretation:
"I said you mean . . . like a baby is inside its mother." But a different
understanding might feature the theme of merger—the child Evelyn
joined with the longed-for parent, not in a sexual or reproductive way
but rather as a means to achieving emotional reinforcement. (This, too,
would speak to her outsider status—and to her wish for parental closeness of a sort that she seems rarely to have experienced.)

In a third session, Evelyn and Ritvo engaged in a game of tying
each other up. First Evelyn tied Ritvo's hands, and feet, together—then
quickly "cut the bonds and set me loose." Ritvo noted that "she seemed
to lose interest" in the game, and pushed her to explain why. She replied, "I wasn't a bad man; a mistake had been made; I was a good man

instead." This led to a further round, in which Evelyn was the one tied; but "she quickly burst the tie with a laugh." Ritvo persisted with his questioning: "I said she seemed to think it was not a good game to play." In response, Evelyn "shrugged her shoulders, and broke off the game." In his summary of the session Ritvo pondered the matter once more: "she quickly loses interest and seems to need to drop it." Exactly so! Her off-and-on engagement with this line of play, and her abruptly shifting affect, could be understood as signaling some particular discomfort. Ritvo's puzzlement, and his notion of her "losing interest," missed her chronic concern with being found "bad" (not "good . . . instead") and an accompanying fear of punishment ("tied up") by her parents.

There is a further, more general point to be made about many of the interactions described in the notes. To put it simply: again and again Evelyn seems to have wanted from Ritvo a kind of straightforward affirmation—what clinicians nowadays commonly refer to as "mirroring." His own instinct, however, frequently went in a different direction. He sought to probe, to question, to bore in on sometimes tangential details—much of which Evelyn would find intrusive, or simply off the mark. In one instance, Evelyn was writing on a blackboard and asked Ritvo to "copy . . . [her words] in my own handwriting." He complied, but then reverted to their discussion of several minutes before about a figural "ornament" she was wearing that day. She, however, "was very intent on her [writing] and did not respond to any of my proddings about the figure . . . around her neck." A few minutes later he pressed forward with questions about her seemingly friendly demeanor. "I tried [various] approaches to get at . . . her attitude, but she was very intent on writing and having me copy. She also drew pictures, and let me copy them."

On another occasion Evelyn made "a series of paintings," and asked Ritvo "to tell her which paintings are exactly alike and which are close 'disalike.'" He probed for content instead, and inquired about the "story" told in the paintings—whereupon "she flatly and peremptorily told me 'there is no story.'" She then put him "on the other side of the easel, painting as well," whereupon he "complained that she wanted to get rid of me, and with a smile she protested that it was not so." (Her smile acknowledged that, this time at least, he was right.)

Yet another time, in another painting sequence, she again moved him to "the other side." As before, he objected that this meant he "was out of things ... [and] it seemed she wanted me [there] ... so I wouldn't ask questions and be curious." Back and forth it went, in these and similar episodes: Evelyn working away (most often painting) in "a very busy fashion," hoping for a mirrored response—that is, simple confirmation of her interest and effort—with Ritvo offering something quite different. Thus she repeatedly sought, for the most part without success, to supply a major deficit in her experience of life at home.

This is a good point for reiterating the largest difference between the theoretical grounding of the original Yale study and that of the newer viewpoints. Underlying the Yale study was the belief that deep fantasy and underlying drives guide the intrapsychic process—that wishes and attitudes, while they are certainly conditioned by a child's home environment, tend to take on a life of their own. In newer paradigms, home, family (parents and siblings)—one's actual, and evolving, life circumstances—come fully to the fore. The transference, such as it is, has a far more immediate relevance: it is less about the oedipus, more about "self"-organization; based less on instinct, more on actual trauma; less on fantasy, more on current reality. Perhaps the distinction can be captured in a pair of clinical terms: "experience-distant" versus "experience-near." This is not a matter of polar opposites, however. Both sides, or elements, have traction; the key is to get them into proper focus and balance.

We come back, finally, to history. For the process notes from the Yale study reflect their era in many very broad social and cultural aspects as well. The 1950s were, preeminently, a time of familism. An important study of family culture in that period bears the title "Homeward Bound"—and the term does seem apposite, on several levels. The predominant social mode included a virtual "cult" of domesticity, which was inwardly turned and demanded a great deal of personal conformity;

a "baby boom," with a concurrent new emphasis on (and anxiety about) child nurture; exaggerated notions of gender difference, and deeply asymmetrical sex roles; and the various accoutrements of a suburban lifestyle. All this was, in turn, framed against a dark view of the world at large, especially in relation to the Cold War and the threat of nuclear annihilation.[4]

This general climate appears here and there in the notes, sometimes very strongly. The members of the Olsen family were certainly "familistic"—enmeshed with one another, striving to engage as fully and deeply as they could—while at the same time struggling against this, as if avoiding a kind of emotional suffocation. Evelyn's preoccupations, as they emerged in her activities with Ritvo, were wholly family-centered. She made almost no mention of other influences on her life—of school and neighborhood, of playmates and friends—at an age (up to eight years) when, surely, such elements were at least formally present for her.

In addition, nothing in the process notes seems more prominent than Evelyn's preoccupation with gender. Time after time she struggled to comprehend the boundaries, and meaning, of male-female difference. To be sure, some parts of this can be understood as expressing her own idiosyncratic (and intrapsychic) identifications, while other parts may reflect the probings and proddings of Ritvo (who was himself, of course, a representative of the era). Still, such sustained appearances, and reappearances, of a single theme suggest at least a degree of cultural shaping. Moreover, the specific configuration of gender presented by Evelyn conformed closely to 1950s norms. She created play scenes in which she cast herself as a determined homemaker—preparing meals for Ritvo, cleaning up the space they shared, and so on. (At one point Ritvo hopefully volunteered that "I suppose [her] Mommy liked a cleaning-up activity"—and Evelyn confirmed this.) When she looked ahead toward adult life, she imagined herself as an actress—one of the few careers in which women of the time were readily visible—and wrestled with the problem of combining that pursuit with the role of wife and mother. At one point, she declared the two to be wholly incompatible:

according to Ritvo, "she said, 'No, you can't do both' . . . [Thus] she won't have children." At other points she hedged her bets, and hoped for some strategy; yet even there the possibilities seemed severely limited. All of this mirrored her cultural surroundings, in which the ideal of woman-as-homemaker remained paramount.

Another recurrent theme in the notes, related but different, embraces all manner of personal transformation. Male-to-female is part of this, but there is much else as well. Humans and witches; clowns and witches; Ritvo as monkey (and then as goulash); it is as if Evelyn lived amid a crowd of changelings. This, like her constructions of gender, can be seen as reflecting both cultural and intrapsychic factors. On the psychological side lay a fear of changeable others, perhaps most especially of her father with his sudden, unpredictable "rages"; on the cultural side a deep undercurrent of anxiety about containing difference and conflict, potential or actual. (The period-specific political strategy of "containment"—that is, holding the threat of Soviet aggression in close check—can also be referenced here. Indeed, some of Evelyn's play refers directly to armies, to battle "campaigns," " forts," and other things military.) If firm boundaries could be carefully maintained, if limits were accepted and old verities held high, if change itself were kept to a minimum—that way lay "security," not to say basic survival. One feels this concern—combined with a partially suppressed fascination—in Evelyn's world, as a reflection of its presence in the world at large.

The Yale study was, in many respects, a product of its time. Its very structure and coloration reflected, at least implicitly, the broad-gauge culture of the age of Eisenhower. (The comforting political persona of "Ike," as he was known, seemed itself a bulwark of containment—and a safeguard against threats posed by incipient change.) By the same token, the Yale study reflected the professional culture of psychoanalysis at a key point in its own evolution, when the original Freudian precepts held sway in an as-yet-unmodified "classical" form. (The reputation of Freud—the influence of Freud—had never been higher, before or since; and this group of therapists, it should be noted, were particularly influenced by Anna Freud and her work with children.) None of this time-boundedness should be surprising. All of history is rooted in a particular irony: both the evidence it leaves us, and the perspectives we use to order and understand the evidence, are marked by a kind of doubled process—the shaping effects of then and of now.

NOTES

1. See Linda Mayes's description of the conceptual and theoretical framework of the Yale Longitudinal Study in Chapter 4.

2. It is important to note that there is (or was) a methodological school of thought that privileged "laboratory" studies over every other setting, arguing that more "naturalistic" influences were not only imperfect but also "contaminating" because they effaced the better controlled, purposefully neutral, institutional setting; see, e.g., John B. Watson, *Behaviorism* (New York: W. W. Norton, 1925).

3. Although the archival records are missing these elements and the generalizability is limited, this does not mean that issues of recruitment and selection were not considered. We just do not have the full record to be able to adequately assess the question.

4. See Elaine Tyler May, *Homeward Bound: American Families in the Cold War* (New York: Basic Books, 1988).

৵ 6 ৵

Archiving the Records of the Longitudinal Study of the Child

DIANE E. KAPLAN

Milton Senn came to Yale University in 1948 as Sterling Professor of Pediatrics and Psychology and as the first director of Yale's reorganized Child Study Center. Having received his M.D. from the University of Wisconsin in 1925, Senn had spent two years as a Commonwealth Fund fellow studying to become a psychoanalyst. When he arrived at Yale, he already had an abiding interest in bringing the insights of psychiatry to bear on the health care of children.

By January 1949, Senn had already outlined a program of research on the personality development of children from birth to adolescence. He wanted to study a variety of problems in the field of human behavior stemming from infancy and childhood and to modify practices in child rearing, child care, and education to address some of them. In his outline, he proposed a study that would employ a long-term appraisal of the same group of children beginning with prenatal interviews of parents and continuing through direct observations of children made in infancy, and in nursery, primary, and secondary school. In hopes of receiving outside financial support for this ambitious interdisciplinary study, Senn submitted a two-page proposal to Dr. Katherine Bain at the U.S. Children's Bureau.[1]

It would be more than a year before the Yale Child Study Center's longitudinal study of the child commenced and along with it, the accumulation of a voluminous assortment of records that are now housed in Manuscripts and Archives in the Yale University Library. The archivists at Yale, in trying to understand and describe the materials in their keep, sought to learn about their context and explain why the records were created and the purposes they originally served. Quite often records of projects speak for themselves; they include organizational minutes, plans of work, periodic reports, and the like. This is not the case with the records of the Yale Longitudinal Study of the Child. The records in the Yale Library comprise methodical notes of research observations of study subjects, but surprisingly, the records do not include administrative documents concerning the founding of the study. In order to piece this history together, the archivists were dependent on a small number of documents in personal papers housed at the National Library of Medicine and the Library of Congress as well as a substantial trove of records at the Rockefeller Archives Center.[2]

In the spring of 1950, Senn learned that the Children's Bureau would probably not be able to fund his proposal for at least another year, but he continued to develop his ideas for the study in discussions with others at Yale. Among those involved at this formative stage were Ernst Kris, Katherine Wolf, Sally Provence, and Edith B. Jackson. With the exception of Jackson, these participants had come to Yale within a year of Senn's arrival.[3]

Edith Banfield Jackson, like Senn, had trained first as a pediatrician, receiving her M.D. from Johns Hopkins University in 1921. Jackson held various teaching positions at the Yale University School of Medicine from 1924 to 1929. After a brief hiatus in which she underwent training and analysis with Sigmund Freud, she returned to Yale in 1936 as a professor in pediatrics and psychiatry. She was a pioneer in family-centered maternity and infant care and parent-infant bonding and is best known for her work on the Yale Rooming-in Research Project, which she directed from 1946 to 1952. She developed the rooming-in plan to allow parents to have an increased role in the care of their newborn children within hospitals.

In 1949, Ernst Kris received an appointment as a lecturer in psychology at the Yale Child Study Center. Kris had worked with Freud and had become a member of the Vienna Psychoanalytic Society in 1927. From 1930 until 1938, when he fled from Austria, he was a member of the faculty and a training analyst at the Institute of Psychoanalysis in Vienna. He escaped to England where he was a lecturer at the London Institute of Psychoanalysis. He came to the United States in 1940 and joined the New School for Social Research. During World War II, he was also a lecturer at the New York Psychoanalytic Institute and the City College of New York. In 1945, he helped found the journal *The Psychoanalytic Study of the Child.*

Katherine Maria Wolf received her Ph.D. in psychology from the University of Vienna in 1930. Between 1930 and 1938 she was a research associate there, working with Charlotte Buhler and Hildegard Hetzer. One of her early achievements was to aid in the development and standardization of the Viennese developmental scales for the first year of life. After the outbreak of war in 1939, she relocated to Geneva, where she studied sociology and worked with Jean Piaget. She emigrated to the United States in 1941 with her companion, Annemarie Leutzendorf. In New York, Wolf taught graduate psychology at the City College of New York. In 1949, she was invited to lecture on a regular basis at the Yale Child Study Center.

The youngest among the four, Sally Provence, was born in East Texas in 1916. She completed her undergraduate work at Mary Hardin College and received her M.D. from Baylor Medical College. As a practicing pediatrician, Provence became interested in child development and in 1949, she began to work in the Yale Child Study Center.

Kris realized the opportunities that Jackson's rooming-in project provided. It was already collecting data on the personality of expectant parents and on the early relationship between mother and child. The project staff could contribute the benefit of its experience and data on

cases. While the rooming-in project limited its focus to the infancy period, however, the proposed child study project would be directed to the
collection of material for a longer-range study. In order to proceed, additional families would have to be recruited. Given the projected length
of the study, new services beyond those required in infancy would also
be required.[4]

It is not clear from the documentary evidence when Senn decided to
submit his more robust proposal for the study to funding sources other
than the U.S. Children's Bureau, but by April 1950, Dr. Charles Warren
of the Commonwealth Fund had reviewed Senn's idea. In a memo, Warren recorded that he had met with Senn to discuss "a research program
which he [Senn] has been organizing in his mind for some time. He said
that the focus of it would be on the problems of child rearing and child
care and how to improve them. He said that parents' 'emotional blocks'
make for difficulty in the optimal handling of their children, and he is
anxious to study these and find out how to relieve them."[5]

Senn's early thinking about the study, which reflects his experience
as both a pediatrician and a psychoanalyst, is recorded in a May 3, 1950,
letter to Dr. Lester J. Evans at the Commonwealth Fund, following a
visit that Evans made to New Haven. Senn wrote,

> There is yet no science of child development or child rearing.
> Scientists working in the fields of psychology, anthropology, so-
> ciology and medicine are aware of the lack of validated data. . . .
> It is the aim of the Child Study Center to carry on research in
> this field, with a continued interest in the methods of training
> professional people so that they might practice in an effective
> fashion the knowledge brought to them through research. . . . If
> parents and professional people ever had a body of facts which
> might lead to what has been called a science of child rearing,
> there would be available to the parents serviceable information
> on how to treat the child.[6]

Senn elaborated on what needed to be studied: "infant feeding, scheduling versus non-scheduling, training for cleanliness, methods of dealing

with aggression, and interpretation of the anxieties and frustrations involved in growth" in order for there to be fewer behavioral difficulties confronting parents and professionals.[7]

The Commonwealth Fund leadership was obviously impressed with Senn and his ideas.[8] In June 1950, Senn received more than $37,000 from the fund for a one-year pilot study, chiefly methodological, with the understanding that he could come back with a proposal for a longer term of support. The post–World War II optimism about the potential of science to improve the lives of individuals is reflected in a response to Senn's initial conversation with the Commonwealth Fund: "They [Senn and his colleagues] have the hypothesis that certain behavior disturbances can be predicted if enough is known about the attitudes and emotions of the parents. His idea, further, is that with such information these disturbances can be prevented. . . . He thinks that somehow a reasonable amount of preventive therapy can be combined with objective observations on the attitudes and behavior of the parents and children without jeopardizing the validity of the study."[9] That is, Senn saw this research as being interdisciplinary, with social science joining medicine in the service of research in child development.

In its original conception, the children were to be followed through their first five years of life, ending when each child began attending regular school. In fact, however, the study commenced with a focus on the pregnant women and their husbands, including their feelings about pregnancy and attitudes about child care and childrearing. Each parent was to "be interviewed separately for as many times as possible, beginning as early in the pregnancy as one may" in hopes that understanding the "emotional climate or the life-space of the parent-child unit (family)" would lead to a construction of personality types and the ability to predict certain kinds of infant behavior "in eating, sleeping, social behavior, learning difficulties, anxieties etc."[10]

Senn was overly optimistic about the number of families that the study could follow: "It is contemplated that from three to five new cases monthly would constitute a caseload that could be followed without too much difficulty (ie. 36–40 cases yearly). Whether this number should

be increased would depend on the volume of work entailed in the follow-up in the succeeding years of the study." He then projected a cost
of $33,500, mostly to cover the costs of three and a half staff positions
needed for the first two years of the research.[11]

In July 1950, the researchers began recruiting expectant mothers as
potential participants. They may have been piggybacking on the recruiting efforts still under way for the Rooming-in Project. The mothers were
to be white, married, between the ages of eighteen and thirty-five, ex-
pecting their first child, and having no severe physical or mental health
complaints. The recruiters also looked for mothers who expected to live
in the New Haven vicinity for several years. Initially, they succeeded in
attracting twenty-two families.

In the first year, as planned, the project staff interviewed expectant mothers, though they had less success getting fathers involved in
the interviewing process. In this first phase of the project, Charlotte
del Solar, a psychologist, and social workers Jeanette Mohr and Laura
Codling did the initial interviewing, and the accumulation of data on
the families began. The investigators interviewed the expectant parents,
focusing on their feelings and attitudes about pregnancy, child care,
and childrearing. Before the birth, a researcher interviewed the mothers several times. Along with standard demographic queries, mothers
were asked about their family history, relation to people currently in
their environment, attitude toward pregnancy, expectations about their
future child, and their plans for child care. Most mothers were given
psychological tests.

The second phase began when the first child was born in January
1951. This phase focused on the child until he or she entered nursery
school. Observers were with the mother during delivery to record her
feelings. Pediatricians Sally Provence or Rose Coleman were present at
the delivery and submitted detailed reports of the newborn's first medical examination. Katherine Wolf observed the newborns twice daily for
periods of about five minutes. She believed that only in the first few
weeks after birth was it possible to distinguish clearly between constitutional and environmental factors that affect a child's development.

Over the following months, the social workers visited the home at approximately six-week intervals to continue the dialogue about child care and parenting begun in the prenatal period, to observe the physical home environment, and to meet other family members, including extended kin. The pediatricians saw both mother and child at well-baby clinics, administered tests at regular intervals to assess the child's general developmental level, and visited the home when the children were sick. The pediatrician thus became an observer of the child and family and would continue to assess the child's maturation and development. This phase of the project ended when the children turned two.

The Commonwealth Fund, pleased by the talent of the assembled staff and the progress of the research, continued to underwrite the costs of the project with an additional grant of $67,410 in May 1952 and $5,000 in May 1953. All the observations and note-taking generated a tremendous amount of data. The time-consuming process of indexing, coding, and sorting this data led to a backlog of material, and by early 1952 the study researchers had decided to admit no new families. Already in the first year, the project staff realized that they could not keep up with the original plan of bringing in three new cases each month. They would only add children to the study by following births of siblings.

When in the third year the children entered the Yale Child Study nursery school they were observed by psychoanalysts and nursery school teachers, as well as pediatricians during periodic examinations in the well-baby clinic. From ages three to five the children were also seen by an analyst in the therapy room. The analysts also initiated individual exploratory play contacts. Originally intended for purposes of observation and exploration, in some instances these interactions became therapy and child analysis sessions as well. The team studied three children intensively through play therapy and via interviews three times a week by a child psychiatrist. Three other children were studied somewhat less intensively through one session with a psychiatrist every other week. Ernst Kris was principally in charge of this phase of the work.

Kris convened weekly staff conferences to review the collected data. Kris would lead these discussions, which all members of the research team attended, when he came to New Haven from his home in Stamford, Connecticut. Later Kris would also host Friday evening meetings in his home to discuss the psychoanalytic treatment of specific children. Study staff members were anxious to establish the relationship between the observational data and the interview materials. The unique aspect of their analysis of the children's behavior and emotional adjustment was that it could be compared not to the parents' recollections of their children's early behavior, but with their early development as observed by the pediatricians and others on the research team.

Although the longitudinal study was a group endeavor (with all data considered, correlated, and analyzed by the group), it became increasingly apparent to the members of the research staff that their interests, which were oriented toward psychoanalysis, child psychology, or sociology, were so divergent that a division of the study would prove more fruitful. In July 1953, they agreed to officially divide into independent investigations. One group, led by Katherine Wolf, would study personality development through the prenatal, neonatal, and infant stages. Another team, composed of Al Wesson, John Mabry, and Jeanette Mohr, planned to analyze the data to understand the process of integration of the firstborn child into the family. The Kris group, the third and most successful group, focused on later personality development. The researchers in this section, who were psychiatrists, pediatricians, social workers, and nursery school teachers, were to study the emotional behavior of the children in their relationships with mothers and others in situations in which anxiety, aggression, withdrawal, and various types of defensive behavior would be observable.[12]

If one searches the bibliographic databases, one can find any number of books, chapters, journal articles, and papers attributed to Ernst Kris and those who worked with him (Marianne Kris, Rose Coleman Lipton, Sally Provence, and Samuel Ritvo) on the data that covered the children through their first five years. The research by the other two investigative teams was never published.

For her team, Wolf invited two postgraduate students in psychology, Martin Kohn and William Kessen, to assist her in analyzing the collected data. One of Wolf's major contributions to the study was her method for systematic and exhaustive observation of the mother and newborn. She developed an ingenious system of "motor shorthand" with sketches, to record the range and intensity of the infant's activity. She described her research as the study of overt manifestations of the basic physical and psychological equipment of infants.[13]

Wolf detoured into a content analysis of the voluminous interview material on the mothers during pregnancy. She intended to publish two volumes: one a study of ten mothers during the prenatal period, and the other an analysis based on the neonatal observation of the infants. By the end of 1956, she had submitted for review a manuscript of the first volume, which included lengthy biographies of the ten babies. The reviewers' comments on the manuscript, tentatively entitled "Origin of Individuality: Evaluative Observations on Ten Children in Their First Two Years," were mixed, and Wolf did not have time to address them before her untimely death on September 15, 1957. Although several junior members of the research team expressed interest in finishing the book in the years following, this part of the study ultimately languished. Wolf's notes and manuscripts were preserved by a member of the team and donated to Manuscripts and Archives.

In reading the data to understand how a firstborn child was integrated into a family, the team of sociologists Wesson and Mabry and social worker Mohr looked at family background, the emotional atmosphere in the home, environmental happenings, parents' experiences, their childrearing practices, and information regarding the child's activities. Their efforts to analyze the interviews and observations made during the first two years of life were slowed when Mohr left New Haven in 1954 to accept a position as a professor in the Simmons College School of Social Work. Work proceeded through correspondence and occasional visits. Wesson had a full teaching load and the analysis and writing fell to Mabry, who apparently left Yale by the fall of 1955. (Both Wesson and Mabry went on to teach and research in the field of medical sociology; Wesson at the University of Washington and at Brown University, Mabry at Syracuse and then at the University of Kentucky.)

Though we know that Mohr, Mabry, and Wesson completed a book manuscript titled "The New Family," it was never published, and there are no records available at Yale documenting their analytical work.[14]

Previously housed in various offices at the Child Study Center, the accumulated notes, reports, photographs, interviews, and analyses generated by the study were transferred to Manuscripts and Archives beginning in 1996. Several separate gifts or accessions from various faculty members and project staff members now comprise the Records of the Child Study Center, School of Medicine, Yale University, concerning the longitudinal study, circa 1951–1965 (inclusive). The Department of Psychology, at the behest of William Kesson, had transferred to Manuscripts and Archives in 1989 what was then thought to be the personal papers of Katherine Wolf. When archivists realized that her records complemented and in some cases duplicated those records coming from the Child Study Center, they determined that the Wolf materials should be kept as part of the records of the study.

The accumulated day-to-day records of observations, results of tests, and notes of interviews by pediatricians, teachers, and therapists present a detailed accounting of the moment-to-moment activity of the child subjects and an unusually rich description of family life in the 1950s in urban America. Figure 2, drawn from a Commonwealth Fund report, outlines the assorted types of material that study investigators created.[15]

Even when the records were being held at the Child Study Center, researchers had begun to mine this material for their historical studies. In transferring the records to Manuscripts and Archives, the donors intended to preserve this valuable resource while continuing to make it available to scholarship. Their goals paralleled the mission of the department, which is to collect and preserve materials of historical value. The archivists want these records to be used rather than stored away, never seeing the light of a reading room lamp. The repository also provides a safe environment and promotes proper handling of the documents in order to ensure their long-term survival. To promote these goals, the archivists followed standard archival practice.

In order to make records accessible, archivists arrange and describe them. Whenever possible, they organize the records according to their original order and filing systems. A group of records that are related as the result of being created, received, or used in the same activity are described as a series. The Yale archives staff established five series within the fifty-three linear feet of the longitudinal study records: I. Family Data; II. Administrative Files; III. Photographs; IV. Katherine Wolf Records; and V. Data on Families (duplicates).

In keeping with standard archival practice, the archivists also created a finding aid to serve as a guide to the records. It is somewhat analogous to the preface, table of contents, and index to a book. In it, the researcher can find information on how and when the records came to the archives, their provenance, and any restrictions on access or specific terms governing use. The finding aid will also include information on the organization that created the records, as well as a description of the collection's size, contents, document types, arrangement, and subject matter. It provides the researcher with a container list or inventory, which itemizes the contents of a box or a folder in summary fashion; archivists seldom describe individual documents. The container list allows the researchers to select specific materials that they wish to examine further. Previously available only on paper, Yale's finding aids are now online and often can be found using search engines such as Google.

Figure 3 provides a listing of the document types found in the research records.[16] These types of records now comprise the files included in the first series, Family Data, which can be found in the first twenty-two boxes of the records and which make up more than half the material in the records. Study staff wrote their own notes and observations, which researchers will find as revealing about professionals' attitudes as they are about the subjects they studied. These were reproduced, some as typed carbon copies and others as mimeographed copies, and filed in notebooks to be shared with other project staff. The archives received multiple copies of these notebooks and selected the most complete, most legible copy of each volume for inclusion in the first series. The duplicate copies were placed in the fifth series.[17]

The family data are organized by family name. (See Figure 4 for a sample page of the finding aid from the first series.) There are compiled records for ten families who were followed for the duration of the project, as well as six families who discontinued their participation before the project ended. The names listed in the finding aid are not the families' real names; rather they are code names developed by the project staff for use in their research discussions. They used a third set of names when referring to family members in the publications that resulted from the study. Some of the earliest data may contain a family's real name and other personally identifiable information.

The data cover the years of each family's participation in the study, generally from 1950 through 1959. The narrative notes and other documents are arranged in chronological order for each family. There is one box of data for the six discontinued subjects. By contrast, the data for nine of ten families fill approximately one box per family. For one family the record is much more extensive, with twelve linear feet of records covering the years 1951 through 1964, and includes notes on work with both parents and three siblings. Additional data that pertain to individual families are included in the third series, Photographs, and the fourth, Katherine Wolf Records. The photographs include posture pictures of the nude children taken to augment the project's textual data.

William Kessen preserved the records of Wolf's research and writing, and it is through his efforts that we know of her role in the study. These records include study data for approximately twenty-four families. Her observations in the hospital, including her drawings in "motor shorthand," and in the early well-baby clinics, document the first child in the ten families who participated fully in the longitudinal study as well as the six who discontinued participation and several additional families. For the discontinued subjects there may be only two data folders, but for families who went on to full participation in the project, there are as many as thirty-six folders of observations. The Wolf records also include her correspondence and drafts for her writings about the study participants.

Surprisingly, there are few administrative files included in these records. There are no drafts of grant proposals, correspondence with funding agencies, financial accounts, or agendas for meetings. There are, however, some notes on research meetings detailing the issues raised there, as well as evaluative observations for nine of the ten fully participating families and records of follow ups with participants from the 1970s and 1980s. These records are in the second series.

Because the Yale Longitudinal Study took place in an era before research protocols had been established for the use of human subjects, participants were never asked to sign release forms granting future researchers access to their records. These files contain medical records, therapy notes, and personal revelations of study participants who never expected their lives to be the subject of the scholarly magnifying glass. Interviews with expectant mothers, for instance, contain discussions of their health history, religious beliefs, and feelings about their husbands and other members of their families, as well as their views on marriage and childrearing. These subjects are of historical interest.

In order to make these records available to research, the archives staff needed to consider how to balance the scholar's desire for access to sources with the subject's right to privacy and confidentiality. Archivists have been dealing with these issues for a long time, but our basic position is clear: "A repository should not deny any researcher access to materials, nor grant privileged or exclusive use of materials to any researcher, nor conceal the existence of any body of materials from any researcher, unless required to do so by law, institutional access policy or donor or purchase stipulations."[18]

This statement alludes to the guidance provided by institutional policies on access to its records. Yale Corporation regulations, for example, restrict access to university records for a minimum of thirty-five years from the date the records were created. Some categories of records are given more stringent access restrictions. Student records (defined as credentials, grade sheets, correspondence, reports, notes, applications, and all other records pertaining to past and present students) are closed for the life of the student plus five years or for seventy-five years from the date the student graduates or withdraws from the university, whichever is longer. Similarly, personnel records of the university's faculty and staff, including search committee and tenure review files, are closed for the life of the person plus five years or for seventy-five years after an individual's retirement or departure, whichever is longer.

These restrictions on access are obviously designed to protect the individual's right to privacy. The time limits imposed ensure that a student or personnel record is released only when the individual concerned is deceased. There is then no problem in opening confidential records since the right to privacy ceases upon the individual's death. The Yale Corporation's regulations recognize the need for exceptions that would allow earlier access to documents for scholarly purposes. These must be authorized by the university secretary after consultation with the university archivist.

Deciding how to give access to the child study records would have been easy if we could have adhered to these regulations. These policies and regulations, however, do not apply to confidential data files received as part of a donation from an individual investigator or his or her heirs. When the archives receive data files from an individual, as is the case with the longitudinal study records, the staff must work with the donor to establish the most suitable means to administer the use of these files. The donor of data files for research involving human subjects should be able to explain to the archivist how the data were collected, whether subjects provided releases, and if the data divulge personally identifiable information. This information will help the archivist determine adequate terms to govern the use of the records so as not only to protect the privacy and confidentiality of the subject but also to provide fair and equitable access. The archivists must not be placed in the position of determining who has a "legitimate" research need to see the papers.

If the donor feels that without exception no research project is so important as to outweigh the subject's right to privacy, then no one can have access until a period of closure, similar to that for the university's student or personnel files, has elapsed. We did not consider this possibility with the Yale Child Study records. Since the donors had already given some researchers access to these files when they were still housed in the offices of the Child Study Center, some cats, so to speak, were already out the bag.

With the donors, we considered the possibility of some less drastic means of restricting access. Could we, for instance, remove the personally identifiable information from the files, a process referred to as redaction? The Health Insurance Portability and Accountability Act of 1996 (known as the HIPAA Privacy Rule) identifies eighteen elements that could be used to identify an individual or the individual's relatives, employers, or household members. While some of these elements, such as Internet addresses or facsimile numbers, did not exist in the 1950s, reading through the HIPAA list does suggest how labor-intensive and costly the redaction process could be.[19] First, someone would have to read each page of each document. If personally identifiable information was found, the original page would need to be removed and copied. Where needed the text would be blacked out on the copy, which would then be copied again to ensure that eradication was complete. This copy would be placed in the papers, which could then be opened. Similarly, facial features would be blackened in photographs to protect the identity of the individual. Redaction is a process that can only be undertaken when the quantity of the material to be redacted is small. In some cases, the researchers are asked to pay for the redacting process, though one could argue that imposing such fees for access fails the equitability test for researcher access.

Because the quantity of data in the child study records was so large, we could not contemplate reading each page. The earliest data do include forms completed by family members, and the redacting of these would not have been an insurmountable task. Reading through narrative notes and summaries of conversations is another matter indeed. Though we know that at some point the staff creating the data started using code names for family members, without extensive reading we could not be sure when in the records this happened.

At one point, we investigated the cost to digitize the entire data series. Digitization sounded attractive because it would allow researchers to search key words relevant to their subject, such as "aggression" or "breast-feeding." Theoretically, too, the archives staff could have searched the digitized material and located the instances where actual family names appeared. This information then could have been redacted in the digital copy, which could then be opened to all researchers. Unfortunately, while digitization was possible, if expensive, the optical character recognition (OCR) needed to turn pixels into letters and words was not. Records created on faint carbons, with differing typewriters and on various colored papers on a mimeograph machine, proved to be too great a challenge for the existing OCR software. Our tests of these documents returned gibberish.

We have sometimes employed a nondisclosure agreement that includes a waiver signed by the patron. This waiver states that although the patron will be allowed to see confidential records, he or she cannot disclose names or other information that could be used to identify an individual, and that violations of this agreement could lead to legal action. The patron must also agree to hold the repository harmless if legal proceedings are instituted.[20] Not all donors are willing to accept such an agreement. William Kessen, who donated the Katherine Wolf materials in the Yale Child Study records, was of this mindset.

Proposals for research with human subjects currently must be submitted to some form of institutional review board (IRB), which ensures the ethical treatment of human research subjects. The donors of the longitudinal study records did not feel that access to these records could be governed by Yale's IRBs. While any research conducted by a Yale-affiliated researcher that involves the use of human subjects must be reviewed by one of the four Yale institutional review boards, not all of those seeking access to the records would be Yale affiliated. Approximately half of the registered readers in Manuscripts and Archives have no connection to the university. Further, the review procedures concern the collecting of new data and its impact on subjects rather than the repurposing of previously collected data.

The donors and the Yale archivists eventually agreed that the best solution was for the files to be restricted until 2050 (one hundred years from the study's inception). This date would presumably ensure that all the participants were deceased. But the donors had not wanted a complete closure of the records and were, in fact, eager for the records to be used. We thus needed a way to decide, on a case-by-case basis, who has a legitimate need to use the records. Since many of the records' donors were now deceased, we needed to find an authorizing agency that was currently active in the field and would presumably exist for the duration of the restriction. Consequently, researchers are now informed that in order to use the records before 2050, they must secure written authorization from the coordinator of the Anna Freud Centre Program at the Yale Child Study Center, who has the expertise required to make this determination.

In fact, so far we have had few requests concerning these records. The archives staff has asked for permission to show a sample from these files to classes in the history of science and medicine and to classes in women, gender, and sexuality studies. On each occasion, permission has been readily granted. Should students wish to pursue further research, they would need to obtain permission for their individual projects. Any requests to publish from the records would, likewise, require the written permission of the coordinator of the Anna Freud Centre Program at the Yale Child Study Center.

We have made our finding aid as widely available as possible so that the research community will know that the records exist and can be used by those given the necessary permission. These records clearly offer materials of interest for those studying the post–World War II American family and serve as a record of psychoanalytic practice of that era. As we make information about these records available, we anticipate receiving inquiries about them from students and scholars in a wide range of academic disciplines including history, psychology, women and gender studies, the history of science and medicine, American studies, and urban studies.

Investigator	Duration of Contact	Type of Data and Function of Investigator	Type of Document
SOCIAL WORKER (Family Interviewer) Miss Jennie Mohr Miss Audrey Talmage Miss Laura Codling	Continuous from pregnancy period.	1) Home Visit - Interview of mother and/or father. Mostly "unstructured" in the sense that it is not a "questionnaire" interview. The spontaneous offerings of the mother are supplemented by obtaining information in areas deemed important by the staff. Though the interview is focussed on the parents, observations of the child at home are included. 2) Observer of Mother at WBC During the first two years, the family interviewer functioned as a "behind the screen" observer of the mother at every third WBC. After two years, home visitor observes mother at each WBC. 3) Observer of Child (and Parent) at Nursery School Home visitor sees the children briefly at nursery school sessions, usually timing this so that parent is also seen. These are informal, casual contacts.	1) Narrative document - Recording of details of interview. 2) Observations recorded on a form worked out by entire staff. 3) Observations transmitted on the day of observation to the recorder of the nursery school day or recorded in brief form independently.

PEDIATRICIANS
 	
Dr. Rose Coleman
 	
Dr. Sally Provence
	Continuous from pregnancy onward.	1) Home calls to sick children
		
		2) Telephone contact
		
		3) Developmental and physical exam of child and interview of mother at Well Baby Clinic
			1) Narrative account of visit.
			
			2) " " " " phone.
			
			3) Pediatrician's WBC Document
			  a) Physical Examination including measurements
			  b) Interview with mother
			  c) Developmental Examinations (Test records and profiles)

Investigator	Duration of Contact	Type of Data and Function of Investigator	Type of Document
NURSERY SCHOOL TEACHERS Miss Eveline Omwake Mrs. Alice Faulkner	From entrance of child to school (age 2-2 1/2 yrs.)	1 and 2) As teacher of child in a group - teachers are expected to function as they would in any nursery school as educators of the child and parent. This involves knowing the child individually but also as he is in a group of peers. 3) As leader of parent meetings held in conjunction with nursery school.	1) Daily nursery school record on each child which is set up as a check list showing materials used, type of play, contact with adults and children, etc. 2) Summary (every 2-3 mo.) of each child's experience in school and teacher's contact with parents at school. 3) Summary of parent meetings (held at monthly intervals) including the major points of each mother's participation
PSYCHIATRISTS Dr. Grace Abbate *Dr. Ernst Kris Dr. Marianne Kris Dr. John McDevitt **Dr. Samuel Ritvo	Two from beginning of study, as consultants and observers-- Three added when children started to nursery school. Direct contact starts when child enters school.	1) In Nursery school as observer of individual (assigned) children in the group. This will lead to the following: 2) Individual Play Session Contact to start at age 3 to 3 1/2 years. (The child's second year in nursery school) Modeled after therapy sessions. 3) Interviews with Parents after psychiatrist becomes a familiar person. These are at present represented by the precursors (informal conversations with parents) 4) Observer of Child and Mother at WBC	1) Recording of relevant observations, independent of the nursery school teachers' recordings. 2) Documentation of sessions (Technique of recording is not yet crystallized.) 3) Narrative recording 4) Recorded on same form used by Social Worker at WBC.

* Dr. Ernst Kris serves as study leader and has been a part of the study since it was planned in 1949-50. He is familiar with the data on all cases.

** Dr. Ritvo has undertaken the psychiatric treatment of one of the mothers in the Study.

Figure 2a–d: Types of material created by study team

Investigator	Duration of Contact	Type of Data and Function of Investigator	Type of Document
SPECIAL OB-SERVER fully trained in techniques of detailed behavior observations. Miss Gladys Lack	From the birth of the first child.	1) Observer at WBC "Behind the screen" observations of child. The documents represented by item 12 b in List of Documents, which follows this chart are not continued after the child is two years. Substituted for this is an observation of the child which is recorded on a form which represents the staff's "distillation" of the crucial areas and items of the more detailed observations previously used. These are recorded by the observer both on the older child and on the siblings. 2) Observer at Nursery School - The special observer is asked at intervals to make written, detailed observations of the child in school. Interval is irregular and is reserved for special situations (times of stress, first introduction to a new activity, etc.) 3) Recorder of Nursery School Conferences - The special observer is one of the persons who knows all children. Thus she is asked to synthesize and summarize the pertinent facts discussed in the Nursery School conference immediately after each nursery school session.	1) Revised Observation Form containing summary of relevant areas of the more detailed method used previously. 2) Detailed Observation Record with summary. 3) Summary of Discussion of Current Nursery School situation.

Investigator	Duration of Contact	Type of Data and Function of Investigator	Type of Document
Organizer of Data Miss Lottie Maury	No contact with families	1) As summarizer of Documents of "The Family Team" the chief function of this person is to keep the staff up to date on each child in order that the research staff meetings are productive and that the important data on each child may be discussed at the time they are current. This alerts the staff members so that the data are enriched by more sensitive observations. 2) As recorder of hypotheses and problems.	1) Summaries of Research Meetings - (including procedure as well as case discussion) Summaries of Case Presentation 2) Recording of hypotheses. Problem File.

appendix II.

2. List of Types of Records and the Documents of the Research Records.
The following is a listing of the documents which are found in the
research records. Those starred apply to the first two years of the
child's life only and are not found in the continuing study. Those
found below the line are "new" documents present from the time each
child was two years of age (when the method of observation was extended
and modified).

a. General or large Record

   (1) Ante partum interviews of mother by the social worker

   (2) Psychological examinations of mothers.

   (3) Pediatric Ante Partum interview (one interview only).

   (4) Labor and delivery record by pediatrician.

          "   "   "   " of nurse or obstetrician (from
          hospital record.)

   (5) Interviews with mother by social worker during lying-in
          period.

   (6) Pediatrician's examinations of infant during lying-in period
          and interviews with mother.

   (7) Pediatrician's records on activity and reactivity of infant
          during lying-in period.

   (8) Home visit records of social worker

   (9) "   "   "   " pediatrician.

   (10) Well Baby Clinic Documents of Pediatrician including

        (a) Physical Examination including simple anthropometrics

        (b) Developmental Examinations

            Gesell and Viennese Test records with both

            quantitative and qualitative evaluations.

        (c) Interview with Mother.

Figure 3a–c: Document types in research records

(11) Photography - (Stills) - (1) Of child during well baby
clinic (used to illustrate the observations) (2) Nude
photographs used for now measurement and later for
somatotyping.

(12) Documents of Observations from "Behind the Screen" (WBC)

    (a)   Evaluative Observations by Dr. Katherine Wolf
        (for first two years only).

 *(b)   Detailed behavior observations on mother and child.

    (c)   Observations of mother by social worker.

**(d)   Observations of mother by psychiatrist.

    (e)   Observations of mother and child by special observer.
        (as designated on page 5)

(13) Documents of Observations in the Nursery School Setting

    (a)   Daily records of Nursery School teachers.

    (b)   Summaries of nursery school teachers.

    (c)   Records of psychiatrists working in nursery school
        group, assigned to specific children and mothers.

    (d)   Very brief notes of pediatrician and social worker as
        they are in nursery school, and incidental observations
        of psychiatrist on children not assigned to them.

    (e)   Observations (detailed behavior observations) by the
        special observer as indicated in the list of her
        contacts.

(14) Documents Summarizing Staff Discussions.

These are brief documents summarizing the discussions of
the staff members involved on a particular nursery school
day or after a well baby clinic. Pertinent observations,

---

  * Not a part of general record.
 ** Irregular up to age 2 - Regular thereafter at each WBC

not previously recorded by the individual observers
(teacher, special observer, psychiatrist, etc.) are thus
added to the record.

(15) Reports of Psychiatrist on Individual Sessions with Child -
These will be begun during the child's second year in school
and will become a vital part of the study from that point on.

(16) Reports of Psychological Testing after age 3.
Psychological testing (Stanford-Binet, Merrill-Palmer,
Arthur Performance and the Projective Tests) will be added
at age 3.

b. The Summary Record -
This record, which exists solely for the purpose of keeping the
staff up to date on each child, contains digests of documents of
the larger record. Its purpose is to permit the entire staff to
be aware of the current situation in each family in order that the
weekly research staff meetings can be fully utilized for discussion
and evaluation.

c. "The Problem File"
This contains a formulation of problems related to procedure and
methodology and also of problems related to the content of the
data - (i.e. problems related to the individual child and his development). It contains the hypotheses which are evolved and the
predictions which are made both general and specific.
Over a period of time this will contain the nuclear material derived from the study.

Series f. Family data   Child Study Center
                                                Yale University

COLLECTION CONTENTS

SERIES I. FAMILY DATA

Description   Date(s)

Series I. Family data   1950-1990s
    Restricted until Jan 1, 2050.
        Dunn
            1950 Dec-1952 May
            1952 May-1953 Feb
            1953 May-1954 Aug
            1954 May-1955 Oct
            1955 Nov-1956 Dec
            1958-1959
            Categories
            Summary record   1953 Mar-1957 Jun
            Follow-up   1965
            Follow-up   1982-1984
            Writings   1959, no date
        Korwich
            1951 Jun-1952 Nov
            1952 Dec-1953 Nov
            1953 Dec-1954 Jun
            Category record   1951-1953
        Kuhn
            1950 Dec-1952 Feb
            1952 Apr-1953 Jun
            Prenatal evaluation sectors
                Staff
                Except staff
        Meredith
            1950 Dec-1952 Jun
            1952 Jun-1953 May
            1953 Jun-1954 Oct
            1954 Nov-1955 Apr

Figure 4: Sample page from series 1 in Online Finding Aid: Guide to the Child
Study Center, School of Medicine, Yale University, Records Concerning the
Longitudinal Study (RU 282), Manuscripts and Archives, Yale University Library

NOTES

1. Letter to Katherine Bain, January 11, 1949, Milton Senn Papers, MS C 280a in the History of Medicine Division, National Library of Medicine, Bethesda, Md.

2. Milton Senn Papers, MS C 280a in the History of Medicine Division, National Library of Medicine; Ernst Kris Papers, Manuscript Division, Library of Congress; Commonwealth Fund Records, Rockefeller Archives Center, Tarrytown, N.Y.

3. Letter from Sybil Escalona, May 2, 1949, Milton Senn Papers, MS C 280a in the History of Medicine Division, National Library of Medicine.

4. Memo by Ernst Kris, November 23, 1949, "Rooming-In Service and Child Study Center," Milton Senn Papers, MS C 280a in the History of Medicine Division, National Library of Medicine.

5. Memo by Dr. Warren concerning an interview with Dr. Milton Senn, April 12, 1950, Commonwealth Fund Records, Rockefeller Archives Center.

6. Milton J. E. Senn to Lester J. Evans, May 3, 1950, Commonwealth Fund Records, Rockefeller Archives Center.

7. Ibid.

8. It is interesting that neither the Warren nor the Evans memos mentions the role of Kris or any of the other participants in the formulation of the project.

9. Memo by Dr. Warren concerning an interview with Dr. Milton Senn, April 12, 1950, Commonwealth Fund Records, Rockefeller Archives Center.

10. Senn to Evans, May 3, 1950, enclosure of supp. data, p. 5.

11. Ibid., p. 9.

12. Senn to Evans, May 3, 1950.

13. Notes by M.C.S., January 12, 1954.

14. Memo from Dr. Warren to Dr. Crane, October 1, 1958, and Memorandum for the files of Dr. Crane, May 21, 1959, Commonwealth Fund Records, Rockefeller Archives.

15. Milton Senn, "An Over-all Report of the Longitudinal Study of Personality Development," December 7, 1953, appendix 1, Commonwealth Fund Records, Rockefeller Archives.

16. Ibid., appendix 2.

17. A box is equal to between one and one and a quarter linear feet of material.

18. ACRL/SAA Joint Statement on Access in Research Materials in Archives and Special Collections Libraries, June 2009, available online at www.ala.org/acrl/standards/jointstatement (accessed January 5, 2014).

19. Elements include name, all geographic subdivisions smaller than a state, all elements of dates directly related to an individual, telephone numbers, social security numbers, account numbers, and full-face photographic images.

20. Manuscripts and Archives employs a waiver for access to the Florence and Henry Wald Papers, which include information on the terminally ill patients whom Florence Wald studied in developing her ideas for the first hospice in the United States. The waiver states: "I agree to preserve the confidentiality of the individuals documented in these records. I will refrain from making any disclosure that would identify any person as the subject of these records. No names or other information making possible the specific identification of an individual will be used in any formal or informal oral presentation or conversation, nor in any teaching exercise, nor in any disseminated product that results from my research. I understand that failure to comply with this agreement may result in legal proceedings being initiated against me. In such a case, I agree to hold harmless and to indemnify Yale University, its officers, agents, or employees, for any loss or damage to them, including any associated legal fees."

❧ 7 ❧

Selected Process Notes
and Research Summaries from the
Yale Longitudinal Study

LINDA C. MAYES AND STEPHEN LASSONDE

In the next pages we present sample materials from the Yale Longitudinal Study records, housed in the Yale University Library's
Manuscripts and Archives department. We offer these records to
give readers a chance to make their own interpretations of the materials and to present just a small sampling of what is available to scholars
for study. We begin with notes from Samuel Ritvo's sessions with Evelyn around a three-month period in 1956. The session from April 11,
1956, is one of three that we refer to in Chapter 8. The other three, from
May and June 1956, illustrate the continuity and discontinuity of themes
from the selected April session.[1]

Following the notes from these sessions in 1956, we jump to commentary on two sessions in 1958 and one in 1961, each of which is also
discussed in our interpretive chapter, Chapter 8. The materials from
these sessions, conducted three years apart, provide a glimpse into the
evolution of themes across time as both Evelyn and Ritvo learned and
grew across the decade of her involvement with the study.

Finally, we provide one example of the investigative team's "conversation" about the study's progress in a report from 1952, predating

Ritvo's work with Evelyn. Here again is a glimpse into how the group was formulating, and struggling with, the enormity of its task and ambitions. These records are a window on a particular approach and theoretical frame for clinical research by investigators who were deeply engaged with the families recruited to the study while being immersed in the culture of their times.

NOTES

1. "Evelyn," the primary subject discussed in this book and represented in these materials, provided permission for the reproduction of the sessions.

McD

p. 1
Summary Record
Therapy Notes SR
4-11-56

When I came down to the nursery school ▇▇▇ was busy playing
with blocks in the far corner. She left the blocks to come in
where the other children were. As she did so she saw me, smiled
and we started upstairs. She announced on the way up that she
wanted a coke because both ▇▇▇▇▇▇ an▇▇ had had one. On
our way up in the elevator she asked me to lift her and I remarked how big she was getting and she told me her daddy is
strong and he can lift her. Her daddy is strong but I am fat.
I reminded her that I had seen her mother on Friday. She said
she knew about it. I told her that her mother had told me that
recently ▇▇▇ has been afraid of witches again and I said I
would like to help her with that fear. She said she is not afraid
any more and when I asked when she had gotten over the fear, she
said, "last night". I said I was glad that it was not bothering
her any more but I would be interested to hear what the fear
used to be like. She told me it involved clowns and witches,
that the clowns chased the witches. When they caught the witches
they tied them and when they got all the witches they changed
clothes and places with them and became witches themselves. When
I asked about the sex of the witches and clowns she told me the
witches were men and the clowns were woman. The witches were men
who wore witches' wigs.

She wanted to go into the playroom to play with the messy stuff.
We had a little difficulty assembling all the materials because
some of them had disappeared, and at one point she became cross
with me because I brought a stick instead of a spoon. She sent
me downstairs to get the spoon and carton she had taken down
with her last time. I talked with her further about the clowns
and witches changing roles and changing the sex and she told me

Figure 5a–b: Process notes for Ritvo's work with Evelyn on April 11, 1956

██████████ p.2
Ther. Notes SR 4-11-56

that women can change into men and I showed an interest in how
and when this takes place. She intimated that it takes place
when a girl is very very small, that it has already taken place
in ██████. ████████ is a boy who has hair like a boy but she does
not have a penis yet. ████████ only pretends that she is a boy.
About herself, ████████ says that there are times when she would like
to be a boy but she is not going to change. When she grows up
she is still going to be an actress but is going to be married
too and have children too. She says that I told her an actress
could do this, that is, be married and have children in addition
to being an actress.

She took the messy stuff she had mixed downstairs with her.
Later when ████ came back to the nursery school with a coke because he had forgotten his and I had to get him another one she
remembered that she had left hers upstairs. When we came upstairs to look for it Miss Lack had thrown it out and so I had to
get her another one too. On this she was insistent.

                         SR:bmt

p.1
Summary Record
Therapy Notes SR
5-11-56

I was with ■■■ when ■■■ came in today around ten o'clock with her mother. She had her appointment for a psychological examination. When she came in I was on the way upstairs with ■■■ and we stopped on the balcony to watch the concrete mixer. ■■■ came out there and actively engaged me while ■■■ was there. She left to go upstairs for the test. When I saw her later after testing she came eagerly with me. We went up to the Blue Room. She selected pie and chocolate milk and we took it into the small side room while she ate. She wanted me to get something for myself saying the pie was all for her. As she was eating and we were sitting close together she told me to move away. I moved away and wanted to know why I had to. Was she angry with me or didn't she like me. She replied that she liked me but wanted me to move away so that she wouldn't hit me. I said I thought that was funny – does one person hit another one when they like them? She indicated, yes, but then trailed off into one of her unintelligible sequences. When she had eaten as much as she wanted she went over to the coke machine and asked for a coke, not for herself but to bring downstairs to Martha and Mary Anele. I tried to find out why she needed to bring something to them, did they have someone to give them things like Doctor Solnit or Martha's daddy? I wasn't sure, however, that she wasn't asking really for herself and only saying that it was for someone else. We had to stop as it was time to go back to nursery school. The hour had been shortened somewhat because she had been delayed at the psychological and I told her we would try to have longer next time.

SR:bmt

Figure 6: Process notes for Ritvo's work with Evelyn on May 11, 1956

████████ p.1
Summary Record
Therapy Notes SR
5-16-56

I saw ███ first again today because both children were quite
late in coming to school, but ███ arrived first. If I had
waited for ███ it would have meant I would have had no time for
him at all. We went up to the playroom and got a chocolate milk
and roll. On the way up I commented on what ███ was wearing.
She was wearing a coverall with ruffles around the shoulders that
look like wings. She said she was a butterfly and I said, "Oh,
then you can fly like Peter Pan". She said, no she cannot really
fly. I asked if they were like fairy wings. She reacted strongly in the negative and answered in a somewhat scolding fashion
that she did not like to talk about fairies now. When I tried
to find out further why not now, she continued in an angry tone
and ran on ahead of me down the corridor.

On the way back to the playroom she told me she wanted me to read
the book about Jiminy Cricket. When we got there she found the
Robin Hood puzzle and we worked on that a while. I got to talking to her about witches and fairies and said I didn't quite
understand last time what fairies changed into. She said they
changed into witches by the magic wand. When I wanted to talk
further about witches and asked whether they were still bothering her she again turned on me peremptorily and told me not to
think about them. I asked if she thought not thinking about them
would make them go away and if that is the advice her mother gave
her. She nodded. She sat down to eat and wished me to read the
book. I said I thought she wanted to keep me busy reading so
that we wouldn't talk and she finished the sentence with the
question "about witches?" I said yes I thought she wanted to
keep me busy so we would not talk about witches, that she thinks

Figure 7a–b: Process notes for Ritvo's work with Evelyn on May 16, 1956

██████████ p. 2
Summary Record
Ther. Notes SR 5-16-56

that by not talking about them and not thinking about them they
will go away but that is not likely. Not thinking about them
does not make them go away but I knew a better way, that if we
could find out how and why the witches came into her thoughts
then we might be able to really make them go away.

I read the book while she ate and mixed flour and water. An
episode in the book calls for singing. She criticized my singing
and mentioned another child who does not sing well and said she
has a good voice and can sing well like her daddy but that ██████
cannot sing well. She interrupted from time to time to order me
to get something for her and kept doing it quite steadily. I
remarked that she was scolding me a lot today and maybe it was
because I brought up the unpleasant subject of witches. She said
I make you get things and get you all tired out.

We left so she could go to ██████ birthday party.

SR:bmt

McQ

■■■■■■ p.1
Summary Record
Therapy Notes
6-13-56 SR

■■ came in with her mother and the sisters this morning. The mother was bringing ■■ to see Dr. Provence. They had missed Monday's appointment because of ■■■ illness. ■ was carrying ■■ diaper in a bag. This morning there was no difficulty about leaving the others. She came very readily to the playroom with me, carrying a book which she had picked up in the waiting room and which she had apparently wanted me to read to her.

When we got to the playroom she asked for the flour. When I brought it she filled the pail and before going any further in her play asked me for some chocolate milk. I discussed the getting of chocolate milk with her and said that I did not think that she wanted it because she was hungry. I think she wanted it more because it was nice to have me get something for her and because it gave her a chance to move around and wander through the building which she likes. I told her I thought it would be best if we stopped it and we would have to stop it soon. I began this discussion with her after we had already started out for the milk. On the way she looked for her mother in Dr. Provence's examining room. Dr. Provence was not there. We went down to the end of the hall to look. When she saw the scales she wanted me to weigh her and I also weighed myself. I told her she weighed 44 lbs. and she was very angry with me because this was not true, her mother said that she weighed 43 lbs., and her mother is never wrong, besides 43 is more than 44.

In the Blue Room while she was sitting on the couch drinking her milk she had her legs drawn up with her genitals exposed and was masturbating while drinking her milk.

Figure 8a–b: Process notes for Ritvo's work with Evelyn on June 13, 1956

████████ p.2
Ther. Notes 6-13-56 SR

When we returned to the playroom she picked up the flour and began to spread the dry flour on the floor. First she was paving
a sidewalk this way, then it turned into making a trap. At first
this was a trap which would catch me. I had to walk through the
flour and as my shoes touched the flour I was trapped. I could not
find out from ████ whether anything was supposed to happen to me
after I was trapped this way. When I tried to draw her out about
it she changed it to a fish trap and I was then supposed to be a
fish who was to be trapped. We played this game until her time
was up. She enjoyed it very much, laughing more each time I got
stuck and could not move.

SR:bmt

The mother was waiting with all three girls when
I came down.   dashed up carrying a baton.
She dashed right into the room, walked over to
the doll house, picked up one of the family dolls,
and said this doll was stupid and she was going
to throw it out the window. The window was wide
open, she missed however with her first throw,
picked it up, made another attempt and this time
was successful. I asked first what the doll had
done to be thrown out the window and she replied
the doll was stupid. I wondered what the name of
the doll was. Her first response to this was
"Matilda" which was the name I had given to the
bad mother person in the story I made up yesterday. She resisted my inquiries to find out further
what the doll Matilda had done. She screamed
back at me and I said maybe Matilda had made
too much noise and that's why she had to be
thrown out.   continued shouting, looking
fierce and angry at me and although this was
always in a mock and playing way, the feeling
portrayed was extremely intense.
This seemed to set the tone for almost the
entire hour. She was very bossy and angry with
me, she went into the play where she was the

Figure 9a–c: Process notes for Ritvo's work with Evelyn on November 6, 1958

11-6-58   Thurs.   SR   2.

teacher and I was the bad boy. She complained to
my mother about me, scolded me, hit me with the ruler, tied my hands, made me stand in the corner,
 shot at me and finally burned me. Every motion
and sound that I made was immediately shouted down
while she glowered at me ferociously and kept attacking me. As the child who was being beaten, attacked and scolded, I said that I thought the teacher
was being very mean to me, that she was behaving
like a witch, and that I was frightened when she
looked at me with that horrible, angry expression
on her face. The name that she gave me as the bad
boy was Bob. Near the end of the time, she wanted
to go downstairs and outside to find the doll she
had thrown out, however, when we got down there,
she barely looked at it and played for a while,
climbing the jungle gym, doing tricks, and twirling
the baton that she had brought. She wanted to know
who was the boss of the whole place after I had
said that Miss Omwake was the boss of the nursery
school. She insisted that the boss of the whole
place must be a man who must be older than anybody
else. We talked about who is the boss in various
places. Her aunt is the boss in the school because
she was born before everybody, and her father is
the boss at home because he was born before the mother. Thus there seemed to be a contradiction as
to who was boss. At first it was the man; then it

seemed to be the oldest one.

Just before she left, I talked with her directly about her behavior today and said that it
seemed to me she might be behaving this way because
maybe her mother had been angry with her and scolded her. I wondered whom the mother gets angry at
and scolds at home, and she told me that it's not
very often at   , but most often at   and
sometimes at herself. I said I thought sometimes
it might frighten her, even when mommy is very angry at   and not at   .

SUMMARY:

It seemed to me that this hour related to the
mother's temper and anger at the children may be
currently particularly   , especially as   was
the one the mother attacked yesterday before the
hour. In the hour   then becomes the angry, violent attacking mother.

Interview SR
November 17, 1958   Monday 7A

I found ▮▮ and sisters with mother in the
crowded waiting room. Mother looked to me more
tense than she usually does, and this may have had
to do with the waiting room being so crowded. On
the way up ▮▮ asked me if I noticed anything
new. I noticed that her hair was curled, but this
turned out to be not what she wanted to show me.
She had on new shoes. She seemed to dismiss her
hair being curled as inconsequential. I remarked
that the shoes were handsome, whereupon she jumped
on me, saying that one doesn't use the word handsome in relation to girls; that handsome has to
do with boys. For girls, one says pretty. But in
fact the shoes were handsome because I couldn't
tell them from boys' shoes. We talked further a-
bout some of the differences between boys and
girls, whereupon she more and more insistently
took up the girls' or women's attitudes toward me,
which included my assisting her in physical things,
carrying a chair for her when she wanted to stand
on it to reach the pencil sharpener, fetching
flour, salt and cocoa from the nursery school. In
general being the women seemed to, as she portrayed it, mean not that things are voluntarily or
loving done for her by the man, but that a certain
homage was due, and carried out with a bossiness
by the woman. As this went on, she slipped into
the role of the teacher; she wrote a list of names
on a piece of paper, read them off, and asked me

Figure 10a–c: Process notes for Ritvo's work with Evelyn on November 17, 1958

to choose one for myself. I chose the name Sal.
Earlier the talk about women's things being pretty
seemed to lead associatively to a question about
my young adult women patient, whether she was coming today, why she came, does she come every day,
etc. The way this came out, it seemed to imply
that ▨ felt quite competitive with this young
woman, who in fact dresses rather nicely though
does not appear in a really dressed-up way.

When I had gotten the stuff from the nursery
school, ▨ played again that she was the restaurant lady and ⊥ was a sixteen-year-old boy who
worked at the G&O (where her father works). But I
was not just a boy, I was a boy witch, and I came
to the restaurant to get something to eat hiding
or disguising the fact that I was a witch. This
play with me as the witch is always accompanied in
▨ by smiling and not with any overt signs of
fearfulness. It was during this play, actually,
that we talked about my other girl patient, the
young woman, and I said that it seemed to me that
▨ wondered who was my favorite, whereupon she
became insistent in asking me who was my favorite.
I said this sounded like the mommy or daddy who
might be asked such a question, and that I could
say, like a mommy or daddy, that I am interested
in all my patients and didn't have one that was my
only favorite. Then we got to talking about favoritism in her family, and she said that ▨ is

her mother's favorite,   is the father's favorite, and first she said that she was the father's favorite, but then changed it and said that
she was her grandmother's favorite. When I asked
her about this switch, she said that at one time
she was her father's favorite, but the father preferred boys and therefore preferred   because
she plays like a boy. When I asked what is playing like a boy, I think she put the emphasis on
the physical activity and the noisiness. In the
play with the messy stuff she went on to smear it
on my fingernails, saying that she was making me
into a girl, and then went on to put brown stuff
all over my hand, and said that she was making me
into a Negro girl. When we went down at the end
of the hour, her father met her. He asked about
the red paint smeared on her dress, but was quite
good-natured about it and did not scold her.

Summary:

In this hour   starts out by showing me
something new and attractive. She takes a feminine attitude toward me, but this seems to be at
the same time very much modeled after her image of
the mother as a demanding, bossy person which the
mother of course is with the children, and the
question is does   see her that way with the
father too. Her rivalry and competitiveness with
my woman patient is overt again in this hour, and
she gives a rather remarkable summary of the cleavage
lines in her own family.   SR

The whole family was 15 minutes late.

2   ████ was wearing a patch over one eye. The
father, who was with them, indicated to me

4   that she was pampering it and wanting to show
it to Miss Omwake. ████ told me about it up-

6   stairs. ████ bumped into a door yesterday and
hurt her eye, a patch was put on it though ap-

8   parently there wasn't much of an injury. It was
better today but in school something happened -

10 I didn't catch it quite clearly from ███.
She got some sand in her eye - this made her

12 put the patch on again. ████ seemed to feel
too that it wasn't a serious injury but some-

14 thing that ████ was pampering. She went on
to tell me that this injury became the basis

16 for some doctor and hospital play at home among
the three of them. I gathered this is a game

18 they play not infrequently. ████ is the
doctor - ████ and ████ are the patients. ████

20 would like to be a nurse but ████ doesn't
always permit it. One form of the play is that

22 there has been an auto accident; an ambulance
comes and brings the patients to the hospital

24 and the doctor takes care of them. ████ also
imitated how ████ sometimes limps around when

26 she is imitating a patient. Sometimes they
include other children in this play. I wondered

28 how it happened that ████ couldn't be the nurse
if she wanted to and I tried to get at what it was

Figure 11a–d: Process notes for Ritvo's work with Evelyn on January 17, 1961

Interview with SR
Tuesday 1-17-61 4:45
p.2

that made it difficult for her to go against ████████'s wish. She tried to shrug it off by saying it's not that much of a problem, that sometimes she does get to be the nurse.

I forget how she got to it, but she told me that they had no gymnasium in her school and have no gym classes. She then asked me if she could change her day off from Thursday to Wednesday – a private gym class is being formed at the Community Hall in Branford and she would like to attend. When I began to explore in more detail how this might be arranged, what it would mean in terms of mother changing her schedule, she suddenly withdrew her request and said she didn't want to, that it was not that important. I tried to take up with her this apparent quick and ready giving up of something she had a moment ago presented as something important to her that she would like to do. She kept insisting that it wasn't important and that she really didn't want to do it anyhow. I had an impression that she might have presented the request in order to show how good, yielding and accommodating she is in her willingness to give it up. However I did not say anything to her about this; it only occurred to me later. Talking about gymnastics seemed to suggest to her that she show me some of the feats she can do. She did

some pushups and situps and really showed
a very creditable physical fitness, I thought,
better than many girls her age. She finally
exhausted herself and suggested that we get
some refreshment. I called her attention to
her abilities in these gymnastics and said
that even though she had told me that
is supposed to have the best shaped body, I
guessed she felt proud that she had perhaps
the strongest body. When we got to the
machines she noticed the peanuts and apparently
wanted them, but started out by asking me
whether I liked peanuts. This was again
getting something for herself by making it
appear that she was getting me something I
wanted. I pointed this out to her and said
how hard it seemed to be for her to say she
wanted something, letting another person see
she wanted it, she behaved as though she felt
this was not the right thing to do, that she
must make it appear she is getting them for
me as much as for herself. When we got the
peanuts she shared them very carefully. We
got a second bag of peanuts and she shared
those. The first time she was left with
3 peanuts, she gave herself 2 and me 1. The
next time she was left with 3 peanuts, she
gave me 2 and herself 1. When we got back
the time was up. We went downstairs.

:   was already on her way down. The

2 two girls had brought homework.   told

me she had a book report to do. I waited

4 inside the receptionist's office where I did

some work of my own until the mother came.

6 <u>Summary</u>: Tells about patch over   eye.

It's not a serious accident but   shows

8 off the patch. They play hospital at home.

    is the doctor.   and Beth are the

10 patients.   would like to be the nurse

but   doesn't permit it. Asks to change

12 her day off so she can go to a gym class, then

withdraws the request, giving the impression

14 that she wants to show me how good she is by

giving up something. Puts on a gym performance;

16 is really quite fit physically. I remark that

though   might be said to have the best

18 shaped body,   certainly can say hers

is strong. Getting peanuts, tried to make

20 it appear that I want them and she's getting

them for me. Divides the peanuts very accurately,

22 the first time giving herself the odd one, and

the second time she gave me the odd one.

24

26

28

May 27, 1952   p.1

Present: Dr. E. Kris (EK)   Miss Gladys Lack (GL)
          Dr. K. Wolf (KW)   Miss Laura Codling (LC)
          Dr. J. Mohr (JM)   Miss E. Hobart (EH)
          Dr. S. Ritvo (SR)   Miss Mary J. Gold (MJG)
          Dr. S. Provence (SP)   Miss Audrey Talmage (AT)
          Dr. R. W. Coleman (RC)

The meeting followed the plan suggested a few weeks
ago, that after the observation from behind the screen
each person would give the impressions they had of the
mother and child. This method has proved most fruitful.
Other elements were added and the discussion developed
according to the nature of the material and the discretion
of the members. As a result, writing up the meetings
becomes less and less a recording of the minutes and
more a presentation of the case. In consequence more
liberty is taken in the re-organization of the various
contributions. In this instance I have attempted to
start on a descriptive level and proceed to a more dynamic analysis following only roughly the sequence of
the actual discussion. Essential statements I believe
are attributed to the correct person, but some details
may be incorrectly assigned or remain without authorship.
Naturally others are omitted. It is hoped that most
statements remain in context in spite of this re-shuf-
fling. (MJG)

I. Description of the mother and child

    A. Mrs. O. is a shy reserved young woman. EK
    There was some difference of opinion as to her
    attractiveness. She has a certain distance about her.
    One would not imagine her cuddling up to anyone.(RC)
    She relates to members of the staff loosely except

Figure 12a–n: Investigative team discussion notes, May 27, 1952

when situations in which she is asking
for help. (SP) She has a great degree of detachment when looking at SP or GL. At times
during "play contact" her mind seemed to wander
as if day dreaming about the child. KW but her
head would startle and turn quickly at the sound
of SP's voice. The body is contained, the eyes
sad and quiet. The only part that seems to move
is the mouth, even when she is not talking. (AT)
But at times the lips are pressed sternly together
(KW) a suggestion of "Sweet Melancholia". EK

    1. Difference in behavior at home and during
        observation: At home she appears shy but
        resolute. (EK) The face is more expressive. (JM)

            a. The company manners and artificial
               voice is not used at all. (JM) She
               even holds the baby differently and is
               not so hesitant in her actions. (CDS
               & JM) nor in her handling of the child.
               Here she hardly talks to ████. (JM)
            b. She is extremely self-conscious and is
               afraid of being watched. She knows
               there are people behind the screen.
               She may unconsciously identify these
               unseen observers with the inhibiting
               figure of her mother. (EK) When the
               screen was closed both she and the baby
               talked jargon. SP

c. The Play Contact situation   Research Meeting p.3

she may feel is child centered.   5-27-52

SP being a pediatrician comes under the same
category. Both CdS & JM feel she talks more
freely to them as they are interested in her.
Mrs. O. probably finds it is good to have
someone to talk to and the interviews and
visits with JM continue this possibility:
Little rapport has been lost in the shift from
CdS to JM. (EK)

2. Compared to last July she appears older, sadder,
less animated and darker complected. SR

B. Description of ____, the child.

____ is an attractive child, a little under developed
for her age, considering she should have a very good natural
endowment. She is like her mother in many ways. ____ too
is not cuddly, she paid very little attention to her mother.
She would smile a little at the observer but inexplicably
and not from anything she or the observer were doing. KW
The smile kept the observer in place rather than being out-
going. (GL) There seemed to be a pathetic quality about
her, something of sadness and longing, a lack of satisfaction
and lack of radiance (KW) that was very appealing. (GL) She
seemed hesitant and inhibited in certain areas, but knew what
she wanted in others. Like her mother also, she seemed to be
under a strain during the observation, did much more mouthing
here, and took some time to become exploratory. JM (She may
have also identified GL with the prohibiting grandmother GL.)

III. Mrs. O. and the other members of the
      household.

A. The husband is small blond soft spoken and has a receding
hair line. He is pleasant to speak to. SP We know little
about him except:

    1. Mrs. O. accuses him of being irresponsible because
        he does not wish to become an art teacher.

    2. He does not have the airyness or aloofness ofMrs. O.
        (EK) and <u>does not appear inhibited in physical contact.</u>
    <u>with</u>   . He enjoys rough housing with her (Mrs. O. does
    not approve nor understand this and says, "strangely
    enough she (goes to sleep afterwards."

    3. Mrs. O. appears interested in CSC. We should try and
        have more contact with him.

B. <u>Mrs. O's mother we assume is an inhibiting figure both</u>
    on Mrs. O. and on   . JM   Mrs. O. also probably feels
she is competing with her mother in raising the child. JM

C.   , her tough bomber pilot <u>brother-in-law has all</u>
    <u>Mrs. O's admiration.</u> EK

D.   the dog, is a bad tempered unfriendly animal
    to which Mr. O. is very much attached. Mrs. O. feels
she is jealous of   .   once crawled up behind   ,
<u>surprised her, and was bitten on the lip causing a small</u>
<u>abrasion.</u> SP (<u>however is not afraid of the dog.</u>) Mrs. O.
would like to get rid of her but says Gretchen is so "nervous"
it would be hard to find her another home. SP has suggested
having the dog vaccinated as a precautionary measure. <u>Mrs. O.</u>
<u>does not like this dog.</u>

III. Mrs. O's bottled sexuality:

A. From discussion of Mrs. O. in General Research
Meeting June 13, 1951, we already noted that Mrs. C.
did not have a very good relationship with her husband.
This was referred to as "her darkest area" (I B 6 Relation
to husband) Repression of libidinal instincts and evidence
of unconscious masturbatory fantasy with concomitant guilt
and anxiety were mentioned There was undue concern in
regard to a vaginal discharge which was shifted to anxiety
over discharge from baby's umbilical cord "In general
Mrs. O. tries to repress all evil and suppress emotion.
She may be priggist". (See IB Psychological picture 5,
6 & 7 of General Meeting June 13, 1951) SP predicted she
would be anxious when child's sexuality became manifest
(same meeting)

B. At present her relationship with her husband is not
good either.

    1. She offers the information that he is ill
       tempered JM

    2. She appears to disapprove of his rough housing
       with ____ (see above IIA)

    3. She says they no longer have sexual relations.
       (although she also says she wants another child
       soon, and another two ten years hence)

    4. Some months ago the relationship seemed so
       strained that we considered the possibility
       that they might separate.

C. She is restrained in sensuous matters and has imposed
inner inhibitions on herself which she wants to handle

Research Meeting p.6
in her own way. This is also apparent ▨▨▨   5-27-52
in her lack of erotic stimulation of ▨▨ and the
prohibitions of autoerotic activities in ▨▨ .
(See Relationship to ▨▨▨ below)

D. As indicative of the type of conflict that goes on,
this delicate and frail young lady with the dreamy
eyes falls for the Herculean he-man-bomber pilot.
He is also her brother-in-law. She suffers and at
this point wants another child. EK

IV. ▨▨▨ behavior in Play Contact (see running record
May 27, 1952)

    A. She seems to prefer objects to people. SR

    B. Separableness from mother (noticed by all)

        1. She pays little attention to her mother relating
            easily to G.L. She did not bring toys over to
            her mother nor did she try to get to her mother when
            put down on the floor (The mother is self effacing
            also, and tries to keep out of the picture KW)
            After the accident ▨▨ crying was minimal.
            Usually children go on crying to get more comfort
            as a secondary gain. One had the impression in
            this instance that she stopped crying almost before
            the pain stopped. KW

        2. She also seperates from toys with great ease.

    C. Easy contact with GL but not a very emotionally
involved one. She enters into the game of handing the
doll back and forth and appears to ask GL for help
while reaching for saucepan.

    D. Hesitancy in touching small objects, especially when

she was on the table.   She seemed more Research Meeting   p.7
5-27-52

self motivated on the floor. KW This may be explained by:

1. Barricade around the television table at home
    to prevent her from touching small objects
thereon.

2. Small objects have been removed from her play
    things at home since Mrs. O. feared choking
(See below E "Differention large and small)

3. Her grandmother is quite prohibitive at home in
    what she allows the child to handle and   may
identify GL with this prohibitive figure.

At any rate GL appeared to have considerable influence
influence on her contact with objects

    a. When GL touch an object it became the focus
    of attention.

    b. She would reach towards objects on GL's side
    of the table but would not go over to them.

    c. She would roll the large truck as GL had done
    but not pick it up.

    d. She only came for saucepan after GL had
    touched it.

E. However her own preference was marked in her attach-
    ment to teddy bear, saucepan and doll, and her rejection
at one time of the clay. She did not touch the doll bed,
cards or train. GL

    1. Marked preference for teddy bear was noticeable
    as she brought this up to her face she had more
of an expression of genuine pleasure than at any other
time. GL She even cuddled it a little. SP At home

we know she throws her other

toys out of the crib before going to sleep

but sleeps with a Panda. SP It will be

interesting to know at what point she discards

this fetish. EK

F. She seems to differentiate between objects as to

whether they are large or small.

    1. Some few months ago Mrs. O. complained of

       excessive mouthing (which was true) and she

      took away small objects lest ▓ choke on them.(SP)

    All the objects she is seen playing with at home

    recently have been large. JM

G. Marked preferential possibilities in choice of

objects but less differentiation than one might expect

especially in mouthing technique which was less specific

today. KW RC would tend to see more specificity and

oral contact with objects than KW.

    1. ▓ hesitated to mouth the teddy bear, perhaps

      because of sensuous pleasure in the texture of

    the fur offered. R.C.

    2. Extreme mouthing was concentrated on small

      doll where she popped its head in her mouth. R.C.

    3. Hesitates to mouth clay. Has a funny lost

      expression when it is removed. KW Never

    mouths saucepan.

    4. Differentiation between teddy bear and doll

      was more marked before accident, differentiation

    however seemed to depend more on emotional conno-

    tations of the objects rather than their objective

nature as before (KW) (See Fvaluative
observation 4-14-52 KW)

H. <u>Rythmical movements with objects tend to dis-
appear</u> (Rythmical movement with truck could be a
functional interest in its operation)KW

I. <u>Alternation between mouthing and shaking objects
marked.</u> KW

J. <u>Sound addiction still noticeable.</u> One got a
different feeling in regard to her handling of the
saucepan. Although she pulled and pushed at it
<u>there was a definite pleasurable re-action to this
self produced noise.</u> EK

K. <u>She is very orderly.</u> KW

    1. Picks up anything that falls on the floor
       even if she is not very interested in it and
    is unsteady on her feet.

    2. Puts doll to bed and puts things in their
       places (as a tentative explanation she may
    be reluctant to have things disappear but not
    to let them go. KW)

L. <u>Still remarkably little vocalization</u> (remarked by
    all)

M. <u>Lack of bodily fear.</u> Even after the accident
was not afraid of falling (Her mother was not upset
either)   appears awkward but strong. This is
deceptive. It is rather that in her lack of fear she
steps beyond the limits of her acquired strength and
skills. This impresses one as being awkward. KW

N. Development in "body" is age ade-   Research Meeting   p.10
quate but one would expect more from   ı 5-27-52
a child with such a bright mother.   is too
preoccupied to develop well now.KW This relative
physical underdevelopment is related to lack of
physical stimulation and prohibition of autoerotic activities. (See below IV Mrs. O. relation
to   A, B & C)

O. Additional data other than "Play Contact".

　　1. Few illnesses. Slight colds no fever.
　　　　Thrush when neonate.

　　2. Accidents.

　　　　a. The dogbite (see above II D,

　　　　b. A shampoo bottle fell in her mouth and she
　　　　　　coughed blood.

　　　　c. Choking proclivities. (see above IV F and
　　　　　　below V B Prohibition of auto-erotic ac-
　　　　　　tivities) Mother removes small objects.
　　　　　　　　is inclined to choke on her food.

　　　　d. Masturbation by activity of thighs. Mrs. O.
　　　　　　was very worried about this sometime ago,
　　　　　　(although she does not mention it as being
　　　　　　masturbation.) We do not know at present
　　　　　　whether   still does this.

IV. Mrs. O's Relationship to   .

A. Mrs. O. has been described as having a loose not
very intimate physical contact with the child.
appears independent of her also. She, Mrs. O. is self-

p.11

effacing during observations and   Research Meeting
doctors' visits, usually waiting for a sign to   5-27-52
take   up. This might be formulated as the
uncertainty of the immediate physical relationship.

    1. She is shocked when father plays roughly
       with   Surely Mrs. O. herself does
nothing to stimulate her erotically.

    2. She stimulates and comforts   after the
       accident as if she were a much younger child. KW

    3. She is somewhat aware of her problem of physical
       contact as she even puts a bath towel in the
bathinette so   won't slip instead of holding
on to her. EK

B. Prohibition of auto-erotic activities.

    1. We will recall her disturbance at   !
       masturbatory activity thru stiffening of the
legs and thigh activity.

    2. She asked at WBC if   should be allowed to
       suck her thumb. This sucking has been very
much interfered with although Mrs. O. probably does
not realize that she had done so. EK

    3. Mouthing objects is preferable to sucking
       your own body. The condition under which
putting the finger in the mouth is permissable
is when a tooth is coming. An objective reason
is all right but not for reasons of pleasure.
(This is the reverse of   who is allowed
to suck but not put things in her mouth. Mrs. K's

Research Meeting
5-27-52

p.12

contact is also more intimate and physical and less vocal, the reverse of Mrs. O.

4. If such strong prohibitions in this area continue _____ may well show a more definite under develop-ment. Mrs. O's attitude to these activities stems of course from her own guilt and anxiety in this area. (See above III Mrs. O's bottled sexuality)

5. Mrs. O. does not appear to be afraid of body damage from falling. _____ courage reflects

   a. Instead of hitting on the immediate contact level (EK) Mrs. O. appears to handle here on a much younger level as comforting her after the fall, or relates on a much older level as exempli-fied in: KW

      1. The marked separateness of the pair.

      2. Our assumption that she probably talks to _____ on an older level at home. KW

   b. We can understand the problem of anxiety and prohibitions but do not know why she relates on this older level. EK. We anticipate she will stimulate _____ to build and encourage her in other activities and accomplishments at about three years (EK) or later (KW.)

   C. Mrs. O. is very meticulous about her material care of the child.

VI. _____ in this Environment.

   A. Within the rather strict limitations of a large number of restrictions, retouching certain objects

and the auto   Research Meeting   p.13.
    and the auto-erotic prohibitions, the   5-27-52

child is relatively free.

  B. Some of the libidinal and physical needs are
     being met by the father's closer physical play
     with

  C. In spite of the mother's disinterestedness and
     restraint   has identified with her mother
in the mouth play and determinedness.

  D. However if the strong prohibitions of auto-erotic
     activities continues, her over all development
will continue to drag.

VII. Areas of Further Investigation

  A. At what age will she discard the Panda.

  B. Will the increased specificity of the object
  (discrimination) be the criterion of her development?

  C. At what age will Mrs. O. adequately stimulate
    the child?

VIII. Predictions

  1. Continuation of strong prohibitions of auto-
     activities will cause her over all development
     to drag. KW

  2. Mrs. O. will adequately stimulate child when she
     can build, paint and show accomplishments at about
    2 or 3 years. EK Adequate stimulation will come after.

  3. Three years unless the prohibitions interfere
     with even these possibilities. KW

IX Methodology.

p. 14

The system of each observer and   Research Meeting
                                        5-27-52
tester reporting on their personal impressions
during "Multipli Observation" when child comes in
on Tuesday morning as basis or point of departure
for General Research Meeting has proved most
fruitful.

                        jhp/bmt

8

Looking In and Seeing Out

STEPHEN LASSONDE AND LINDA C. MAYES

I n the thousands of pages of process notes by the Yale Child Study
Center clinicians on Evelyn and her suburban five-member family,
we learn that Evelyn's mother grows restless at devoting all of her
time to raising three children. While the children are still young, she gets
a job, first as a waitress and then as a substitute grade-school teacher.
In her own therapy, she also reveals her diminishing interest in sexual
intimacy with her husband. Much of the family's focus in therapy is on
the stormy and disruptive willfulness of the middle child, "Wendy"—
our subject's younger sister—who supplies the impetus for the family
to seek a comprehensive therapeutic treatment for their unhappiness.
While the parents' difficulty with Wendy is referred to throughout these
records (and indeed, Wendy ultimately runs away from home as a teenager), one of the few comments by the parents that speaks to their motive in committing the entire family to therapy is uttered by the mother
early on: "All our family are coming apart at the middle."[1]

The turn to psychotherapy itself signifies a rising tide of middle-
class introspection, on one hand, and, on the other, growing faith in the
expertise of psychologists, psychiatrists, and pediatricians in refining

childrearing techniques.[2] As we have already suggested, an intense optimism underlay the assumptions of the longitudinal study in particular. Even so, we cannot fail to observe that such optimism permeated much of American life well into the 1960s.[3]

We offer unabashedly, then, a "world-in-a-grain-of-sand" approach here, for the material not only provides vivid descriptions of everyday life—the complex interactions of a growing family during its children's entire early years of development—it also records what they (and their therapists) *thought* about their lives with one another as they were living it and speaking about it with the therapists in the study. Historians, unlike scientists in any field, must rely on what shards of evidence we can find—we cannot manufacture it. In this instance the most compelling feature of the study's process notes is that they display a multifaceted subject emerging in "real time" and in this instance, under a special lens of psychoanalytically informed therapy. Both the family and the therapist were using the psychoanalytic lens to look closely at their lives as these were lived, felt, and reflected on. However flawed by the imperfections of the study's design or the loss of Ernst Kris's guiding hand—however shaped by the individual intellectual biases and predispositions of the clinicians who worked with these families, these materials offer not only a compelling view of the *behavior* that forms a fine-grained, moving picture of change over time, but also an accompanying "soundtrack" with commentary on their exchanges.

The lure of these materials for historians, then, is the substantiation of cultural change evident in the details of ordinary people's everyday lives. A similar lure is present for "clinical historians" who seek evidence about their patients' internal transformations in their stories about the ordinary, and sometimes extraordinary, events and relationships in their day-to-day lives. Such detail is rendered lavishly—indeed, overwhelmingly—by the case records of the Yale Longitudinal Study. Yet what makes this collection so extraordinary is that we have the privilege of "listening in" on what children (and their parents) thought about their exterior worlds—family, neighborhood, school—as well as their interior lives: how children, especially, perceived themselves and others;

what they *did* with the way adults constructed their lives emotionally; how adults equipped them to conquer their fears or feed their fantasies of triumph; and how children armed themselves emotionally against the very adults whose love was the ultimate measure of acceptance and competence. We also are privileged to listen in to how the adults constructed, reconciled, and revised their roles as parents with their own self-identities, how they saw themselves enduring or not in their children, and how as their children grew up, they looked ahead to who they might become after their active parenting roles diminished.

EVELYN'S FAMILY, THE YALE STUDY, AND NEW HAVEN'S ECONOMIC AND SOCIAL HISTORY

Born in 1951, Evelyn began her therapy when she was three-and-a-half years old and her work with her therapist, Samuel Ritvo, continued for over nine years, until she was twelve. Evelyn was the eldest of three girls. When she began therapy, her sister "Wendy" was two years old and "Tammy," the youngest, was a four-month-old baby. Evelyn's parents were lower-middle class. Her father's family were of northern European descent and had migrated to the United States many generations earlier. Her mother's family were from Denmark and solidly middle class. It is notable that much of the father's material in therapy deals with his "feelings of inferiority," feelings that the clinicians periodically referred to when observing his complex relationship with Evelyn. Process notes from his therapy suggest that his low self-esteem was grounded in his relationship with his own parents. His father demeaned him as inadequate and insufficiently masculine, and had deprived him of a college education in favor of his older sister. His mother, with whom he was close, nonetheless inculcated in him a distrustful attitude toward other women.[4]

While factors such as socioeconomic status, religion, ethnicity, and race were not included in the protocol for recruiting subjects for the Yale Longitudinal Study, there was a self-conscious effort to attract a pool of subjects in rough proportion to the city's demographic composition.

Indeed, the new field of medical sociology had been forged at Yale and its medical school during the middle decades of the century. Precedent for the graphic representation of an "ecology" of socioeconomic status in New Haven during the 1930s had been advanced by Yale sociologist Maurice Davie, who had published a small handbook on socioeconomic status modeled on the work of the Chicago school of sociology. Davie composed a statistical portrait of New Haven's population and social status, which he mapped onto the city's political wards. Immediately after World War II, Yale sociologists August Hollingshead, Jerome K. Myers, and Bertram H. Roberts worked with psychiatrist Frederick C. Redlich of the Yale School of Medicine to devise an index of socioeconomic status utilized specifically to correlate social stratification with mental illness.[5] Their efforts pioneered the incipient field of medical sociology. Hollingshead's team carried out a ten-year, two-volume study of mental illness in New Haven's population from the late 1940s to the late 1950s. So again, although the sample size of the children recruited into the study, the expertise of the Yale Child Study Center staff, and the explicit goals of the study diluted any meaningful attempt at fielding a demographically representative child/family study, the social differences of the families' backgrounds (and between spouses and their families of origin, for instance) informed the observations made by its clinician-researchers.[6]

New Haven's population peaked in 1910, when 25 percent of its residents were of Italian descent. It was a city whose economy and population had been built on making carriages, specialized hardware, clocks, rubber, and munitions during the nineteenth century.[7] These industries relied heavily on the kind of semiskilled labor that fueled the demand for immigration across the industrial Northeast and Midwest in the United States during the late nineteenth and early twentieth centuries. By the end of World War II, however, the structure of the city's economy and demography had shifted profoundly. Carriage manufacture, which had been dependent on sales to southern states before the Civil War, never truly recovered the predominance it had enjoyed during its antebellum expansion; and of course with the introduction of inexpensive, mass-produced automobiles by the early twentieth century, carriage-making and ancillary metal-making went into sharp, permanent decline in New Haven. Munitions manufacture ascended in importance, however, as the plant that made Winchester weapons boomed during World War I, becoming the largest employer in New Haven County. The health of the Winchester Repeating Arms Company was sustained through World War II, and though it declined thereafter, the company continued to be an important source of jobs and wealth through the Korean War. With the demise of heavy industry, the garment industry took up the slack during the early and middle decades of the twentieth century, again employing mostly semi-, and unskilled workers, and primarily women. But large-scale manufacturing at mammoth industrial sites was fading and in its place emerged dozens of smaller-scale operations run out of former factories and warehouses. As the garment industry was unionized in New York during and after World War I, so-called runaway shops sprang up overnight north and south of New York City along the coastlines of Connecticut and in New Jersey. Garment makers of all kinds along the Eastern Seaboard employed the cheap labor and skills brought by immigrant women from southern and eastern Europe. With the coming of World War II, male workers were siphoned into the armed services, so jobs previously reserved for nonimmigrant males in New Haven's manufacturing plants like Winchester and Sargent's (the city's prominent lock and hardware manufacturer) became available to adult workers who had not been drafted into military service. Increasingly these were African Americans involved in a pattern of chain migration from the Carolinas, as well as second-generation immigrant women. The Great Migration, which had barely touched New Haven during its most transformative phase (before World War I and the Great Depression) began pushing northward into Connecticut. Munitions and other industries that had previously discriminated against African Americans were forced to open their doors and offer opportunities to employ, and even promote, workers in the most menial occupations into semiskilled and skilled positions. As a consequence, the character of New Haven's population began to shift dramatically.[8] Notably, then, while the very small sample of families recruited into the Yale Longitudinal Study was diverse socioeconomically, educationally, religiously, and ethnically, there were no African American children participating in the study. Clearly "self-selection" played a role in the recruitment process.

EVELYN'S FAMILY RELATIONS

Evelyn's mother seemed like an unhappy woman—she was characteristically described by the clinicians as "tense"—and it was not clear how stable her own parents' marriage had been.[9] Evelyn's mother found Evelyn difficult and hard to understand, though objectively, sister Wendy was far more troublesome and temperamental. In the clinical material, the conflict between Evelyn and her middle sister is most prominent while considerations of the younger sister were in the background. Soon after Evelyn joined the study, the entire family was seen by the staff's psychotherapists, but Evelyn's mother left treatment after a few years, finding it to be too time-consuming with the new demands imposed by a part-time job that she had taken in a restaurant. Her husband remained in therapy, however, even after the family had moved a couple of suburbs away from the Yale Child Study Center and at the cost of considerable effort, for to do so he had to assume primary responsibility for transporting the children back and forth to their sessions.

In general, the father was perceived by Evelyn as volatile and capable of unpredictable and intense anger. While it was never articulated by the parents, Evelyn came to believe over the course of several years that her parents had wanted one of their children to be a boy and that her father in particular was disappointed about having had no sons.[10] He frequently felt and pointedly expressed irritation with Evelyn, whom he identified as most resembling his own inclination toward indirectness and dissembling in dealings with others. Evelyn's mother similarly voiced concern about what she called Evelyn's "slyness" in her attempts to "get her own way." Like her husband, she disliked what she perceived to be Evelyn's manipulative style of gratifying her wants, but she was not as annoyed about this tendency in Evelyn as he was.[11] Clear "favorites" among the children were verbalized by the parents. Revealingly, Wendy, the middle child, who seemed to be aggressive and boisterous with everyone, was the father's favorite; he admired the very aspects of her personality that he admittedly lacked, that is, her assertiveness and straightforwardness. The mother favored the youngest daughter but she appreciated Evelyn's obedient nature and her frequent attempts to understand the mother's feelings. She interpreted Evelyn's efforts to anticipate her desires as mostly genuine, even though these same tendencies irked her at times. The mother also expressed an almost inexplicable fury at Evelyn from time to time. Perhaps as a result, many of Evelyn's strategies in dealing with others appeared as attempts to deflect anger or to "get what she wanted without asking for it."[12]

AGGRESSION AND THE CONSTRUCTION OF GENDER: EXCERPTS FROM THE CLINICAL RECORD

We offer the following three excerpts from Evelyn's clinical record— "snapshots" from Evelyn's therapeutic interactions with Ritvo at ages five, seven, and ten—to illustrate the kind of material available from the study for historical review. These excerpts of Ritvo's original process notes include Ritvo's statements summarizing his formulation of a session. We chose to present the therapeutic process materials because they are the most detailed records in the collection and they comprise the majority of the entire recorded data from the longitudinal study.

While we have chosen to feature sessions illustrating a theme that was particularly strong in the cultural currents of the time—changing gender roles and how women or girls could and could not be assertive and aggressive—Ritvo was very interested in aggression and in gender development. Aggression, in particular, was the overarching theme in his clinical/intellectual work and at the very least, we need to acknowledge that he was more inclined to record this type of material and perhaps to elicit this in Evelyn as he engaged with her on this thematic playing field.[13] Theoretical shifts in psychoanalytic developmental theory and clinical practice with children in the next two decades mean that present-day clinicians might well see the material Evelyn presents in these excerpts through different filters—those dealing with her concern about her relationships and attachments to others and her worry about being left alone, unloved, or rejected in favor of her adored, though fiery, middle sister.[14] The latter emphasis reflects a so-called object-relations perspective that began to influence psychoanalytic work with children by the mid-1960s. Indeed, the family focus of the Yale Longitudinal Study reflects the emerging influence of the object-relations perspective, which describes the process of developing an individual mind or psychic organization in relation to other persons in the individual's environment. Further, the object-relations perspective emphasizes that individuals relate to others and to experiences according to how they were shaped by their family experiences in infancy and childhood. An individual who experienced, for example, a neglectful upbringing might as an adult expect similar behavior, especially from those persons who consciously or unconsciously remind that individual of someone from their childhood. Further, these internalized schemas or representations of people become the templates by which a person anticipates the behaviors and feelings of others in his or her present relationships. Therapists observing through this filter might well have emphasized different aspects of Evelyn's material in their notes and formulations and indeed, might have elicited different material in their work with Evelyn. Hence, this clinical material not only reflects Evelyn's larger cultural and social world; it also is a measure of the larger theoretical and professional world of child analysis and psychotherapy in the 1950s.

An additional caveat is important here. We are presenting only material from Evelyn's work with her therapist, but the value of the Child Study Center's longitudinal study was that other therapists were simultaneously documenting interactions with the children's parents. With a few exceptions—for context—we have chosen not to present parallel material from parents' therapies or interviews so as not to overwhelm our method's objective: to demonstrate how a historian might fruitfully use clinical material such as therapeutic process notes of interactions with a child. Records from more than one family member add to the complexity of the historian's task but do not change its intent or focus.

A word about the "normative" developmental arc for a child five to ten years of age will be helpful here. Children of this age are starting to enter a broader social world with their entry into school. They encounter other children and adults beyond their family. Indeed, for children from Evelyn's time, entry into school represented an even more dramatic shift in peer relations than is currently true, inasmuch as many fewer children in the 1950s and 1960s first attended preschool programs or out-of-home child care. Children of this age are also developing cognitive skills for more logical and complex symbolic thinking. They begin to take on the values and beliefs of the adults around them and start to struggle with complex feelings like shame, guilt, and disgust. They come to understand that others have a different point of view and different knowledge than they have, and that these differences have consequences for how others behave and for their interactions with others. They become curious about what others think and feel, that is, about the mind of other persons in addition to what they can directly observe about others' behavior. During this developmental period, children begin to develop a more defined sense of self and compare themselves to others. Their widening peer group in schools facilitates exposure to social comparison and competition. They begin to recognize disparities and differences in their abilities relative to other children, and self-esteem and self-worth become important developmental themes. In this comparison of abilities, gender is key—children are investigating the typical or expected gender roles for boys and girls. In each of these respects, Evelyn appears to be a typically developing child.

The records of the Yale Longitudinal Study afford us a closer look at Evelyn's internal world—and especially how she is defining who she is vis-à-vis others—than might be available by typical observational studies in middle childhood. The first passage we highlight is from the process notes and comes from the spring of 1956, after a year-and-a-half of therapy. Evelyn is struggling with what it means to be angry and aggressive. She is just five years old now and is more often using imaginary play as a way of conveying her worries and thoughts.

> [Evelyn] says she's no longer afraid of witches . . . She told me that she had gotten over them "last night," that it [her dream?] involved clowns and witches, that the clowns chased the witches. When they caught the witches they tied them up and when they got all the witches they changed clothes and places with them and became witches themselves. When I asked about the sex of the witches and clowns, she told me the witches were men and the clowns were women. The witches were men who wore witches' wigs. . . . I talked with her further about the clowns and witches' changing roles and changing the sex and she told me that women can change into men and I showed an interest in how and when this takes place. She intimated that it takes place when a girl is very, very small. That it has already taken place in Tammy. Tammy is a boy who has hair like a boy but she does not have a penis yet. Wendy only pretends she is a boy. About herself, Evelyn says that there are times when she would like to be a boy but she is not going to change. When she grows up she is still going to be an actress but is going to be married too and have children in addition to being an actress.[15]

In this excerpt, Evelyn's play about very fluid gender—a boy can be a girl and a girl can become a boy—is typical for her age but also for Evelyn. Only a few months earlier, it should be noted, Evelyn had expressed the opinion that a woman could only do one *or* the other, but not be *both* a mother and an actress/breadwinner. She had also remarked in earlier sessions that she wanted to be an actress when she grew up but did not think that it was compatible with being a mother. Again, gender roles in her family tend to be fraught with difficult choices—being one gender means giving up some behaviors, feelings, and even desires. Also, as in her later material, aggression as with witches is a male trait, though the clowns are able to subdue the witches and then steal from them—they become witches in clown's clothing and fool everyone. Recall too that this is Evelyn's personal struggle in her family—her sister Wendy torments her and, in her eyes, "takes" from her. How can she subdue her sister and at the same time recover some of her assertiveness to win back her mother's admiration? Is it possible, too, to see this material as reflective of the broader cultural dilemma for women of this era? Can they take on the career and professional aspirations of their male partners and at the same time seem feminine? If they continue to appear feminine, even stereotypically so, can they fulfill their silent, assertive aspirations without the world seeing them and branding them witch-like and surely not sufficiently feminine or attractive?

We turn now to a second excerpt. This comes from three years into Evelyn's treatment, during her visits in November of 1958. Evelyn is seven years old, Wendy at the time is five, and Tammy, three. For several weeks Evelyn has been playing about aggression and fighting, angry feelings, and how to deal with being angry. She has also struggled with the prohibitions she seems to perceive about girls fighting, feeling angry, or being assertive—this is the province of boys and men or of very evil women (witches and so on) who perhaps in the totality of their evilness are not *really* women but a heinous, genderless mix.

Evelyn picks up the doll, says it is "stupid," and throws it out the window (after two attempts). The therapist asks why she did this and she says because "it's stupid." "What's the doll's name?" he asks. She replies, "Matilda." (This is the name he had given the "mean aunt/witch" the day before.) She wouldn't answer further inquiries about what the doll had done. Her therapist writes:

> She screamed back at me and I said maybe Matilda had made too much noise [reference to Evelyn's singing the day before, causing the mother to react furiously] and that's why she had to be thrown out. Evelyn continued shouting, looking fierce and angry at me and although this was always in a mock and playing way, the feeling portrayed was extremely intense. . . . She was very bossy and angry with me, she went into the play where she was the teacher and I was the bad boy. She complained to my

mother about me, hit me with a ruler, tied my hands, made me stand in the corner, shot at me and finally burned me. Every motion and sound . . . I made was immediately shouted down while she glowered at me ferociously and kept attacking me . . . I said that I thought the teacher was being very mean to me, that she was behaving like a witch and that I was frightened when she looked at me with that horrible angry expression on her face.

She asked who was "boss" of the Child Study Center. She insisted that the "boss of the whole place must be a man who must be older than anybody else." We talked about "who is the boss" in various places. Her aunt is the boss at school [she was her school's principal] because she was born before every body and her father is the boss at home because he was born before the mother.

Age has its privileges, and remember that Evelyn is the oldest in her family. Thus there seems to be a contradiction as to who is the boss. At first it was the man; then it seemed to be the oldest one. The therapist wonders,

[W]hom the mother gets angry at and scolds at home? . . . and she told me that it's not often at Tammy [the youngest] but most often at Wendy and sometimes at herself. . . . It seemed to me that this hour related to the mother's temper and anger at the children . . . especially as Evelyn was the one that the mother attacked yesterday.[16]

The next week Evelyn continues her explicit play about gender and aggression as described again by her therapist:

In the [role] play she is again the woman who performs and is the one who is running a business. It seems to me that this may have connections with the mother's having done some outside work for money in recent months [she works in a restaurant now]. It is as though the woman now is not only the boss but an important provider as well.

Her therapist remarks:

> [S]he gives a rather remarkable summary of the cleavage lines
> in her own family: she said that Tammy is her mother's favorite,
> Wendy is the father's favorite, and first she said that she was the
> father's favorite but then changed it and said that she [Evelyn]
> was the grandmother's favorite. When I asked her about this
> switch, she said that at one time she was her father's favorite,
> but the father preferred boys and therefore preferred Wendy
> because she plays like a boy.[17]

In this material, Evelyn's therapist is keenly tuned into his patient's concerns about being assertive and about defining her role in
her family—who likes whom better, does standing up for oneself make
a girl more or less likeable, is being the boss a privilege for boys only,
can she boss her therapist around and still have him like her and see
her? From the clinical perspective, Evelyn is able to represent these
questions symbolically in her play and in direct questions/conversa-
tions with her therapists—at least from these records, she seems developmentally age-appropriate. Is Evelyn's attention and worry about
how girls can be assertive particularly heightened in her as she sees her
mother turning more toward her younger sister—and by her mother's
belief (as she stated in an interview before Evelyn began her therapy)
that boys are "brutal and attacking by nature"? Or were we to have had
the advantage of this high magnification in the lives of many school-
age girls from the late 1950s, would we have seen similarly intense worries and confusions? Does Evelyn mirror only timeless, age-expected
efforts to understand the essence of being one gender or another? Or
are her efforts granted a particular urgency not only because of her
own family's concerns, but also because of the cultural overtones of
the time?

Our third excerpt comes near the end of Evelyn's therapy in January
of 1961. She is nearly ten years old. Her style of dealing with irritation
and anger was to hide her feelings, pretend that she was not upset, while
at the same time subtly working out her way. Her mother had taken
a job outside the family in a restaurant, and her middle sister Wendy

seemed more and more like their mother, at least according to Evelyn, who was still preoccupied with gender-specific behaviors.

> Evelyn tells how the girls play doctor at home. . . . Wendy is the doctor, Evelyn wants to play nurse but often Wendy doesn't let her. Evelyn asks her therapist if they can "change her day off so she can go to the gym class [her school doesn't have a gym], then withdraws her request, giving the impression that she wants to show me how good she is by giving up something. . . . Getting peanuts, she tried to make it appear that I wanted them and she's getting them for me." This was again [acquiring] something for herself by making it appear that she was getting me something I wanted. I pointed this out to her and said how hard it seemed to be for her to say she wanted something, letting another person see she wanted it, she behaved as though she felt this was not the right thing to do.[18]

Evelyn has developed sophisticated and effective strategies for disguised assertiveness—she gets her way by appearing to nurture and care for others, a stereotypically feminine role that would only a few years later be repudiated by the early feminists. Her adaptation is a fragile one, for it is not always so effective with her middle sister or her mother. Nonetheless, it is a practiced and already integrated part of her personality. Again our questions—can we view this material both as an individual and a cultural narrative regarding gender differences in assertion, aggression, and the expression of any negative or angry emotions? May we view this narrative as a window on the cultural themes of the time and the dilemma facing many young girls as opportunities were beginning to widen for women in the workforce and as more women were becoming better educated?

Clifford Geertz has written that "societies, like lives, contain their own interpretations. One has only to learn how to gain access to them." Putting aside the "only" in this epigram is of course an impossibility. For gaining access to interpretations, whether they inhere in societies or lives, is the entire point in trying to understand the past or children's development. Indeed, each of our collaborations seeks its opposite in Geertz's simile.[19]

Our method is to "read out" from a life—or more accurately, the representation of a life—to the society that shapes, supports, and tears at it. Our "sample," such as it is, is miniscule. Yet the authors of the process notes that constitute the text, which now stands for that life, produced an enormous amount of information for us to interpret. If only we can learn "how to gain access" to the interpretations this life/text contains. So our method is also to try to understand how this developing girl (and her family) made use of the cultural discourse available to her to make sense of her self and of her world. How did she understand what was possible for her? How did she comprehend her future—its limitations and its promises? Much of how she understood was through the lens of gender. She grew up in a world in which females were portrayed as both the victims of men and the objects of their protection. Males were direct, active, aggressive, and even violent; females passive, yielding, surreptitious, and even sneaky.

The cultural discourse of the day—the "tool kit" of her consciousness—was, as we have suggested, a paradox, for the era that glorified marriage at a young age, self-fulfillment through childrearing, homeownership, consumerism, and asymmetrical gender roles was perhaps the briefest "period" in America's cultural history. One could realistically cite the years 1954 to 1958 as precisely those that most closely resembled the ideal of family life held out to upwardly mobile white Americans after World War II, when all the ingredients of family building came briefly into alignment. Marriage was seemingly stable, home ownership at an all-time high, divorce at a decades-long low, the proportion of male breadwinners was historically large, parents were young, and children were born and raised in close sequence during a very narrow span of the family's life cycle. These were the mythical 1950s but the cultural ideals they enshrined were understood as very real for girls learning how to accommodate themselves to the expectations of their gender, not just during these few years of the mid-1950s but also for many years afterward.

In Evelyn's material as processed by her therapist, we see those cultural ideals as lively constructions in her mind and her development. Her mother embraced these ideals and passed that legacy on to her daughter. Evelyn struggles, sometimes agonizingly, to decide what she, as a girl, could do and be. How assertive and demanding could she be before she would lose this ideal of femininity and if she crossed some invisible cultural, family line, would the price nonetheless be worth the gain? Perhaps a young girl today worries about the same questions in general, but chooses other cultural icons to represent them and the lines are not between feminine and non-feminine stereotypes but rather motherhood-career boundaries. How will she raise her children in a corporate, increasingly global, world and a world in which education looms large in determining so many outcomes related to definitions of success among contemporary middle-class Americans? Will she choose to raise children at all and how does this choice affect her sense of self and her visions of personal fulfillment? In other words, how will she advance in her work and begin her family? For a young white, middle-class girl today, it's not whether she needs to give up an idealized feminine role but when or if she assumes motherhood alongside a profession. Across the generations, the developmental issue is the same; it is just expressed or represented using the cultural material most at hand.

So why is this observation important and why does it define the nature of the collaboration between historians and developmental clinicians? We suggest first that this collaboration goes beyond those skilled in each field learning the basic language and premises of the other—it is more than professional appreciation and respect. Rather, looking at lives up close to understand culture is like the prospector sifting patiently through a plate of ore looking for the gold flecks as clues to the lode that must lie upstream. How children and adults talk about their lives in and out of the clinical setting provides the gold flecks that lead us to the social-cultural vein. It is neither that cultural currents shape developmental themes nor that developmental themes exist outside of culture. There is an interaction—one shapes the other—and to understand and study this phenomenon, we need a lens that moves from the fine-grained detail to the large picture and back again. The records of

the Yale Longitudinal Study offer us one way to use that lens to consider both a time of great sociocultural change in American family life
and an era of transformation in our understanding of child and family
development.

NOTES

1. Yale Child Study Center, Longitudinal Study YRG-37E (96-A-082), box 1
(October 31, 1955), 2, Yale Manuscripts and Archives, Sterling Memorial Library, New Haven. The interest in the parents' sexuality was not unique to
the psychoanalysts in this study but rather was part of an emerging "enlight-
enment" about human (and specifically female) sexuality during the postwar
years. Recall that the Kinsey Report on human sexuality had been published
only a few years before this study began, and as mentioned earlier in this volume, opinions about men's and women's divergent perceptions, experiences,
and knowledge of sexuality varied greatly. See Alfred C. Kinsey et al., *Sexual
Behavior in the Human Male* (Philadelphia: W.B. Saunders, 1948); Kinsey et al.,
Sexual Behavior in the Human Female (Philadelphia: W.B. Saunders, 1949);
and Betty Friedan, *The Feminine Mystique* (New York: W.W. Norton, 1963).
For historical accounts of sexuality of the era, see John D'Emilio and Estelle B.
Freedman, *Intimate Matters: A History of Sexuality in America* (New York:
Harper & Row, 1988), chaps. 11–13; Elaine Tyler May, *Homeward Bound: Ameri-
can Families in the Cold War Era* (New York: Basic Books, 1988); Linda Gordon,
The Moral Property of Women: A History of Birth Control Politics in America
(Urbana: University of Illinois Press, 2002), chap. 11; and Stephanie Coontz,
*Marriage, a History: From Obedience to Intimacy, or How Love Conquered Mar-
riage* (New York: Viking, 2005), 251–52.

2. See, e.g., Julia Grant, *Raising Baby by the Book: The Education of American Mothers* (New Haven: Yale University Press, 1995); Barbara Beatty, Emily D. Cahan, and Julia Grant, eds., *When Science Encounters the Child: Education, Parenting, and Child-Welfare in Twentieth-Century America* (New York:
Teachers College Press, 2006); on the possible moral/philosophical implications of this trend, see Philip Rieff, *The Triumph of the Therapeutic: Uses of
Faith after Freud* (New York: Harper & Row, 1966).

3. For survey data on postwar optimism, see, e.g., John Modell, *Into One's
Own: From Youth to Adulthood in the United States* (Berkeley: University of
California Press, 1991), 219–20.

4. See Chapter 9.

5. See Chapter 3, David Carlson's essay in this volume, on the role of Redlich in particular in the emergence of Yale Child Study Center as a focal point of psychoanalysis in the United States during its heyday.

6. Maurice R. Davie, "The Pattern of Urban Growth," in G. P. Murdock, ed., *Studies in the Science of Society* (New Haven: Yale University Press, 1937), 132–61; August Hollingshead and Frederick C. Redlich, *Social Class and Mental Illness: A Community Study* (New York: Wiley, 1958); and Jerome K. Myers and Bertram H. Roberts, *Family and Class Dynamics in Mental Illness* (New York: Wiley, 1959). See Chapter 3, as well as the research note by Hans Pols on the significance of the relationship between social stratification and mental illness by Hollingshead and Redlich: Hans Pols, "August Hollingshead and Frederick Redlich: Poverty, Socioeconomic Status, and Mental Illness," *American Journal of Public Health* 97, no. 10 (October 2007): 1755; and Julia Adams and David L. Weakliem, "August B. Hollingshead's 'Four Factor Index of Social Status': From Unpublished Paper to Citation Classic," *Yale Journal of Sociology* 8 (Fall 2011): 11–20.

7. Famously, the major weapons maker in New Haven, the Winchester Repeating Arms Company, had descended from the Eli Whitney gun manufactory, where Whitney had refined the concepts of interchangeable parts used to such revolutionary effect on his more famous invention, the cotton gin; see Douglas W. Rae, *City: Urbanism and Its End* (New Haven: Yale University Press, 2003).

8. See ibid.; on Italian immigrants and the rise of the garment industry in New Haven, see Lassonde, *Learning to Forget*, chaps. 3–5.

9. For more background on both parents, see Chapter 9.

10. See "Evelyn Olsen," Yale Child Study Center, "Yale Longitudinal Study," January–February 1956, YRG-27 E Yale Child Study Center Collection, box 1. It was common for Italian immigrants and their children to favor male over female children; see Lassonde, *Learning to Forget*, chaps. 4–5.

11. YRG-27 E Yale Child Study Center Collection, 96-A-082, box 1.

12. Evelyn's therapist raised this issue repeatedly over the course of the nine years he treated her; see ibid., boxes 1–7.

13. Marianne Kris and Samuel Ritvo, "Parents and Siblings—Their Mutual Influences," *Psychoanalytic Study of the Child* 38 (1983): 311–24; Samuel Ritvo, "Object Relations," *Journal of the American Psychoanalytic Association* 10 (1962): 102–17; Samuel Ritvo, "Correlation of a Childhood and Adult Neurosis: Based on the Adult Analysis of a Reported Childhood Case," *International Journal of Psycho-Analysis* 47 (1966):130–31; Samuel Ritvo, "Late Adolescence—

Developmental and Clinical Considerations," *Psychoanalytic Study of the Child* 26 (1971): 241–63.

14. See, for instance, the observations of Virginia and John Demos in Chapter 5 about changing therapeutic and theoretical lenses since this era.

15. Yet a few months earlier, Evelyn had revealed to her therapist that she at first thought that *he* was scary and resembled a clown. See YRG-27 E Yale Child Study Center Collection, 96-A-082, boxes 1–7 (April 11, 1956).

16. YRG-27 E Yale Child Study Center Collection, 96-A-082, boxes 1–7 (November 6, 1958).

17. Ibid., 96-A-082, boxes 1–7 (November 14, 1958).

18. Ibid., boxes 1–7 (January 17, 1961).

19. Clifford Geertz, "Deep Play: Notes on the Balinese Cockfight," in Geertz, *The Interpretation of Cultures: Selected Essays* (New York: Basic Books, 1973), 453.

ᎧᎾᎮ 9 ᎨᎬ

A Dynamic Biography, Based on
Direct Observation and Psychoanalytic
Treatment in the First Ten Years with
Follow-up to Age Fifty-Five

SAMUEL RITVO ET AL., WITH A FOREWORD BY
DAVID RITVO AND AFTERWORD BY "EVELYN"

FOREWORD
DAVID RITVO

Completed two months before his death and published posthumously here, Samuel Ritvo's "A Dynamic Biography" represents the capstone of a remarkable sixty-year career as psychoanalytic clinician, educator, and researcher. Perhaps nowhere did his acumen in all three areas cohere more than in his work in the Yale Child Study Center's Longitudinal Study of the Child. The story of Evelyn told here comes from observations made in the course of psychoanalytic treatment from ages three to eleven, and, most remarkably, from follow-up interviews and correspondences at ages fifteen, thirty-four, fifty-three, and fifty-five.

As one reads through it, one comes to appreciate the power both of what is abiding—the influence of early childhood experiences—and what is in flux: emotional shifts that accompany changes within the family (the arrival of siblings, parental discord, moves), developmental phases, the psychoanalysis. Perhaps most curious to the reader, we also see here the power of Evelyn's relationship with her psychoanalyst.

Evelyn seems to have been fortunate that her mother and she were "a pair well suited to one another"; that her mother, in her ambition for her daughter and trust in the institution and treating physician, supported her daughter's treatment; and that the apparent failure of the father to imbue her with a positive regard for herself as a girl was able to be made up for in the analysis and through the person of the analyst.

The period in the nation's history during which Evelyn was in the study, the Eisenhower era, was a time of great confidence in the country and faith in science. I can remember getting my first polio vaccine at the Child Study Center from my pediatrician, "Doctor Sally"—that is, Sally Provence, M.D., the pediatrician involved in the study. I can also remember where I was when the news of Sputnik came on the radio and the subsequent tracking of we students so that the "fast learners" could be the vanguard of a new generation advancing our nation.

It would be understandable that, in this atmosphere, the Longitudinal Study of the Child would be undertaken with great excitement and optimism. Testifying to the sense of importance that those in psychoanalytic circles had about their work, my father worked twelve hours a day six days a week. Ritvo family trips to New York City and western Massachusetts on Saturdays were planned so that we children could have precious time with him in the car as he traveled monthly to all-day meetings of the New York Psychoanalytic Institute and Western New England Psychoanalytic Institute. (Our mother would take us to musicals and museums in New York and ski areas in the Berkshires while Dad was in his meetings.)

The prevailing belief within the psychoanalytic community was in psychoanalysis as a science. Dad held strongly to this view throughout his career, as evidenced by his adept use of psychoanalytic metapsychology, especially the structural theory, to understand and explain Evelyn's emotional life. The ruling ego psychology seemed fitted to Dad's faith in people's capacity for mastery—or, in psychoanalytic terms, in their ability to manage the vicissitudes of the instincts and the harshness of the superego. Helping people who struggled in their attempts at mastery was, of course, where psychoanalysis came in.

This present account, written almost half a century later, is more a biography, an account of a life, than it is a case study. The descriptor "dynamic" in the title is a double entendre—perhaps intended to suggest more the liveliness of a story than a psychoanalytic metapsychological theory. And the story is really about the relationship between two people, my father and Evelyn, not just in the course of an analysis but all the way through to Evelyn's grandmotherhood and Dad's last years. Of course there was, as Hans Loewald wrote, a "developmental gradient" in the relationship by virtue of its professional nature. But as Dad mentions more than once in the account (and in keeping with his beliefs expressed in 1978), the benefit that Evelyn gained from her treatment was not just from the interpretive work but also from his role as a person in her life, "a new object" in psychoanalytic parlance.[1] Yet he seems to be apologetic in his observation of this phenomenon, perhaps, ironically, feeling that it makes the work less scientific, a view more in keeping with the orthodoxy of post–World War II American psychoanalysis: "*Though not a basic aim of the technique of psychoanalysis* [my emphasis], the analyst's becoming a new object may play a significant role in the psychoanalytic process and make an important contribution to the therapeutic effect of psychoanalysis, particularly in childhood, when meeting a developmental need makes it possible for the child to come closer to realizing his or her potential." Thus we observe him in 2008 struggling to stay loyal to the precepts of the psychoanalytic world of a half-century earlier when psychoanalysis, just like America, was in ascendancy, and anything seemed possible if we only applied ourselves with scientific rigor and American know-how.

In the letter Evelyn sent to my father when she was fifty-five in her last communication with him, she described him as "trustworthy" and empathic ("you always heard me"), "kind and supportive," and "loving." What better person to have had as an analyst . . . or a father.

A DYNAMIC BIOGRAPHY

SAMUEL RITVO

(WITH R. LORD, A. NAYLOR, S. PROVENCE, AND A. SOLNIT)

In 1949, Ernst Kris and Milton J. E. Senn organized a longitudinal study in child development at the Yale University Child Study Center. The study has been described in detail elsewhere.[2] For the purpose of this presentation it will suffice to say that the original study focused on the first five years of life. The purpose of the study was not to verify psychoanalytic theory but to address the expectations of clinicians and theoreticians that such studies would supply essential data for the understanding of personality and for the early diagnosis and, hopefully, prevention, of personality disturbances.[3] Historically, the study was initiated at a time when psychoanalysts expected that direct observational studies could lead to a reexamination and refinement of psychoanalytic theories of the emerging and functioning person, which would supplement the contributions that psychoanalysis had already made for the retrospective study of human behavior. In this study the retrospective and prospective outlooks were combined: educators, pediatricians, psychoanalysts, psychologists, and social workers collaborated as expert observers of child life in various settings and as specialists in their own field, making direct observational data available as a basis for predictions that could also be examined retrospectively.

Although it was an observational study, it was interventional, providing pediatric, educational, and psychological services for the children. The act of rendering service was an essential variable of the research, making possible continuity of observation and access to relevant data that might otherwise be missed or be difficult to assess. The professionals and clinicians were aware that their service and intervention influenced the observation. To protect the validity of the data, this fact was taken into account and precautionary measures were taken.

In return for the families' cooperation, the study provided complete well and sick baby care in which the pediatrician served as the child's physician, as an observer of the child and family, and as the administrator of periodic developmental tests. On the basis of all these data, the pediatrician made assessments of the child's maturation and development.

Another principle of the study was to adapt itself to the growth of the child, ensuring the acquisition of data that would be relevant to the formulation and description of a dynamic life history of each child. Thus, in their third year the children entered nursery school where they were observed by psychoanalysts and nursery school teachers while involved in an appropriate educational experience. From ages three to five the children were also seen by the psychoanalyst in the therapy room. This step, originally intended as a modification of the usual therapeutic situation for purposes of observation and exploration, was in some instances (based on the need of the child) expanded to include therapy as well. In the case of Evelyn, the subject of this presentation, psychoanalytic treatment was undertaken.

It was envisaged that the combination of prospective and retrospective viewpoints could provide the data for an understanding of genetic and dynamic factors, of endowment and environment, of nature and nurture. This combination would permit the systematic study of life histories necessary for understanding in what way certain personality characteristics arise and how they persist—that is, how the sameness of personality manifests itself despite developmental changes. The nature of the data gathered by these multidisciplinary observers would make it possible to demonstrate the interactions among the child's growth, his or her changing instinctual needs, the differentiation of various ego functions, and the vicissitudes of object relations.[4]

In addition to the multidisciplinary observations in the first five years, Evelyn, who started in analysis at three years, four months while in the nursery school, remained in analysis until her eleventh year, except for a period of one year at age seven when she was in psychotherapy once a week. These data, together with interviews during adolescence and adulthood to age fifty-three and a letter from her at age fifty-five, provide a unique opportunity to study the issues outlined earlier.

FAMILY BACKGROUND

At the time of Evelyn's birth, her father, a man with mechanical and managerial talents, was in his late twenties, seven years older than her mother. He had reacted to two factors in his life situation by shunning his active male self-image. The first was the great love his father had for the eldest child, a daughter two years older than Mr. P. An early idea was that if he had been a girl he would have been the loved object of his admired father, rather than the butt of his repeated criticism. Mr. P. bore a great resentment toward his older sister. He felt that she had not only preempted his father's interest and affection but had also deprived him of the opportunity for a higher education, since the family's limited resources were wasted on the failed education of his sister. Mr. P.'s hostility was transferred to Evelyn when she became the older sister at the age of two. The second factor was the quality of mothering that Mr. P. received from a most aggressive, overprotective mother who warned him all through his childhood and until her death when he was in his mid-twenties to trust only her, and especially not to trust girls, who usually "drain" a man. He accepted her attitude and had never really separated from her emotionally, so that at her death he was left with the unconscious need to replace her.[5]

After the death of her father when she was ten years old, Mrs. P. grew up in an all-female household consisting of her mother, her older sister, and a spinster maternal aunt. Mrs. P. always considered herself ugly compared to her sister. Her mother once told her that she had reacted to her as a newborn with the wish to hide her from the world because of her ugliness. The sisters had been very close while growing up, with physical contact playing a part in their relationship. The sister apparently functioned as the pretty female in this couple while Mrs. P. considered herself far superior in intelligence, unconsciously representing the active male in the twosome. Mrs. P. married shortly after her sister had married and moved away, replacing her sister with her husband and dodging her fear of being left alone with her mother and aunt. Mrs. P. had musical and artistic interests. She had been enrolled in professional training but had stopped just short of fulfilling the requirements for certification. The realization that she had not married a superman, perhaps a condition for more fully experiencing her femininity, led to disappointment.

By the time of Evelyn's birth, Mrs. P. gave the impression of suppressing any show of emotion and regarding both libidinal and aggressive impulses as "evils." Envy and rivalry of her sister, as well as criticism of her mother and husband, were repressed or otherwise defended against. Deep dependence on her mother was replaced by a protective attitude toward her and a surface independence that became an outstanding feature of her contact with the staff of the study. Basically an obsessional character, Mrs. P. had times of crisis in her struggle against evil, especially during subsequent pregnancies. While she emphasized doing things correctly and being fair and just, she also described herself as having "sneaky ways which nobody would suspect." Isolation was one of the main mechanisms by which she dealt with the opposing tendencies and deep ambivalent conflicts in herself. In this way the conflicting sectors of her life were kept well separated. Later, in the nursery school and the treatment, Evelyn showed a preference for the same mechanisms. Mrs. P. was an introspective, imaginative person who characterized herself as a dreamer and whose relationship with Evelyn was imbued with mental stimulation and fantasy.

INFANCY

Although born ten days before the expected date, Evelyn was a mature infant at birth. The parents had both hoped for a boy but were very happy and satisfied with the baby. Mrs. P. chose to carry out most of the baby care herself, very eager to do everything just right and feeling that she was handling the baby quite well. The bottle, used as a supplement to breast feeding after the first week, was fully substituted for the breast at one month when Evelyn developed an oral monilia infection and Mrs. P. felt the breast was more irritating to the mouth lesions than the bottle.

Evelyn and her mother appeared to be a pair well suited to one another. This sensitive, introspective young woman who had earlier established a balance between action and control of impulse was paired with an infant who was receptive to the mother's care, easily satisfied and pacified. The mother had a strong empathic tie to Evelyn and constantly tried to be aware of the infant's feelings, carefully observing and responding to her needs. Through all the feeding the mother gave the impression of trying to gauge the optimal degree of pressure to exert on Evelyn and to find the right combination of permissiveness and frustration. At five months when Evelyn liked the fruit but not the first vegetables offered, Mrs. P. did not experiment with other vegetables but persistently offered the same few. When Evelyn refused to open her mouth and turned away from the spoon, the mother persisted in offering it until Evelyn finally accepted it. Mrs. P., apparently troubled by her own aggression, was then concerned whether this was "forced feeding" and would harm the infant. Mrs. P. also regulated the amount of food she allowed Evelyn to have. She watched how much Evelyn was eating and tried to give her what she thought was enough, concerned that Evelyn would get too fat.

Between seven and nine months Evelyn became much more active in her orality and was unusually preoccupied with mouthing, biting, and chewing. She persisted in biting the rim of the cup when milk was offered. Here the mother exerted her counterinfluence by holding Evelyn's chin so that she could not bite. Evelyn responded by continuing to take solids well but refusing to take milk from bottle or cup for a period of several months. At one year the teaching and training aspect of the feeding took a more moralistic turn. The mother reported that Evelyn would eat something she did not like if rewarded by something she did like. At fourteen months Mrs. P. could accept to some extent Evelyn's feeding herself messily with fingers and spoon, but by sixteen months mother and child had made another deal: Evelyn was permitted to mess and feed herself one meal daily, and Mrs. P. fed her the other two without messing.

Thus throughout the early feeding history the mother exerted varying degrees of pressure on Evelyn to mold the child in the form the mother preferred. Evelyn seemed to adjust quite well to the mother's pressure, aided in this by her marked capacity for receptivity, relaxation, and relatively easy pacification in the feeding.

In the toilet training the mother was much more ambiguous in her demands. When Evelyn did not respond readily to mild pressure, the mother was unable to make a more forceful demand partly because of her guilty feelings, which the child manipulated with great skill. Another factor in the mother's ambiguity was the pleasure she derived from inspecting and handling the stool in the diaper. Evelyn's sluggish, inactive gastrointestinal tract may have been a contributory equipment factor in her not yielding as readily to the mother in toilet training as she had in the feeding.

The receptivity that was noted early in response to her mother's care was a prominent feature of Evelyn's endowment. In her early motor development she was receptive and reactive in her response to the adult rather than the active initiator. She did not use activity for discharge of tension. The mother contributed to the relative underdevelopment in the motor area by her preference for visual contact over physical handling. Consequently Mrs. P. presented the face, eyes, and voice in her contacts with Evelyn rather than other modalities. This contributed to an early visual alertness and discrimination. During the first several months the observation was repeatedly made by the mother and others that Evelyn was particularly interested in the human face, an interest that not only persisted but became more pronounced with time. In the latter part of the first year and in the second year this interest could be seen in her preference for toys with faces and in her ability to discern faces even when they were only faintly outlined.

In her third year, upon entering nursery school, a glance at the face of another person accompanied by a smile was Evelyn's chief way of contacting adults and children. The face also assumed importance in her fantasy play as well as in outbreaks of anxiety and the formation and content of phobic symptoms. In her fourth year her interest in and fear of faces played a prominent part in her therapy. This interest in the face was part of her unusual ability to be keenly aware of the mood and affect of the people around her, especially the mother. Evelyn's preference for visual contact was related to the mother's preference for this way of contacting her child. Bodily contact, though not grossly lacking, was less frequent. The relative paucity of physical contact was thought to play a part in Evelyn's lack of motor skill in the third and fourth years.

Evelyn's interest in dolls and toys with faces, encouraged and shared in by the mother, was followed by fantasy play with imaginary companions in which Evelyn assumed many roles herself. The fantasy play went quite beyond the domestic mimicry usually seen in the second year. Evelyn used the highly advanced fantasy role play as one means of coping with the new sibling and the separation from the mother at age two.[6] By pretending and role playing she was able to bridge physical separations.

A relationship among lack of physical discharge, early autoerotic activity, and early fantasy development was also suggested in Evelyn's reaction to the mother's absence every evening for three weeks when Evelyn was six-and-a-half months old. Evelyn began to fuss before going to sleep, and rocked and banged her head rhythmically in the crib. Much to the mother's discomfort, she also began to masturbate by thigh pressure. Characteristically, the mother worked at distracting her from this activity by offering a feeding or a play contact. The feeding pleasure was now less dangerous in the mother's eyes than masturbation. If interrupted without being offered this kind of substitute, Evelyn became angry, cried, and repeated the activity. At this time the mother also reported that if Evelyn toppled over from the sitting position in her crib or lost the toys out of her crib, she resorted to the autoerotic activity rather than cry or ask for attention from the adult. These behavioral changes persisted when Evelyn was brought to the well-baby clinic three weeks after the mother had stopped her evening work. The pediatrician found that Evelyn's gross motor performance was relatively poor though adequate for her age. She refused to support her weight on her lower extremities. At the time Evelyn was subjected to two stresses: the first was the partial loss of the mother; the second could be called the stress of mastering a newly emerging function, that is, supporting her body weight on her legs. In this function, as in a number of others, Evelyn refused to attempt something new until she was completely ready. Learning seemed to take place silently, with little visible practice. When she took the new step, it was on her own initiative, and when the new activity or function was fully formed.

In this situation, as in the feeding, the mother applied a steady pressure on Evelyn until the masturbation and the disturbance in going to sleep disappeared. The mother restrained Evelyn in bed in such a fashion that she was able to turn over but could not rock in the crib. The restraint probably also impeded the masturbation. During the next two monthly visits, the mother described Evelyn as much more satisfactory to her, more "consistent" and more "eager to please" the mother. The pediatrician had the impression that the mother again showed a greater closeness and empathy with the child. With recovery from this crisis Evelyn made a spurt in her development. In this way the mother again conveyed the moralistic outlook just as she did throughout the feeding. Evelyn's own receptivity facilitated her acceptance of the mother's attitude. We learned years later from the mother's analysis that she felt very guilty because as a teen-age babysitter she had "masturbated" a baby girl.

Evelyn's interest in the face played an important part not only in her fantasy life but also in coping with outbreaks of anxiety. At two-and-a-half her great aunt frightened her at Halloween by appearing as a ghost in a white sheet with eyes and nose cut out. Shortly afterward, at the easel in the nursery school, Evelyn painted a large circle; added eyes, nose, and mouth; and announced, "Halloween!" This was the start of an impressive attempt to cope with the frightening experience, not merely by active repetition in play of the passively experienced terror, but also by imaginative paintings of what she feared. These strategies demonstrated a capacity for richly elaborated fantasy and sublimation that had one source in the identification and object relationship with her gifted, highly introspective mother who missed no opportunity for mental stimulation.[7] For many months after Halloween, Evelyn was afraid of pictures in books or on television of clowns, people in masks,

Santa Claus, knights in armor, even people wearing eyeglasses. She returned many times over to drawings of knights as if, again, to master her passively experienced fear through active repetition of a fantasied representation.

When Evelyn entered the nursery school, her precocious ego development was evident. She was the most mature and predictable child in the group. Although the other children were important to her, she was demonstrative and energetic in her independence and was the least forlorn child when her mother left. She was highly advanced in all her intellectual achievements. Though not especially sociable, the richness of her fantasy was far more advanced than that of her peers. The group got on better when she was there as the initiator of dramatic play. She was unusually determined and persistent as she devoted herself to learning to ride a tricycle uphill or mastering the jungle gym—difficult tasks for her since her motor skills were limited. Yet because it was very important to her to do things the right way, she would refuse certain challenges about which she was unsure, for example, some of the items in the developmental test.

Evelyn's easy separation from her mother in nursery school was a narcissistic blow for Mrs. P., who remarked, "She misses me so little it almost hurts." In what appeared to be identification with the mother's isolation mechanisms, Evelyn was unable to handle more than one relationship at a time, a characteristic that lasted into early adolescence. Mrs. P. also employed isolation as a defense in a physical-spatial sense by keeping the children apart in later sibling conflict and rivalry situations.

EARLY CHILDHOOD

Toward the end of the first year Mrs. P. had mastered her ambivalence and her struggles with aggression and depression enough to develop a strong empathic tie with Evelyn and find genuine pleasure in her child. Despite this empathic tie, Mrs. P. perceived Evelyn's independence as a separation. At the twelve-month well-baby clinic examination she did not look once at her mother, not even for comfort after falling down, and the mother, in turn, hesitated to pick her up. This early separateness was discernible again later in her capacity to remain independent from both her parents.

Toward the end of the first year, Mr. P. grew closer to his daughter. Pleased that her first word was "Daddy," he appreciated her responsiveness and her evident enjoyment of the roughhousing in the evening, after which she went to sleep quickly, much to her mother's surprise.

The feelings of both parents, particularly the father's, changed strikingly with the birth of another daughter, Wendy, when Evelyn was two. The parents' unconscious identification of the children with figures from the past and the children's particular individual qualities played an important role in the change.

Mr. P.'s shame and disappointment in the birth of another girl was so great that he did not announce her arrival. But he soon identified Wendy with himself and saw her as a symbol of the masculinity he wished for but could not fully allow himself, often calling her by boys' names. Wendy's constitutional makeup supported her masculine idealization by the father. From the beginning Wendy was an extremely active, energetic infant in contrast to Evelyn who, except for the early, energetic masturbatory activity, was slower and more muted in her reactions.

Mrs. P., too, had had a strong, conscious wish for a boy during the pregnancy. In contrast to her happiness with the first baby, her reaction to the second was observable gloom. A reflection in the newborn's eyes was seen by the mother as crosses that indicated an early death for the child. Tragically, this proved to be true as though Wendy was destined to enact the fate forecast by the mother.

Within months after Wendy's birth, Mr. P. completely shifted his affections to her from Evelyn who had been loved as an only child, but now, as the elder one, was identified by the father with his own disliked older sister. He transferred the main focus of his affection to Wendy and later to the third sister. Though he continued to respect Evelyn's independence and persistence, he was critical and resentful of her awkwardness compared to Wendy and viewed her protection of her rights and interests as selfishness. Not surprisingly, her reaction to the abandonment by her father was usually to side with her mother, contrary to expectations for a girl during the oedipal phase. Evelyn's relative closeness to her mother was also fostered by Mrs. P.'s conscious attempt to counteract the father's negative ways by paying more attention to her.

The conflict precipitated in the parents by the birth of a second daughter and the changes in the dynamic relationships in the family were aggravated by the striking constitutional differences between Evelyn and Wendy. Extremely well-endowed in looks, vitality, and intelligence, physically graceful, boisterous, daring, and even dangerously reckless in her activity, Wendy stood in vivid contrast to the receptive, adaptable, superficially compliant Evelyn. Overshadowed by her sister, Evelyn tried to gain attention by imitating her, but these efforts were responded to by the parents as clumsy and irritating. Wendy, commanding the attention of both parents, created another problem for Evelyn. Over the years, the parents' rising anger and frustration at Wendy's increasingly provocative ways were displaced unfairly onto Evelyn. As a result, Evelyn often chose to play alone. By distancing herself, as she often did in nursery school as well, she could hope to avoid punishment for Wendy's sins.

The advent of another girl, Tammy, two years after Wendy, again frustrated the hope for a male child. Nevertheless, Tammy was regarded as a most satisfying child from the beginning. She was selected by Mr. P. to be the achiever. Both parents related to her as if she were the boy, and as she grew up her sisters joined in thinking of her in this way. In her analysis Evelyn communicated a fantasy shared by the three girls: the younger the child, the greater the chance it still had to become a boy, even if not born one. By then, at age seven, Evelyn had already given up that hope for herself and for Wendy, but Tammy might very well still achieve it. From Evelyn's analysis we also learned that in all their fantasy games her sisters gave Tammy a male role. In their doctor play Wendy was the doctor, Evelyn the nurse and Tammy, usually a royal personage, was the patient. Mrs. P. did not have the same need for physical distance from Tammy as she had for the other two. A comment when Tammy was three illustrates her attitude: "Even when Tammy's hands are sweaty and dirty they are sweet to hold." The father had the same high admiration of Tammy and so much needed her to be a boy that he denied the existence of her rather severe speech defect for a long time, as did Mrs. P. Evelyn's fantasies and the sisters' play reveal how accurately the children perceived the parents' wishes, fantasies, and feelings about Tammy and how the sibling relationship was influenced and molded by it.

These complex, shifting, emotionally charged identifications in the family, and their changing images and expectations of one another, were being lived out in a tiny, crowded two-family house in which Mrs. P.'s mother lived upstairs. A degree of disorganization due to sexual stimulation and excitement was a prominent feature of the family life. The nature of the mother's reactions conveyed a continuous sexual excitement. Evelyn and her sisters often exchanged beds or shared beds with their parents. There was little privacy; parental fights and the primal scene were frequently observed and overheard by the children. As became evident in the analyses of Evelyn and Wendy, many of their games were principally for mutual masturbatory activities.

Evelyn's statement to her analyst at six illustrated the children's reactions to their sexual excitement after one of their many observations of the primal scene: "Mommy and daddy do what married people do— love. Mommy gets all the love from daddy, and he gets all the love from her. Wendy and Tammy get all the love from me. This is done by kissing. Wendy and Tammy do this to each other while I am at school."

The sexually and aggressively charged atmosphere was viewed as having far-reaching effects on Evelyn. Her awkwardness and the male and female identification were considered in this context. The awkwardness was now viewed not only as a result of her body build and early minimal physical stimulation, but also as a reaction to Wendy's charm. Furthermore, Evelyn's particular awkwardness in approaching her father was seen as an imitation of her mother's condescending feeling that a man must have allowance made for him or be approached at just the right moment, when he is "in the mood." A further contribution to Evelyn's awkwardness was the mother's long-standing ambivalence toward her own and Evelyn's femininity, seen very early in the mother's marring of the child's attractiveness by some tasteless detail of her clothing. Evelyn seemed to be especially inhibited in her motor behavior when being observed, a sign of conflict over her exhibitionism, as confirmed in her analysis. Her awkwardness, like that of other children, also reflected a variable level of anxiety.

Nevertheless, Evelyn still experienced a good deal of pleasure in motor functioning. She was still persistent in mastering physical feats at nursery school. She sustained her investment in difficult physical activities, such as jumping rope and basketball, until she mastered them. This characteristic very likely had roots in the very early autoerotic component of the motor activity of the lower limbs, which had persisted up to the present as a preferred mode of tension discharge. This view was based on a proposition formulated by Ernst Kris in relation to Evelyn's early autoerotic activities. His formulation was that early sexualization exerts a positive or constructive influence in terms of attaching libidinal pleasure to certain activities, which may lead to a tenaciousness of function, given certain situations, whereas in other situations early sexualization may lead to the disruption of or an inhibition of development. Evelyn's early ability to sustain pleasurable investment in an activity until she was able to master it was now considered to have become a character trait.

LATENCY AND PREPUBERTY

In an attempt to improve the family living conditions and buttressed by his increased masculine self-esteem as a result of his analysis, Mr. P. was able to use his father's tools as his own and he set to work building a family room in the basement. During this moratorium, when Mrs. P. was less critical and interfering, there was less strife and also less sexual activity between the parents. The effects on the children were dramatic. Evelyn, then eight, produced some of the best and least messy paintings in her treatment at this time. During more disturbed phases, and well into latency, she would mix all sorts of colors with flour, water, and paste to produce a mess, expressing underlying fantasies of badness, sexuality, and violence. Similarly, Tammy's speech improved considerably while the moratorium was on.

In contrast, Wendy, six, became intensely excited and uncontrolled, related directly to an increasingly close contact with her mother, who, during this interval, discharged not only her hostile aggressiveness on Wendy, but also expressed her loving interest, for several nights sleeping in Wendy's bed with her. Mrs. P.'s relationship with Wendy became progressively wilder and more eroticized as she increasingly identified her with her own poorly repressed, promiscuous wishes and fantasies. The child was an object for her sexual and aggressive strivings, as well as a proxy for enacting them. For these unconscious motivations she did not wish the exciting and explosive Wendy to be changed, and, against explicit advice, took her out of a much needed analysis.

Mrs. P.'s relationship with Evelyn did not have the intensity and sharply conflicted quality of the relationship with Wendy, which was on a level closer to the instinctual drives. She was able to share Evelyn's analyst with her, to delight in her fantasy life, and to foster and participate in Evelyn's unusual capacity for sublimation, by stimulating her drawing and by reading and singing with her.

In reaction to her father's ongoing alienation, Evelyn identified even more with the mother. Like her mother she tended to isolate relationships from one another, had difficulty carrying on more than one relationship at a time, and tended to distance herself. Like her mother she daydreamed and dawdled, and she joined with her in mutual feelings of deprivation.

In contrast to the aggressive and excited interchanges between Wendy and her mother, Evelyn could appeal to the more rational and controlled side of the mother's personality. In fact, reversing what one would expect, the child fostered the mother's self-control. When Mrs. P. became angry, Evelyn typically would hide her feelings or react with a quiet reproach. Such a response, which evoked the mother's guilt and moral reactions, led to more organized, rather than instinctualized, behavior on her part. At times Mrs. P. treated Evelyn as if she were an extension of her own superego, not unlike her own mother. By contrast, she tended to view Wendy more as an instinctual partner. Thus the mother used one child in the service of drive expression and the other in the service of drive control.

When Evelyn was nine the family moved away from the crowded house they shared with the grandmother to a larger year-round house at the shore. The father's admiration and devotion to Wendy began to shift to Tammy, accelerated by Wendy's fear of the water, which handicapped her severely in water sports, the father's favorite pastime. This further disqualified her for the role of the boy who would satisfy the father's longing for a child who would fulfill his own unachieved ambitions. As Wendy's fortunes were sinking, Evelyn's rose for a time when she proved adept at swimming and an eager fisherman. With this shift Wendy became more difficult and obstreperous, eliciting increasingly angry responses from both parents. Here the treatment-research team recalled the mother's very first view of Wendy: crosses in her eyes that foretold an early death. In reaction, Evelyn and Tammy grew closer together and, no longer fearing reprimand from the parents, expressed their own anger toward Wendy more openly. At this point Evelyn took over the parental authoritative role as doctor or teacher in their play together.

Later in latency, with the greater ego resources available to her from the developmental thrust of latency and her analysis, Evelyn achieved a more secure position in the family. She had earned the respect and approval of both parents, had become a mother substitute for Tammy, and had been able to use her own endowments for sublimated activities. Her artistic creativity in school was commended glowingly. Although often awkward there, spilling and dropping things, she had developed as a defense the ability to laugh at herself. Her characteristic ability to tolerate disappointment and gain the ultimate reward of mastery through persistence served her well.

Nevertheless, Evelyn still retained an image of herself as the awkward member of the family who never would be in the preferred position. She was on the periphery, neither making nor being in trouble. In school, where her work was above average, she claimed not to want to be either the best or worst reader, just in the middle. Having learned from her experience with Wendy, she played with only one other child, avoiding the dominating troublemaker who, with her followers, was always being punished. Mrs. P. reportedly had stopped spanking her because Evelyn found this so devastating. Evelyn's middle-of-the-road position can be viewed as avoiding peaks of excitement, both sexual and aggressive, a position consonant with her capacity for sublimation and probably motivated also by her awareness of her mother's battles with Wendy. Although Evelyn had all along looked to her mother for affection and received it, the relationship remained ambivalent. Mrs. P. admired Evelyn's abilities, especially those that represented the mother's interests, but she also identified with Evelyn as the grotesque and unattractive sister. Evelyn could not help seeing that the most intense bond of all, pathological as it was, was that between her mother and Wendy. Mrs. P.'s aggressive, punishing behavior toward Wendy bore out the oft-made observation that the child most spanked and punished is the one most intensely loved.

Evelyn was frightened of her mother at times but displaced much of her fear onto Wendy, who gave her good cause. Should Evelyn, for example, not respond quickly enough to Wendy's demands, Wendy would grab and physically shake her, following Mrs. P.'s frequent practice with all three daughters. Wendy expressed rejection or outright hatred of Evelyn when, abandoned by her father, she felt herself to be alone. This was a striking reversal of the usual situation, for it is generally the older child who, on entering latency, breaks away from the younger. Although Wendy probably initiated the break to avoid further rejection, it is unlikely that Evelyn, aged nine or ten, could see it this way. The jealousy between them was intense. Evelyn told her analyst that Wendy had the more attractive-appearing body, although hers was healthier. She understood from her parents that she played basketball on Saturday mornings to help with her potbelly, whereas Wendy danced to exploit her gracefulness. In these circumstances Evelyn felt herself constantly disparaged.

During latency, Evelyn continued to have difficulty establishing reliable barriers against the breakthrough of instinctual strivings. In the face of derivatives of aggression or sexual excitement in the analytic situation, Evelyn regularly regressed to playing with messy materials, soiling her clothes or the room—a form of discharge that passed her own censorship and that she excused on the grounds that her mother would not object. Despite this, Evelyn was still seen as the family member with the best control and the only one who was functioning well. In her twelfth year, however, on the threshold of puberty, she seemed to be considerably less imaginative and derived little satisfaction from feminine interests, a turn to concreteness frequently encountered in prepuberty as a defense against the derivatives of the early intensification of instinctual drives in preadolescence. Another determinant in the inhibition of her feminine interests was her father's never having experienced her as a delightful and feminine daughter, despite their having achieved a somewhat comradely relationship.

Evelyn's schoolwork was also below her earlier achievement, in part due to the chaos of the household. Attaining academic excellence under those conditions would have required unusually strong motivation. Mrs. P.'s special ambition that the children be well-educated and intellectual was realized all too briefly in adolescence by Wendy. One formulation of this failure was that the mother conveyed her conflicts about her own intellectual ambitions, linked as they were to problems of sexual identity and aggressiveness, more strongly than the intellectual ambitions themselves.

PSYCHOANALYTIC TREATMENT

Psychoanalytic treatment was begun at three years, four months. Evelyn was attending the nursery school and the therapy room was one floor above the school. She was seen three times a week until age eleven except from age seven to eight when she was seen once a week. The first two-and-a-half years of the treatment are presented in some detail because they illustrate the developmental and therapeutic effects of the analysis begun at a critical time when Evelyn was reacting to stress in the family with anxiety and fear. Her fear of pictures of people in masks on television and in books had begun with the frightening Halloween incident with her great aunt. She was also distressed by loud noises like the doorbell, by the aggression of neighborhood children, and by her parents' arguments. New fears kept appearing: she was afraid of the dark and of her bedroom at night; all toys with faces and the paintings on the wall had to be removed before she would go to bed. Projective tests indicated an active struggle with anxiety. The examiner commented on Evelyn's efforts to avoid conflict and unpleasant feelings altogether, a defense that had also been observed in nursery school and remained an outstanding, lifelong characteristic.

In an interview at the start of the treatment, the mother stressed that Evelyn had a mind of her own and that she was slow to anger but could be fierce when she got angry. She was independent going up and down stairs, refusing to hold an adult's hand. By then, quite aware of the shift in her father's affections to Wendy, Evelyn was reluctant to go out alone with her father or remain in the house with him. Mrs. P. was delighted but somewhat awed by Evelyn's very rich fantasy life: she liked to play alone with her toys and to act out favorite stories. But the mother felt the fantasy became too much toward dusk and Evelyn was anxious until the shades were drawn for the night.

In the treatment Evelyn showed the same reluctance to be alone with the analyst as the mother described with the father. She was quite explicit that it was because the analyst was a man. The treatment room was one flight above the nursery school, and Evelyn came upstairs for the session on the days she came to school. For the first six months she refused to come alone with the analyst and insisted on having the teacher remain with her. In her play, her drawing, and her relationship to the analyst, she made it quite clear that she preferred the woman and had no room for the man. Yet there were times when she was coquettish and teasingly contrary.

Being with the man was unsafe and seemed to precipitate a loyalty conflict with her mother. Her first paintings were of mother, sister, and herself. She explained there was no room for Daddy. She warned that if the analyst liked something she would not draw it. She would not let him fix one of her buttons—"Mommy will do it."

Themes prominent throughout the treatment appeared in relation to the analyst in the first few months and kept reappearing in variations consonant with current developmental conflicts and life circumstances. Chief among these were beating fantasies and a fascination with getting wet and dirty when she painted and making messy mixtures that she managed to get on her clothes despite wearing a protective apron. Although often looking shocked, she insisted that her clothes were washable and that her mother did not mind. This behavior was reminiscent of her quiet but firm opposition to the mother's efforts at toilet training. Although she had finally complied, she found other ways to express her opposition.

The beating fantasy first appeared a few months into the treatment when she said that the analyst was a naughty man because he had spanked her mother. This occurred at the same time as the mother announced that she was pregnant with the third child. Evelyn was interested in the prospect of a new baby. She wanted to be a nurse to help get the baby out. During that period she came into her mother's room at night complaining of aches and pains all over her body, and told her a dream in which squirrels and other animals were attacking and eating one another, giving the impression that the news of the mother's pregnancy had stimulated an aggressive reaction. She also had an unusual angry outburst in nursery school. She threw a piece of puzzle at the teacher and was disturbed by this impulsive act. Impressed by her mother's ability to have a baby, she said proudly that her mother was a lady engineer, while her father was not an engineer. He could only make things of wood. Reflecting her parents' wish she said she was going to have a baby brother.

After six months, while still declaring to the nursery school teacher that she did not want to stay with the analyst, she began to be close and cuddly, reading a book with her head in his lap and letting him know she thought about him at home. Finally she was able to tell the teacher that she loved him. Clearly, she had transferred to the analyst her wishes for her father's interest and affection and she could enact these fantasies in the safety of the analytic situation. She was able to use the analyst as a new developmental object for expressing the instinctual needs of a girl in the oedipal period.

When she returned in the fall after Tammy was born (four years, seven months), she interfered with the analyst looking at the baby in mother's arms and told him proudly that she was not afraid of clowns any more, that she was going to be a clown on Halloween. She added that she had not liked him last year but did not feel that way anymore. This declaration ushered in an oedipal transference that became more intense as time went on. Her secret was that the analyst was her best friend. She played marriage games in which a new doll became her new baby. She was content mothering the baby while the analyst was sent out to work. She secretly took a toy home from the therapy room and told mother that the analyst said she could have it. She confided she wanted to have five daughters. At home she was being less truthful and direct and more evasive with her mother, taking things from the other children without permission and showing jealousy of Wendy's being at home with mother while she was in nursery school. The wish for a child and the fantasy of having one were quite strong.

In the family play with the analyst as husband she was very messy preparing the food. The mutual soiling was part of the intimacy and excitement. At home, she said, mother did not get annoyed at the messing but father did. Mother scolded and father spanked when he got angry. In this way she revealed the connection between the beating fantasy, the anal messiness, and getting the excited physical contact with her father. At the same time the mother expressed concern that Evelyn, who had so much to repress and conceal (as became apparent in the analysis), was growing away from her. She felt she knew less and less what Evelyn was thinking. Evelyn went against her mother in sly ways but readily expressed guilt if the mother scolded or punished her.

Evelyn went on to a very direct expression of her romantic and seductive wishes toward the analyst. She expressed her affection as well as her sadness at the thought of leaving him one day. The magic spell will be broken and the analyst will die. She followed this by playing doctor with the analyst. She was the Mommy, excited and giggling, then she shifted to playing with messy stuff and ended by washing her hands, an indication of how the anal messing at this time served as a regressive avenue of discharge for the oedipal excitement. Furthermore, the guilty feelings toward the mother could be easily dissipated with the hand washing, heralding the lenient superego that had been predicted for her.

All this occurred after the mother gave her permission to like the analyst, telling her that he was a doctor who was interested in what children were thinking and helping them with their worries and fears. The mother's positive attitude toward the analyst and the treatment was a critical factor in Evelyn's eventually permitting herself to play out her fantasies and experience her oedipal transference. In this period she was feeling the effects of the father's increasing withdrawal from her, first in favor of Wendy and now in favor of Tammy as Wendy was becoming more troublesome. This issue appeared in the transference displaced onto jealous and competitive feelings toward Jerry, another study child in the nursery school who was in treatment with the analyst.

The idea of gender switches led to Evelyn's fantasy that women can change into men. This happens when they are very small. It had taken place in Tammy, still an infant, who had short hair but no penis yet. This was one of the rare instances when Evelyn admitted that there were times when she would like to be a boy, apparently in the interest of winning her father back. This strong desire to be the favorite was expressed in the transference in the paradoxical statement that if the analyst takes Jerry first he likes *her* better—a reflection of her experience with her father of falling out of favor when the second child came. Her sadness over not being able fully to possess the oedipal object was conveyed in the story of Thumbelina who couldn't marry the swallow because he was too big—he had to leave her behind.

An upsurge of destructive, aggressive primal scene fantasies with cannibalistic, oral-sadistic derivatives led to a disruption of the oedipal marriage play and a resistance. She expressed anxiety in playing that the analyst was the father for fear he would hurt her. She added that Daddy hurts Mommy and breaks things during the night while Mommy is asleep. Then mother and the girls get father up, make a stew and they all eat the father. Also, father could cut up the mother and the girls and eat them too. At the same time, the mother reported that Evelyn was very attached to the analyst and she was very pleased about it. She still had fears of witches at night and wanted her closet door closed. In keeping with her capacity to avoid conflict and unpleasant feelings, her mother observed that Evelyn was very good at reconciling fighting children. She was able to find the right words to restore peace. The mother noted that Evelyn was keen in picking up the mother's uncomfortable attitudes about sex and also about being poor.

Through identification and her capacity for fantasy gratification, Evelyn was able to have a secret closeness with her father. Although her father was very irritated by her awkwardness she prided herself that she had a good voice and could sing well like her Daddy. About the birth of Tammy, the favorite of both parents, she said, "That is when I had *my* baby," the fantasy gratification of her wish to be like her mother and have a child from her father.

The oedipal, primal scene and beating fantasies took on oral-sadistic qualities. At two-and-a-half, Evelyn had feared the white faces with dark eyes that were similar to the ghost costume at Halloween. Now she was afraid of the clowns not only because of their eyes but also because of their big, dangerous mouths. They tied people up, hit them and they died. These fantasies were expressed in the transference. The analyst was a fox with a big tail that was going to tie her up. She confided that she loved to be tied up and played that game with her friends.

She attributed her lack of a penis to her masturbation and felt guilty toward her mother for that. She told a dream about a witch whose nose kept getting bigger and bigger until it was as big as a banana. Then it broke and fell off. Her thoughts about the dream were that men have a penis between their legs and she has a little one. The next hour she said that the nose broke off because the witch touched it and went on to say that she did not want the analyst to see or talk to her mother, a prohibition she had never expressed before.

She was curious about the analyst's steadfast interest in helping her and wanted to know why he never got mad at her (five years, five months) the way her parents did. Did he want to know all about her because she was pretty? It was clear that in addition to being a transference figure the analyst had become a new object for her who gave her a secure feeling of being valued as a girl, an essential experience for a girl in the oedipal phase if she is to feel confident in her femininity. Though not a basic aim of the technique of psychoanalysis, the analyst's becoming a new object may play a significant role in the psychoanalytic process and make an important contribution to the therapeutic effect of psychoanalysis, particularly in childhood when meeting a developmental need makes it possible for the child to come closer to realizing his or her potential.

The experience that the analyst never got angry at her despite her provocations, besides enabling her to feel secure, was, in a sense, analyzing in abstinence, since even to have gotten annoyed would have been to gratify the perverse desires of her beating fantasies and her messing. Nevertheless, she achieved a form of gratification in fantasy by telling her mother repeatedly that the analyst spanked her and by coming down to her mother after the hour with her clothes soiled. Coming down dirtied had the quality of having done something exciting and forbidden and seeking the mother's pardon. She also confided to the analyst that she told mother he hit her in order to keep the secret from mother that she liked him and liked to come. Her next question was whether he was going to get a divorce and marry her or would he get a divorce and marry her mother. That way she could replace her father with the analyst.

She began to show a sexual interest in boys. She declared that boys made her messy by making peepee on her bare bottom. They came at night like burglars. At this time she behaved affectionately and seductively toward the analyst and expressed a wish to stay all night with him the way grownups do. Her mother reported that she had kissed a boy in school and that she was now a "queen" with the boys in the neighborhood (five years, ten months).

ADOLESCENCE

After the termination of the analysis at age eleven, Evelyn was not seen again until she was fifteen. In mid-adolescence she appeared subdued and somewhat depressed. Her comments about her home and school life gave the impression of docility, compliance, inhibition, and a massive repression of adolescent sexuality with no hint of rebellion. She tentatively enjoyed some of the prerogatives of increasing independence but was not about to undertake anything bold or venturesome. Though strongly attached to her family and home, she was on the periphery, with the mother still intensely embroiled with Wendy, and Tammy still the favorite of both parents. Evelyn's attitudes toward herself were reflected in her untidy and careless dress, reminiscent of her nursery school days, which might also have been a defense against adolescent sexuality by making herself less attractive to boys.

At eighteen, after her freshman year in college where she was enrolled in a program preparing for the health profession she had talked about as a child, she initiated a meeting with the analyst. The immediate reason for the meeting was to seek a reference for a summer job that involved living away from home. It became clear in the interview that she was actively engaged in the processes of change toward the end of adolescence that would lead to greater autonomy and that the analyst continued to represent the process of self-examination and self-understanding that facilitates change and adaptation to a new stage of development. She spoke of her "strict superego" and her guilt if she failed to please others and made it clear that she wanted to feel less opposed to her wishes and desires.

Evelyn began to emerge from her drab, muted adolescence in her sophomore year. She achieved a greater degree of independence from her family and attained a leadership role among her peers. Elected to the student government, she was recognized as a person to whom others could turn for help and support. During her junior year, she went on a weekend retreat led by a teacher whose searching theological questions had a strong influence on her, fueled even more by the fact that her husband-to-be, Sandy, then in the service, whom she had admired from afar, was a devout evangelical churchgoer. From this time on, Evelyn believed that through her actions and feelings she was carrying out God's loving will. In effect, this transference of the defense against adolescent sexuality to a permissive, loving superego allowed her to overcome her inhibitions safely and calmly.

Quite in contrast to Evelyn, Wendy, locked in the intensely ambivalent tie to her mother, one aggravated by her provocative and explosive temperament, was increasingly in turmoil. Depressed and desperate, she ran away at seventeen and married shortly thereafter. Tragically, she and her husband met a violent death several years later, leaving behind a newborn infant to be raised by her parents.

The totally opposite modes Evelyn and Wendy responded to and the developmental conflicts of adolescence—particularly those stemming from the intensification of sexuality and aggression and the need to alter the infantile form of tie to the primary objects—reflect their different temperaments. Evelyn's receptivity, easy pacification, and intolerance of anything disagreeable enabled her to moderate and tolerate the tensions and continue functioning adequately while waiting for liberation. In doing so she demonstrated her capacity for self-regulation of affect. Wendy's action-oriented impulsivity, reverberating with the mother's aggression, made a lethal solution all but inevitable in a historical period when turbulence and violence were epidemic among the young.

When Wendy and her husband died, leaving behind Joni, their infant daughter, Evelyn, then a college senior, was able to be supportive to her parents in their grief and in their undertaking to bring up the orphaned child. But she was independent enough to resist the mother's efforts to draft her into being a substitute mother to the baby or, later, to accept the child as a younger sister.

The religious experience marked a pivotal point in Evelyn's transition toward greater autonomy, just as the transference and the real relationship to the analyst had earlier helped her to take developmental steps appropriate to that age. The transference of her "strict superego" defense to a protective, permissive God-father enabled her to loosen the tie to her parents and make the transition to adulthood, that is, to choose a husband, pursue her profession, and establish a new family. In taking these steps, Evelyn drew on the qualities of resourcefulness and independence that she had shown in her early years. In her characteristic adaptive, sublimating way, Evelyn achieved what Wendy, by running away, was unable to do. In the meeting that Evelyn had requested shortly before her religious experience, she had spontaneously expressed the insight that her father could never be close and loving toward her because he identified her with his own older sister. By finding God, loving God, and being loved by Him, she replaced her rejecting father with a loving Father, as she had replaced him with the analyst in the oedipal period. This delayed, sublimated gratification of a desire that had been frustrated enabled her to be independent of both her parents without feeling guilty and thereby fulfill the early prediction that she would develop a loving, protective superego.

ADULTHOOD

Evelyn was seen at thirty-four in two extended follow-up interviews in her home by an interviewer who had never met her before, and in three interviews with her former analyst—one in the office where much of the analysis had taken place, and two in her home. At thirty-four she came across as a delightful young woman—warm, responsive, intelligent, and poised. Pleasant looking, she was fair with brown hair, bright hazel eyes, and a welcoming smile.

Evelyn conveyed a sense of being entirely at ease with herself. For a mother with four young children living in tight financial circumstances, she appeared remarkably serene. She described herself as easy-going and good-natured, with the capacity to enjoy life. Her way of caring for her children reflected these characteristics. She was able to draw on her early recognized talent for fantasy to be attuned to her children's thoughts, feelings, and needs. Intuitive and supportive, she appeared re-laxed, firm, competent, and loving. Her husband shared the same views of child rearing. The two boys, seven and five, were very close despite the usual squabbles. Evelyn was delighted that her third and fourth chil-dren were girls and believed this was the ideal family. She nursed all her children with enjoyment for their first year. She cuddled and crooned to the baby and, quite unlike her own experience with her mother, there was much physical closeness. When Evelyn was hospitalized for her hysterectomy, friends took turns bringing the baby to her. She left the older children with friends, rather than with her mother, who was quite offended. Evelyn had thought this arrangement was really best for the children and had decided to implement it despite her mother's antici-pated negative reaction.

Evelyn was in the ninth year of an apparently good marriage to Sandy, a college classmate and Vietnam veteran, an attractive, quiet man and a homebody like her father. "They say girls marry men like their fathers, and though I never thought of it at the time, it seems that I did." Besides being a homebody, Sandy and her father had other char-acteristics in common: their relatively low educational attainments, and their somewhat limited ambitions. The differences between them, at least in their relationship to Evelyn, were more striking. Evelyn experi-enced Sandy as a nurturing husband and father, in marked contrast to the model provided by her own father. Sandy's and her personalities, unlike those of her parents, were not in conflict. Interestingly, just as Evelyn, when old enough, protected herself against angry confronta-tions with her father by avoidance, she has carried over this behavior into her marriage. When angry with Sandy, she has been able to walk away, to distance herself for a cooling-off period.

Evelyn and Sandy evidently complemented one another. He was in a service industry and, well trained by his mother, knew how to cook and to clean up afterward. True to her old messiness in the treatment room, Evelyn admitted that she simply was not cut out to be a good housekeeper. This was not one of her priorities, but Sandy did not seem to mind. Evelyn indicated that their only real problem at the time was lack of money. She said, "I can put off the trip to Hawaii for a while, but it would be nice to get out every so often." With nothing left over to save, they were reconsidering their careers. After completing her training as a healthcare professional Evelyn had worked in various institutional settings, but she did not like the impersonal climate, nor being on the lower rung of a hierarchical ladder. She was able to find a work setting in which she could have a one-to-one relationship with her clients in their own home. She found the direct relationship and the opportunity to be innovative and creative much more satisfying. She was able to continue this work part-time after her first three children were born.

With the pressure of four young children, Evelyn and her husband were examining the changes they could make to improve their situation. Sandy kept lowering his sights and Evelyn came to terms with this, observing that change was hard for him. She did the same herself, giving the impression that she preferred not to have to cope with the stress and anxiety involved with ambition and competition. She commented wistfully that a colleague had suggested that her true vocation lay in medicine. But on the whole, Evelyn appeared to be cheerfully resigned to her situation and to count her blessings.

Evelyn's tact, intuition, and interest in others have drawn people to her. She valued her clients, who entrusted her with confidences they would share with no one else. She felt she had a gift for establishing rapport quickly, that she was resilient and able to handle hostility well. She had many friends and reported that her friendships "really go deep. We talk, one-to-one, mostly about our feelings and where we're coming from." She believed people turned to her for help because she was nonthreatening, nonjudgmental. She viewed herself as sensitive and a good listener. Able to anticipate danger, she had attempted to warn a friend that an extramarital affair could cause the breakup of her marriage. She implied that she had been able to avoid a similar temptation by anticipating the painful consequences it would produce.

One of Evelyn's regrets was having less time for the church in which she and Sandy had been very active. She mentioned specifically two people in their parish who were in trouble, to whom she cannot now offer help. She also missed the music. Singing in the choir and other groups, occasionally as a soloist, formerly had been a source of deep pleasure. Singing with her mother had been a pleasurable activity in childhood.

Another facet of Evelyn's strong tendency to maintain a cheerfully resigned surface was her avoidance of involvement with persons with pathological emotional disturbances, a seeming paradox in one so drawn to helping others. The early climate of disorganization and the mother's constant struggle with violent feelings toward Wendy that erupted repeatedly sensitized her to situations in which someone might lose control and heightened her own defenses against loss of control. This defensive stance, consistent with her basic temperament, was observed in the nursery school at age three when it was noted that she seemed to learn through experience what she could and could not handle. At that time this quality was regarded as precocity of the ego, an early flowering of an endowment factor. When Evelyn was eleven, Marianne Kris, noting her avoidance of dangers and disagreeable feelings, commented, "Her attitude says, 'I don't want to tolerate anything disagreeable.' This is her main defense." This trait was prominent in adolescence; at thirty-four, she was keenly alert to another's emotional state and could consciously choose not to expose herself unnecessarily to stressful feelings. She was careful to avoid situations and experiences that would generate anxiety or leave her out of control.

Wendy and her fate, mystically foretold by the mother, have deeply influenced Evelyn's emotional life and her relationship to her parents. Her memories of Wendy attest to the extent of her early hurt. She referred to Wendy as "my sister," explaining that a sister is somebody with whom you have a relationship but don't necessarily like. By contrast, she called Tammy by her name. She viewed Wendy, who was "just born different," as a person with a possible genetic disorder and referred to the play *The Bad Seed*. She has often wondered about the role of heredity and mentioned a great uncle who was said to have been psychotic and a sexual abuser of children; she described her maternal grandmother as a "manic depressive" and her mother as having serious bouts with depression. Evelyn pointed out that Wendy, in her self-destructiveness, her inability to anticipate the consequences of her actions, and her tendency to harbor grudges, was very different from herself. Wendy had had a penchant for danger and a morbid streak. As a teenager she had painted her small room entirely black, including the ceiling, and one of her favorite books was *One Flew over the Cuckoo's Nest.* Evelyn's comment about this was, "Who needs that?" Wendy's wildness, which resonated with a comparable element in her mother, strongly affected Evelyn and helps to explain her avoidance of emotionally unstable situations. She talked about mental illness with interest and curiosity, as in her speculations about Wendy's genetic makeup. But she did not want to learn further details of her sister's death, as if further exposure to this hostile and self-destructive personality would be too disturbing. Both Wendy and her mother were associated with the fear of loss of control of her own aggression.

The repercussions of Wendy's fate continue to reverberate within the family. They are kept alive by the presence in the family of Wendy's orphaned daughter, Joni. Evelyn has declined to involve herself with Joni other than as her aunt. She described the child as "already a teenager who says 'I hate you'" to those closest to her. In addition to Joni's aggression, which threatened her own control, Evelyn was frankly envious of Joni's many privileges—dancing, music, and other lessons that she herself never had and that her own children will have to forgo. Even in death Wendy has displaced her once again from her parents, just as she had as a child.

After two sons, the birth of her first much-hoped-for daughter, whom her husband also cherished, was very gratifying. It seemed to free Evelyn further from the ambivalence toward her own mother and from what both parents criticized as selfishness and lack of interest in her niece. She repeated with pleasure and pride her husband's comment that he must cherish his daughter now because some day he would have to give her up to another man. This was a fitting reward for a woman who long ago had resigned herself to the realization that she could never regain her father's love.

Evelyn's lack of lofty ambitions for herself and Sandy may be a reflection of her father's negative appraisal of her and of his own rather modest career. But it has resulted in a common-sense, realistic approach to life and has avoided the stress of ambition. Although Evelyn, like her mother and in contrast to their husbands, completed college, her parents did not set a high educational standard for her to follow. Despite an intelligence well above average, Evelyn was neither motivated nor encouraged to pursue high academic achievement. The message she took from her parents and their own dissatisfactions seems to have been "don't expect or anticipate too much."

Nevertheless, at thirty-four, Evelyn appeared to be leading a satisfactory and fulfilling life. Despite serious financial limitations, she counted her blessings. She had achieved a good marriage and had established an apparently happy family. Her friends have been a source of deep satisfaction. She attributed her capacity for friendship in part to her mother, whom she experienced as a sensitive, attentive listener throughout her childhood. She also acknowledged having learned the art of good listening and communicating from her analyst. Evelyn's work has been a source of gratification as she employs her professional skills with intelligence, judgment, and imagination to help people.

Establishing a functional family, achieving professional success, and having a respected place in the community speak for Evelyn's having attained a high level of integration and maturity in early adulthood. There are indications that these achievements also have served to ward off conflict in relation to instinctual strivings whose derivatives might surface as ambition, lust, or hostility. When her husband was considering retraining for a more interesting and better-paying job, she acquiesced readily to his settling for a lesser, rather than a higher, skilled occupation. These observations suggest that upward mobility may threaten to generate anxiety, guilt, and conflict, and that Evelyn uses her well-established capacities for adaptation, sublimation, and avoidance to achieve a viable compromise that enables her to be quite content with the status quo.

MIDDLE AGE

At fifty-three, Evelyn had two interviews with her former analyst at the Child Study Center, one of which was recorded. She greeted the analyst with a warm, spontaneous hug, obviously enjoying being back in the familiar childhood setting. She was very casually dressed and appeared relaxed and comfortable.

Both of her parents had died. Her mother had died in her late sixties of lung cancer; she had been a heavy smoker. Evelyn looked back on her relationship with her mother as positive. She recalled her surprise as an adolescent when girls would talk of quarrels with their mothers: "as I grew up I remember feeling I had a decent relationship with my mother. I remember in high school people would talk about their mothers and say they couldn't talk to them. I never understood that. I'm sorry. We had our moments."

Her father died at age seventy-nine of heart trouble. Over the years, her father was able to be closer to her. He always appreciated the fine Sunday dinners she prepared when she took over some of the cooking responsibilities while her mother was at work. Her professional health-care expertise also brought him closer to her when his health was failing. Ironically, her father also drew closer to her when his older sister, whom he had always resented and whom he identified with Evelyn, became physically incapacitated: the father was more dependent on and appreciative of his daughter's expertise when she helped him to manage his sister's care.

Evelyn was still working in home healthcare. Her children were all well-educated and either engaged in or on the way to productive careers. The older one was married and has a son, and the younger one had recently married. She was delighted at being a grandmother and very pleased that her sons are best friends. She brought many photos of her children and grandson. Her children live at quite some distance, and she would like to move closer to them, but her husband does not make changes easily. In her understanding way, she was prepared to wait. Religion and the church have been important in creating and supporting spiritual values, which have had a binding effect on the family. At this time the church did not seem to play the same important role in her life as it had formerly, as though it had fulfilled the function of creating and unifying the family. She preferred solitary creative activities like knitting and sewing in her free time.

Evelyn had pleasant memories of nursery school and the analysis:

> I have many memories. As far back as I can remember we came here. I can remember enjoying myself and I didn't think of it as anything unusual. It was a normal thing for me. I thought every child went to the doctor's office. I had no idea I did something different . . . I remember nursery school and playing and enjoying the outside and the big huge exposure to the outdoor playground. It was fun. And playing with real clay, real stuff, not the powdery, and making things. I can remember you coming down to get me, and we would go upstairs and what I remember is sometimes thinking things and you would ask questions about it and I would say things that I didn't think I really meant. You would talk about things and while I was talking, I would also be thinking: "Why would I say that?" But if I said it, I must have meant it.

Apparently, in the freedom and safety of the analytic situation she was able, with the speech action of verbalization, to experience and reflect on thoughts and feelings of which she had not been consciously aware. She continued:

> I remember making hopscotches and you got me magic markers and you got me charcoal. We would eat peanuts sometimes. You got me postcards from some trip you went on and the caption was, "We Like Peanuts." I think I still have that. I remember we would wander around and go on like a tour and going through the labs where the animals were. One of my recollections was chocolate milk with onions because we would go to the place and get an onion roll and chocolate milk. Kind of a combination of flavors you don't forget very easily. We had some good times. I enjoyed myself. I didn't find it to be burdensome.

About ten years later in her development, when the whole family was in analysis, there were tragic events when the family turned to the analysts for support. Evelyn recalled:

I know that you guys were there when we had some incidents in our own growing up years that were tragic. That was like when I was seven and my neighbor's daughter was murdered by her mother. I don't remember being that upset about that. I think my mother was more concerned about it than I was . . . I remember thinking that was something that just happened and she wasn't going to be there anymore. And for a mother to do that has got to be very odd and strange. But, you couldn't do anything about it. . . . I think the biggest trauma was when Wendy ran away and she was killed. I remember coming and talking to you about it, I think. If anything, as much as I benefited from the experience of analysis, I think the person who could have benefited more than I, being in the position I was in, was my sister. She was difficult. She was a hard one to know and a hard one to get along with. I remember loving her, caring about her, but not understanding her. Her mode of operation was confusing. Like, don't you see if you behave this way, this is what's going to happen? I mean, if you upset Daddy, he's going to get mad. Is that a good thing? No! So don't do it. One of the things that I recognize about myself is I get, I guess you could say, intuitions about how things can happen and when a certain thing gets said or a certain behavior occurs, it's like a red flag. So I pull back and observe and temper what I say about those occurrences so as not to mix it up. I want it to be calm. My favorite thing is calm. So if it's going to be rainy, I want it to stop. I try not to incite that. I try to alleviate that in some way if I can. But with her, I couldn't do anything because she was just off doing whatever and her rationale for running away was she was trying to protect the family. That was her thought. Protecting them from herself and from I'm not sure what else. . . . One thing that fascinated my sister was understanding how things worked, like a flame. To her it was an attraction. She was drawn to it rather than repelled by it. Where I would be, like, it was nice, and I would get close and feel the heat and say: I can watch it from there. She would get closer. It wouldn't bother her that it was getting hotter. She was drawn to it.

Evelyn's emphasis on calmness and her vivid description of how she anticipates and avoids danger fully confirms Marianne Kris's conclusion, made when Evelyn was eleven, that her main defense was not to tolerate anything disagreeable. This was observed at age thirty-four and was deemed a factor in her resilience and capacity for relating adaptively at home and at work. Now, at fifty-three, Evelyn was letting us see that it was not a relatively simple defense but already at age eleven a capacity for self-regulation based on her talent for mentalization, for being aware of what the other is thinking and feeling as a guide to her response. This quality, rooted in the receptivity noted in infancy, and in the rich interaction with the face, eyes, and voice of her mother, was made more consciously available as a tool for self-regulation and adaptation by the analytic experience.

About Tammy, the youngest, with whom she is still very close, Evelyn observed:

> Tammy always felt like she was on the tail end of things. Her perspective of events was totally different than mine. I kind of look at myself as being from the family facing outward. I was the emissary from the family. I was the one that experienced things and came back and shared, so that when things would happen to her it was like, oh yeah, Evelyn did this, Evelyn did that. She would have an understanding before she would do something, where I was the first. I didn't turn around too much to see some of the things that would happen. I was just going. Even when I was younger, it was always that way. I was the first.

Here she sees herself as independent, venturesome, and serving as guide and mentor to Tammy, roles that were reminiscent of her declaring, when Tammy was born, "That's *my* baby."

Evelyn, now in her fifties, was enjoying her work and recalled how she decided on it very early:

You know, people would say to me, "what do you want to be?" I remember making a decision about nursing when I was very young, like three or four. It was because of my aunt. She was taking care of me and I injured my toe or something and she just took care of it. I thought, "[T]hat's what I want to do." . . . There were no qualms in my mind that I'm going to do this. The ability to take care of someone's bodily ills brings one very close to the other person and to do it for oneself without mother can be very reassuring and supportive of independence.

She explained further:

The reason I like it is because of the listening, sharing, getting to know someone. I think I learned those things from the analytic experience. You have to be an active listener. You have to pick up on intonations. . . . As you are listening you are thinking about what is going on . . . the feelings and flashpoints make it interesting. I do a lot of ok, ah-ha, just to let them know I heard what they said without saying anything. One of the things that we started about two years ago, we were supposed to bring a computer into the room with us and sit there and do the computer stuff. I was like: uh-uh. This is not what I can do. I want to listen to someone. I can pick up a whole lot more than computer things. I rebelled against it. I don't do that. If they found that out, they would probably have a hissy-fit. I'll do it afterwards. Let me have my visit.

Here, again, is the independence observed in childhood. She focuses on empowering the client to be active on his or her own behalf rather than being their advocate since she will not always be available to them. It's not clear whether it was merely coincidence, but all the clients she described were women.

Her sensitivity to others' thoughts and feelings has served her well in her marriage and in rearing her children. For instance, she is ready to move to be close to their children but "my husband doesn't make changes very fast. So he's not too great with the idea of moving. He's warming up slowly. I have to convince him that if we want to see our kids, we have to get closer." While she waits she is able to content herself with her work and her creative activities.

She gave illuminating examples of how she employed her mentalizing ability in rearing her children:

> I can remember one time when Josh was two or three and he was talking to me and whining. I said, "I really don't understand you anymore. I had no idea what you just said to me. When you can talk to me, come back." So he got himself together and we started talking and he started whining and I said, "there's that whine. I didn't understand what you said." So I didn't have to yell at him for whining. But yet he didn't get what he wanted from whining and it works good.

When they were teenagers and they would get at each other she said to the older brother: "He cares what you think about him and when you give him a hard time, he doesn't like that. So you have to encourage him. Once Josh realized that, the relationship changed. Now, they call each other, they are best friends. And they say they love each other on the phone or to each other. Josh was his best man. It's really nice. They both are interested in the same profession too. It's amazing."

She was able to adapt her interaction with them to their developmental needs: "When my kids were getting older, I remember thinking it's a gradual process. College is a good experience in that, rather than making a decision for them, you want to be included in the decisions and point out the qualities of the decision. But you let them make it so they can make the decision on their own. But then, you also say, well the door is always open if you want to talk to me about it."

She spoke almost apologetically of her artistic activities, as though she were intruding on her mother's tie to her sister and displacing her:

> Another thing I discovered about myself, I didn't realize, because my mother was artistic, and my sister was artistic, I never

really considered myself artistic. Yet I have come to the conclusion that I may not be in the same caliber as they were, but if you put me through the general public I have got a lot more than a lot of people. So I have explored that in myself as well. It's creativity. It started when I was a kid, I didn't realize this was part of it. My grandmother taught me how to knit and crochet so I knew how to do that. As different things would come up for the kids, my mother always made costumes. I just thought, that's what you do. I never really thought anything about it.

One motive for the artistic activity seems to be her need for the tie to her mother and sister. She told how she turned to quilting as a creative activity with a friend who, like her mother and her sister Tammy, had studied art. She also enjoys cooking creatively. In her enjoyment of these activities we see again the capacity for sublimation noted early in nursery school.

Then, as though in loyalty to her old tendency to awkwardness and to her mother's marring of her appearance she added, "But I hate housework. What else is new, I have never been a neatnik. I feel like all the furniture I have in my house is hand-me-downs. There's maybe two or three pieces that are mine, that I bought. But it doesn't go together. It's tough to have that decorative sight. You kind of make do. Because it's not a priority I don't spend time with it." Paradoxically, in view of the messes she often made in the analysis, it was surprising to hear that in college she loved chemistry, especially the laboratory, because of the cleanliness and precision required to insure a reaction, a behavior reminiscent of the pleasure she took in overcoming internal and external obstacles in the mastery of a skill.

She ended the meeting with this self-observation:

Nursing isn't an occupation, it's a vocation. It's kind of who you are. No matter what situation you are in, whether it's a working relationship or nursing, it defines who you are—the nursing process as much as everything I went through in school regarding the nursing process. That is kind of labeling something that I already felt. It's part of the living process to me. I find myself keying in on things not just in a conversation. It is significant in terms of the whole picture.

The metaphor of the key is striking. The face, the eyes, the words are the keys that unlock the mind and feelings of the other and facilitate an adaptive response. These keys were forged very early in the interaction between a receptive endowment and the rich visual experience with her mother and their effectiveness was enhanced in the analysis.

Two years later, at age fifty-five, Evelyn spontaneously sent this letter to the analyst:

Dear Dr. -

I have been thinking about this off and on since our discussions last year. I believe the reason that I have been able to handle the tragedies that occur in the course of life thus far is not so much the influence of my family or some depth within me, but instead, it is because you have taught me how to work through these events. I say this after looking back on our encounters and the various events that could have left me "scarred for life" and have not. I have met many people who are "scarred" from lesser events and had often wondered why I had not responded in the same way. I now realize it is how we dealt with those events at the time and our ability to talk about them in the sense of their reality that allowed me to understand that I was "OK."

I want you to know that you have had a tremendous impact on my life and that I would not be the same if you had not been a part of my life. I knew that you were trustworthy and that you always heard me. To me, hearing is very different from listening; hearing requires a connection in the brain leading to comprehension. I thank God for you. I can also say that I love you as the kind and supportive, loving person that made me "who I am today." Thank you!

I am typing this because, as you know, we in the medical field have illegible hand writing.

Looking forward to hearing from you again,

With love, Evelyn

SUMMARY

In middle age, at fifty-three, Evelyn was in a marriage that has functioned well in raising a family of four children who are all leading productive lives. This is a noteworthy accomplishment for someone who grew up in a family that experienced conflict and trauma. If we ask what personality traits contributed to this achievement and how they arose from endowment and experience, we can identify three traits that played a large role: the emphasis on "calm," which bespeaks a capacity for self-regulation of affect, an important component of resilience; the "active listening," which is her subjective experience of observing her own mind in interaction with the mind of the other person in the service of interpersonal adaptation; and the capacity for sublimation, a feature of her personality that was noted very early.[8] These characteristics, intricately interrelated and integrated into her daily functioning at home, at work, and in the community, have served well in safely meeting her instinctual needs and maintaining pleasurable ties to family and community.

Evelyn's capacity for calming herself had its origins in her mother's fine attunement to her needs in infancy, when the mother responded to Evelyn's receptivity and easy pacification. When Wendy's behavior became the focus of controversy and Evelyn tended to be wrongly blamed, she sought calm in isolation, a mechanism her mother also employed. At eleven, what appeared to observers as a defensive intolerance of anything disagreeable was the behavioral manifestation of the capacity for self-regulation of affect, a capacity that reflected a highly developed capacity for mentalization. The insistence on calmness was particularly striking in adolescence. While Wendy was engaged in the struggle with her parents, which culminated in her running away, Evelyn was able, with the help of what she later called her "strict superego," to suppress or regulate sexual and aggressive impulses and maintain and moderate her behavior until she could take up her adult role.

The "active listening" has its roots in the early interaction between the mother's preference for visual over physical contact and Evelyn's receptivity. This contributed to an early visual alertness and discrimination and an unusual interest in the human face. A glance at the face and a smile became her way of making contact with another person. Observers noted that her interest in the face was part of her unusual ability to be keenly aware of the mood and affect of the people around her, especially her mother. The interest in toys and dolls with faces led to a rich fantasy life in which she played many roles. By pretending and role playing she was able to bridge the physical separation from her mother when her sisters were born. The rich fantasy life provided an intermediate space for the expression of instinctual needs in imaginative play and in sublimated activities like painting. Looking back as an adult, she observed that in the analysis she had learned to listen actively and to reflect on her own and the analyst's words.

Listening to verbalization and tone of voice became and has remained a reliable key to understanding another person's thoughts and feelings. These strongly established traits, which subserve the mentalizing functions, have functioned well as an early warning system of physical and psychological risk or danger, allowing her to employ self-regulating adaptive and defensive measures which provide permissible instinctual satisfaction while maintaining calm. Evelyn's lenient superego, which had been predicted in early childhood, has had an important role in the self-regulating function. A nurturing, protective superego had been predicted based on the internalization of a well-attuned mother protector and regulator.[9]

In keeping with Freud's view that the ego is first and foremost a bodily ego, following the developmental line of Evelyn's relationship to her body reveals the major role it has had in the differentiation of various ego functions, in meeting instinctual needs and in her object relations. The early lag in motor development was judged to be due to body build and the mother's preference for visual over bodily contact. At six months she turned to her body to soothe herself by masturbating with thigh pressure when her mother was away at work. In nursery school, despite the limitation in her physical skills, she persisted at a task she had set for herself until she mastered it. Her resilience and assertiveness in independent activity, which enabled her to maintain a pleasurable interest in the process of mastering a skill, became a lasting trait. At eight and nine, when Wendy's fear of the water lowered her standing with the father, Evelyn gained favor with her father, who loved water sports, by proving herself to be a good swimmer and fisherman.

In her fourth year Evelyn's relationship to her body took on a new significance when her aunt, a nurse with whom her mother was very close, was able to treat her minor wound. Thereupon she decided healthcare was her vocation. If someone other than mother could soothe her hurts, Evelyn could, by a process of identification and internalization, care for her own body and for others, a comforting and reassuring thought.

Cooking, another body-related function, proved a mutually enjoyable link to her mother when, at eleven or twelve, Evelyn prepared the family meals while her mother was at work. It also brought her father closer to her, because he enjoyed her cooking. Whenever she phoned home from college he would ask when she was coming home so they could have a decent meal, proving the old adage that the way to a man's heart is through his stomach. Cooking has continued to be a gratifying creative interest. Her other artistic and creative activities are linked in her mind to her mother, but in declaring them she has to add that her talents are less than her mother's, as though she were trespassing.

The tendency to awkwardness has its origins in her body build and the relative lack of bodily contact in infancy, quite in contrast to how she was observed cuddling her own infant. The image of herself as awkward was reinforced by her father, who wanted Wendy to be a dancer and prescribed basketball for Evelyn "to make her potbelly smaller." A further contribution to the awkwardness came from the mother's longstanding ambivalence toward her own and Evelyn's femininity as seen in her tendency to mar the child's appearance with some tasteless article of clothing. This was reflected in her disinterest in home decoration. However, she has been able to experience aesthetic pleasure in her creative activities.

Evelyn presents a unique opportunity to examine the long-term effects of analysis in childhood. The analysis, which began during the period when her father turned away from her to her sister, provided a transferential father figure and a new object at the crucial point in feminine development when the girl turns to the father in forming a triadic relationship with the parents. At that juncture and at other critical points in the family life during her childhood, the analysis offered, via fantasy play in the setting of an oedipal transference, a safe and trustworthy venue for instinctual gratification and object relations related to the new steps in development. It also provided, as Evelyn described in her recollections of the analysis, the experience of consciously reflecting on her own thoughts and verbalizations during the play when the analyst brought them to her attention. She attributes her talent for active listening to the analytic experience though, of course, it also had deep roots in the early interactions with her mother.

In her most recent communication, the spontaneous letter in which she condensed the time since our previous meeting to one year, she gives her conscious perception of how the analytic experience helped her to cope with conflict and trauma without "scarring." The analyst, she writes, taught her to "work through" troubling events and that it was "our ability to talk about them in the sense of their reality that allowed me to understand that I was 'OK.'" The emphasis on "our ability" implies that the transference to the analyst as a protective, parental figure made it safe to pay conscious attention to the thoughts and affects stirred by the tragic event. This facilitated self-regulation so that she was able to experience a tragic happening as an aspect of reality, a quality of mind that is important for resilience.

The analyst was originally established in her mind as trustworthy when he did not respond critically or withdraw his interest if she was messy or expressed hostile feelings, but instead drew her attention to comprehending the thoughts and feelings that were symbolized by the words that accompanied the behavior. This is what she recognizes when she says she was heard, not just listened to. She ventures into the realm of neuropsychoanalysis when she concludes correctly that brain connections are involved. Thinking of the analyst as "the kind and supportive, loving person that made me 'who I am today'" reflects the parenting (in its meaning of caring for) aspects of the long relationship, which resulted in a bonding based on identification, idealization, and internalization of the mentalizing functions that were exercised in the analysis. But we must bear in mind that the basic building blocks for these functions were formed in the earliest years by the interaction between Evelyn's receptive endowment and her mother's sensitivity and responsiveness to her needs. In retrospect, what was thought, at eleven, to be a blanket defense (not to tolerate anything disagreeable) was already a sign of her capacity for self-regulation as the result of a complex mentalizing process. This view is corroborated by Evelyn's childhood recollections of Wendy's behavior and her conception of the mental state behind it, which then became a determinant of her own adaptive response. She concludes her communication with the wish to meet again and presents her awkward writing as the symbol of the common bond with the analyst—the healing profession.

AFTERWORD
"EVELYN"

As a young girl, I thought of the Child Study Center as the place we would go for Nursery School and to see the doctor for checkups. I did know, however, that it was a unique situation and that some of the children, like me, were being given the opportunity to see a "special doctor" for individual play time. My "special doctor" was Dr. Ritvo. He would come down to get me during Nursery School and we would go up the stairs—or take the old fashioned elevator to the second floor. We would go to a special play room when I was in Nursery School. There was an easel and powdered paints to mix. I remember doing some pretty ugly pictures in terms of color; had a great time mixing all the colors together. We would talk and play. We never had to call each other by name because there was just the two of us.

Our visits continued even when I was no longer attending Nursery School. My mother would drive me to the Child Study Center after school. This routine continued until I was twelve. Now we would meet in Dr. Ritvo's office. We would still play games—like draw and play

hopscotch on his carpet, or create shaded pictures with charcoal on special paper—and of course talk while we were engaged in any activities.

We both enjoyed food. He would share peanuts or chips or we
would go down to the canteen and get an ice cream sandwich from the
machine. One time we walked to a place that had stools at a counter—he
ordered hot Pastrami, I had never heard of it before. He gave me a little
piece to try—YUM! I was sold on hot Pastrami.

He would talk me through how I was actually feeling about events
in my life and help me to see things from a different angle. I am not
sure if he realized this, but he taught me how to listen to people and to
guide people to their own conclusions about problems they were facing. This came in very handy in my role as a nurse. He promoted my
independence by showing me that I could think things through and see
solutions to any dilemma that would face me. As much as I was a part
of a study on childhood development—he was a teacher of how to face
life and its trials and help people along the way.

He will always be my special friend in my heart. I am very grateful
for the experience of the Child Study Center. But most of all, I am grateful for the time I had with Dr. Ritvo and the privilege of knowing such
a great human being.

NOTES

*Essential data on which this chapter is based were provided by members
of the study team, who were expert observers in their fields of social work,
early childhood education, pediatrics, and psychoanalysis. The richness
of the study findings derives from the interdisciplinary team approach
and the skill of the clinicians involved. The author wishes to acknowledge
Ruth Lord, M.S.W., social worker; Audrey Naylor, Ed.D., early childhood educator; Sally Provence, M.D., pediatrician; and Albert Solnit,
M.D., psychoanalyst, for their important contributions to the study and
to the ideas expressed in the chapter.*

1. Samuel Ritvo, "The Psychoanalytic Process in Childhood," *Psychoanalytic Study of the Child* 33 (1978): 295–306.

2. Samuel Ritvo et al., "Relations of Constitution, Environment and Personality, as Observed in a Longitudinal Study of Child Development: Case Report," in *Modern Perspectives in Child Development* (New York: International Universities Press, 1963).

3. Ernst Kris, "Notes on the Development and on Some Current Problems of Psychoanalytic Child Psychology," *Psychoanalytic Study of the Child* 5 (1950): 24–46; and E. Kris, "Some Comments and Observations on Early Autoerotic Activities," *Psychoanalytic Study of the Child* 6 (1953): 95–116.

4. Kris, "Notes on the Development."

5. Knowledge of the parents' conflicts and the family interrelationships was gained through the simultaneous analysis of all five members of the family, a project begun when Evelyn was seven. Ritvo and other members of the study team sometimes referred to the family as "Olsen," their pseudonym in the study and at times as "Parr"—hence the abbreviation here, as "Mr. P." (editors' note).

6. In contrast to the elaborate fantasy play that characterized the direct relationship to the mother, for a long time there was an absence of fantasy play in the treatment.

7. Ernst Kris, "Neutralization and Sublimation: Observations on Young Children," *Psychoanalytic Study of the Child* 8 (1955): 30–46.

8. Ibid.

9. Samuel Ritvo and Albert J. Solnit, "Influences of Early Mother-Child Interactions on Identification Processes," *Psychoanalytic Study of the Child* 8 (1958): 64–91 (esp. 91).

✣ 10 ✣

Back in the Day: Child Psychoanalytic Emphases in the Yale Longitudinal Study Psychotherapy of "Nancy Miles"

T. WAYNE DOWNEY

As Linda Mayes and Stephen Lassonde have pointed out in the Introduction, the zeal of the investigators involved in the Yale Longitudinal Study far outweighed their research skills. In this regard their courageous explorations were more analogous to the Lewis and Clark expedition to explore the Pacific West 145 years earlier than they were to man's landing on the moon twenty years later. But the study has also never been replicated. And by taking the psychoanalytic psychotherapy of "Nancy Miles" as a manageable sample of the data, we can arrive at a new appreciation of the role of siblings and families in the shaping of a child's development.

"Nancy" was the firstborn daughter of a fractious couple with the surname "Miles."[1] Nancy was offered psychotherapy by an experienced child analyst whom I shall call "Molly" at a frequency that varied between weekly and biweekly over a seven-month period. I would categorize the treatment contact as largely psychodynamic with bits of a cognitive/behavioral approach thrown in. As is the case in everyday human communications, much of the impact of an analysis is based on nonverbal factors. All told, these factors add up to a series of connective emotional experiences that attempt to rework, interpsychically and intrapsychically (that is, both interpersonally and internally), deficient and defective object relations. This model of therapeutic action was based, in a manner that appears now to have been quite limiting, on a participant-observation model rather than a more specifically interactive model. Paradoxically, there was scant interpretation of unconscious wishes, conflicts, and defenses, which so bulwarked Winnicott's interventions in *The Piggle* in 1977.[2]

This volume's space limitations precluded my including Molly's original process notes. I am offering the next best thing: my interpretive take on the notes. While Nancy was followed from before birth, her psychotherapy commenced when she was in her fourth year. Among the reasons for treatment were persistent indicators of anxiety and depression over the previous years accompanied by an increasing lag in her cognitive development. In other words she was in increasing psychological pain and her development was flagging. She appeared to be "dying on the vine" as a result of pernicious family influences and somewhat hidden psychological trauma that was only fleetingly apparent to investigators of the Miles family. On reading this material I was struck by the ways in which the raw and undigested data of the life of the Miles family and their struggles to gain economic and marital security came to augment my understanding of Nancy's communications in her therapeutic play. The study data helped to delineate the area of traumatic, unassimilated, unconscious mentation that Nancy was nonverbally and intuitively attempting to work through with her therapist. As with many children, her unconscious mentation consisted of reactions to experience that had never risen to a level of conscious thought and speech in her everyday life. This latent information about determinants of Nancy's state of mind tended to get swamped in the welter of day-to-day details. It turned out to be critical in highlighting the regular appearance of Nancy's older object-related stereotypes, as well as her search for new object relatedness with Molly. I use "old object stereotypes" to denote the frequent, regular attempts to project onto another the early fantasies and psychological attributes of an important other;

these include often frustrating or unsatisfactory characteristics of the primary objects, the parents. In the service of mastery, this involves the repetitive projection of a threatening person from current or past experience. The older object repetition and projection, however, can also be of a "good" object with a soothing or idealized nature. In the latter case, the projections may serve to keep anxious dysphoric stereotypes of "helpers," who are in reality not so helpful, at bay by maintaining the therapist in an idealized "can do no harm" light, cloaking threatening hostility in the supposedly benign garments of a "new object."

THE THERAPEUTIC ELEMENTS OF PLAY

This case review also sheds light on the process of internalization. How do Nancy's temperamental givens—such as her internal proclivity for passivity and withdrawal in the world outside her family—interact with external frictions in the process of internalization? A partial answer would be that the tumult of the Miles family, taken in as dysphoria and depression, was both dramatized at home while paradoxically displayed in public as inhibition and depression. Her public persona contained a wish not to be understood. At home Nancy showed her identification with the hostile aggressor in her angry exchanges with her parents and brother. Outside the home, she showed the deadening ravages of those identifications, inhibition and depression. Structurally the medium of play provided a sieve for straining out elusive elements of her id, sub-ego, and super-ego functioning and bringing them into a more synchronous interaction with her ego.

In situations of neglect or psychological assault, we find mother-infant dysregulation or the overstimulation of hostile affect storms that mimic both the parents' initial conscious or unconscious rage with the child as well as the child's defensive identification with the aggressor. Additionally in Nancy's case there was the narcissistic injury brought about by the arrival of a new preferred male replacement child. Primarily she responded to this intrinsically as a loss of place and secondarily as an interpsychic loss of status. The therapeutic action of play permits the child to achieve some semblance of ego wholeness and mastery that is more consonant with his or her developmental level. In Nancy's instance, Molly's therapeutic contact facilitated a positive shift in her mood disorder that was manifest in her good-naturedly teasing Molly and sticking out her tongue at her, and in gains in intellectual functioning where she became able to do card naming games. But the treatment seems to have had its limits. The end result may have been that Nancy became able to use the nursery school as a safe haven from her chaotic home environment, or to a lesser degree it may have paradoxically contributed to a neurotic character fixation dominated by social anxiety. But overall, Nancy's contact with Molly caused a diminishing of significant amounts of anxiety and depression. Molly's abrupt, unexplained departure, occurring as it did without an opportunity for Nancy to psychologically metabolize it, may have contributed to the persistence in Nancy's character of a state of shy, quiet withdrawal. In the manner that trauma begets trauma, was Molly's leaving a retraumatization of Nancy? Did it inadvertently replicate the narcissistic insult that had occurred when Nancy's mother had shifted her love from Nancy onto brother Eric after his birth? Any feelings of rage at being replaced by a sibling (and a male at that!) were then swamped by regressions to transitional objects (dolls and stuffed animals), muted compliance, and a characterological resistance to being "understood" (resonated with).

THE NATURE OF TRAUMA

In a research meeting when Nancy was ten months and twenty-two days old, Ernst Kris made the comment that outside events rarely constitute major traumata. Years later most clinicians would construe such a statement as stemming from Freud's ambivalence and confusion about whether his hysterical patients became so because of the distorted and forbidden wishes for the important people in their lives or because of real negative, painful, external experiences. As it turned out, many of them had been subjected to incest, violence, and sexual abuse at the hands of family members and close family friends. Kris's perspective in questioning the effects of poor childrearing on children reflected that of the field at the time. It underlines how the investigators were blinkered in regard to the role of trauma in child development, making it difficult for them to fully account for what they were garnering and seeing. What we see now was probably also the case then: most therapists are drawn to the work after having experienced mal-parenting in their own early histories, with its traumatic shifts in object preferences and alliances. Nancy's fall from familial grace with the birth of her brother gives the lie to the idea of trauma being a null factor in child development. As the case information developed, it became clearer that the team slowly and informally shifted its attitude to allow for the greater contribution of external trauma, in the form of the parent's conflicted feelings toward Nancy and the gender bias of the culture at that time.

THERAPY SESSION 1: COMMENTARY
ON THE ELUCIDATION OF LOSS

I will review the transcribed process notes of therapist "Molly," taking into consideration ancillary information provided by other involved members of the study group. Molly's manner of capturing the play narrative is notable in terms of what seems to be missing by modern standards. There are few references in the play and personal exchanges to the interactivity of the minds of analyst and child. What thoughts get stimulated and why? In first sessions we routinely allow for unfamiliarity on the part of child and therapist. The immediate references to "Mary" and "Maria" (girls in the nursery) suggest that in addition to Nancy's prior, at least passing, acquaintance with her therapist Molly, early transference activity is present. The therapist does not engage Nancy by treating the milieu as part of the treatment frame. The basic assumption seems to be that the playroom provides the therapeutic frame. She defers to Nancy's wish to finish her "baking" project rather than more actively insinuating herself into the play. At such an early stage, it is obviously a choice on the part of the therapist as to whether to join the play or wait on the sidelines, so to speak. But similar deferrals happen in subsequent sessions. The therapist's style tends toward the sessile. This raises the question of whether this style dovetails unproductively with a character that in Nancy's case tends toward shy reticence and disengagement. Certainly the analytic standard at the time encouraged silence and watchful passivity on the part of the treater. Did the fishbowl atmosphere of the study contribute to the treaters taking a more laid-back and noncommittal stance? Molly's approach in these sessions seems more observer than participant. In current circumstances, if our reading of the child so indicated, we might opt to sound out, early on, the child's willingness to interact with a strange therapist. As it was, Molly merely watched Nancy play.

Nancy's insistence on finishing her sand bakery project before going to the playroom suggests that she, at times and in certain situations anyway, was not as passive as she often appeared; that she had a mind of her own. Some anxiety may also be involved in her exercise of self-possession when confronted by Molly, a relative stranger. It is of note that Molly spoke with a brogue (this comes through in the word usage and rhythm of the notes). This is not to suggest that an accent would imply a threat, since both Nancy's grandparents spoke heavily inflected English. It may be quite the opposite, making Molly sound familiar like her grandparents, not foreign. It is notable that after finishing her "baking" Nancy attempted to move away from Molly toward a different play area, rather than to where Molly was stationed to take her. Was Nancy feeling disengaged and averting herself from the therapist in kind? This sort of evasive action might raise a flag in the analyst's mind as to whether this was a subtle early sign of either independence or ambivalence and anxiety.

Home is definitely on Nancy's mind as she starts out by stating that she wants to take home the initial perfunctory drawing that she made. Given later events, however, this statement seems to ambiguously subsume the found picture of another child as well. She reemphasizes how much home is on her mind when, following the scribble drawing, she shifts her attention to the doll house. On one level this can be understood as standard early exploratory play, casing the play space and play materials. But then a parapraxis on Nancy's part signals that the play is emotionally charged. She does not see the bedroom on the upper floor of the doll house. The cascade of emotional errors continues as a baby doll is placed in a "crib." She becomes aware of her parapraxis and immediately changes the noun to "playpen." The process continues as the woman doll and baby doll become "Nancy and her baby," instead of mother or Molly and baby. This is followed by Molly's first interpretation within the play as she states that the icebox in the doll house is a Frigidaire with no door. This is an interesting choice of words given that "icebox mother" was a common contemporary term employed to denote an etiological object factor for children with autism. Could Molly have been entertaining some similar questions about Nancy's object relations? In intuitively assigning the category "lost" to the door rather than questioning Nancy further about what may have happened to the door, Molly attempts to both show her understanding of Nancy and to start to frame their contact with contemporary analytic loss theory. Nancy, with a flash of anxiety that may stem from some notion of hers about irreversible bodily damage (castration anxiety to Molly) vehemently denies this. The sexualized and phallocentric term "castration anxiety" has gradually fallen out of usage as a term that connotes female inferiority based on hypothesized genital trauma. It still may be manifest clinically as a specific form of anxiety in males or females where performance anxiety is equated with specific fantasies of genital mutilation that has either occurred or is yet to come. She is emphatic that she wants/prefers the fridge to not have a door. Embedded in this exchange may be the transferential hope/wish/question for Molly as to whether a female can be strong and potent even if genitally different from the "ruling" males; even if her body is lacking a phallic appendage. Is anatomy truly destiny? Or does strength come from some other less obvious sources so that in metaphorical terms it matters not whether the fridge comes with or without a door? In fact without a door we can see into the fridge and view its heretofore hidden mysteries and strengths. This may be an early example of Nancy's tentative curiosity about the hidden strengths of the intact female body. In any event, Molly's first interpretation is vigorously denied by Nancy. She wishes that total completeness is possible without a door!

Nancy proceeds to defensively smooth out this anxious moment, which was apparently too much and too quickly about loss. For her, it seems to be about not just the speculative loss of body parts but also the real loss of self-esteem, status, and standing in the family over the previous two years coupled with the loss of love and attention from significant others. She dramatizes this by populating the doll house with a father, cousin, and friend. That none of these figures extended into the dramatic play suggests further the immediate defensive and reparative fantasy function of these figures. The friend doll with a name so close to Molly's further bolsters speculation that transference developments are looming. Even nowadays the problem with identifying these elements of a treatment process in children is that the therapist is often not prepared to see these elements for what they are. The mindset back in the 1950s and sometimes currently has tended to be that such elements are identifiable and interpretable only much further down the line. The material here suggests that the text of a therapeutic process is determined by what the analyst is ready to see, and when.

While there was a momentary retreat from Molly's sortie into castration anxiety and loss after the Frigidaire episode, Nancy experienced another "anxious moment" around finding a broken chair with a leg scotch-taped back onto it followed by encountering a doll with a missing sock and shoes. It is important to note that this "large doll" is actually Nancy's size. Later on she became "Terri," Nancy's constant transitionally objectified companion. Terri accompanied Nancy everywhere in the nursery school after Nancy rescued her from the playroom, becoming the successor to Nancy's original transitional object, a blue blanket. According to the head nursery school teacher, when Nancy froze into neurotic withdrawal, she would often place Terri on one side of her and any available adult on the other. Nancy made a partial restitution in the play by finding the missing shoe and mandating that the doll did not need to wear socks. This play fragment appears to be an attempt by Nancy to break out of the various conflicting conformities about clothes, appearance, and femininity that dogged her. This segued into exploration of the doctor's kit; a further hint at a preoccupation with restitution and another thrust out from under the shadow of trauma. Molly notes that Nancy liked to carry a suitcase around in the nursery. That might mean that an engaging tie-in comment had been made to Nancy, since many girls of her age carry around parcels. These are often as important for what they may contain in the way of retrieved lost articles as they are for being similar to objects of adult identification and adult power such as satchels, briefcases, and purses. In other words, they reflect early oedipal power issues rather than the later, more popular, oedipal themes deriving from adolescent sexual romance.

At the end of the session, in a coda to her smear art at the beginning, Nancy painted a muddy, apparently overdetermined hue (suggesting feces) that she proceeded to dedicate to her brother. Molly terms him a "newborn," while in fact at that point Eric was about eighteen months old. Finally she wanted to take three pictures home, including the pink papered one of another child that she had discovered on the easel when she entered the playroom. Her wish/parapraxis was that she had created it. Nancy could be read as having at some level been aware of what she was appropriating from another child patient of Molly's. The play stage was immediately set for an enactment of her sibling agita; taking something from another of her therapist's imagined charges and in doing so mastering a rivalry (at least a little bit). Enactments imply the presence of transference. As I mentioned earlier, at the time the existence of transference in child work was being debated. Here, however, as it does with adults, transference manifested itself in the most mundane and everyday of ways. The mention of the brother as the future benefactor of her theft (a reversal), the exploration of the doll house with its broken and/or repaired furniture (capturing Nancy's own bodily anxiety, diminished mental state, and wish for repair by Molly); all these allusions seem in sum to amount to a bit of transferential compensation from Molly for what she had lost with the arrival of her brother. Molly seemingly thwarts this plea for specialness, for a gift from her. She treats

Nancy's wish perfunctorily as if it were literal, without questioning it. She apparently uses her authority to deny her request and Nancy characteristically submits passively without protest. The defensive and aggressive aspects of this dynamic on Nancy's part are not addressed by Molly at the time or as a possible response in the notes. Molly handles the matter operationally with the matter-of-fact suggestion that she leave the pink painting in the playroom. In other words, an instrumental, rather than an interpretive action, is taken by the therapist. Technically it is not that such an instrumental intervention is incorrect. At Nancy's age such an act of authority might be interpreted as dependently gratifying or as firming up the treatment boundaries. With both adults and children now we might handle the answering of a question not with another question, but with an instrumental response, simply answering the question . . . and then following up on the subsequent words or play as though they are part of a free associational response. They usually are. The problem that arises with a command response is that it may be exercised at the expense of increasing insight and self-observation even for a child of Nancy's age. An opportunity may be lost to investigate the complexities of motivation. Such interventions might have helped to thwart the consolidation of Nancy's conflict into her later social anxiety. She might have been freed up, rather than, if not tightened up, left in a state of social inhibition.

Throughout the record there are many recorded statements about how special a male baby is in the minds of the extended family members of the Miles clan. Molly infers that Nancy's discomfort in the first session is not frustration but a reaction to the heat. She assists her in taking off her jacket. Nancy's drawing attention to her "pretty dress" seems in hindsight loaded with her need to replenish her wounded female narcissism by asking for a complement from Molly. There also seems to be in this comment an ironic attempt to give dresses the same or more value as more masculine items of clothing like trousers or slacks. Several observers have mentioned how conflicted the area of apparel was for Nancy. Her father demanded that she wear slacks or overalls. Her maternal grandmother (who bought all the children's clothes) insisted that

Nancy wear only dresses when she visited. And her mother inevitably wore a dress, even if it turned out to be a somewhat shabby housecoat.

Nancy ends the session on notes of homage, restitution, and revenge toward her brother and new rival, Eric. Molly's summary statement attributes Nancy's "defensive reaction to missing objects" to the "castration complex." This may be accurate but it also tilts toward the archaic. Such a formulation seems to spring more from theoretical knowledge than from a creative discovery of poignant anatomical loss in the hour. It captures only a part of a complex amalgam of many losses, which may be only partially grasped by the anatomically based metaphor of castration anxiety. Certainly the culture of the time was phallocentric and, as mentioned, the overt family standards favored boys. But Nancy's loss dynamic also seemed to contain elements of depleted self-esteem, unstable object constancy, and a depressive regression to separation anxiety (the latter manifested in her reluctance to leave Molly). In contemporary terms, "castration complex" can be taken to refer to an intrapsychic closed state of developmental affairs for females in the first three-quarters of the twentieth century. It harks back to a time when anatomy was magically conceived as conferring a subordinate destiny and women and girls were in large measure delegated to wearing a gendered cultural and physical straitjacket. They were defined in fixed passive, depressive, masochistic, and envious terms. They were considered to be among life's losers relative to boys and men with their phallic scepters. Nancy commences her therapeutic exercise, then, expressing through her play actions anxiety, pain, and depression about her gendered fate. She fumbles for a solution in which her brother Eric has not superseded her.

PSYCHOTHERAPY SESSION 2: HOPE FOR AUTONOMY AND INDEPENDENCE

In this session, Nancy, smiling, positive, and expectant in response to Molly's appearance, announces that her mother is at home. This seems to be a marker for her current state of object constancy. She both conveys an understanding of where her mother is located out of sight, along with her calm expectation that her mother will arrive to pick her up at the end of the morning. The concept of object constancy was a dawning idea at the time, introduced in midcentury by Anna Freud and Hans Loewald, among several others. It is a concept that seems to have been easily accepted in child development but whose place and usage has lagged in the field of adult analysis. For a child of Nancy's age, object constancy usually possesses a dynamic, fluid quality, waxing and waning depending on degrees of stress and the amount of separation or stability surrounding the primary objects, the parents. In this session there seems to have been a regrouping of her object constancy, enhanced by a smiling positive transference to the reappearing Molly. Her comments about her mother and then her grandmother, Nana, have a free-associational quality. The mention of her sick grandmother, a cause of great anxiety for her mother, Flo, signals Nancy's own anxiety and confusion about her grandmother's physical state layered with concerns about her own. There seems also a subtle anxiety as to whether Molly is a doctor who used needles. (At the time, Nancy's grandmother's diabetes was being treated with injections of insulin.) The positive emphasis seemed to be twofold: women and mothers can be depended on, and women in need, like grandmother, will be taken care of in their illness, just as Nancy in her distress is being taken care of by Molly. In this session it becomes clearer that the whole nursery school setting, not just the playroom, is being used as a play stage, by Nancy anyway. Nancy with doll and carriage seems a displaced, active dramatization of Nancy's growing passive dependence on Molly. Again, as she did in finishing up her sand play in the first session, Nancy quietly asserts herself, retrieving her doll and carriage from the threat of appropriation by another child. This time, however, her actions are supported by Molly's presence, rather than being an anxious reaction to it.

Once in the playroom, Nancy repeats her focus on trying to bring order out of disarray, this time in regard to the shelves of the refrigerator. Her emphasis on the mother doll in the kitchen and the father doll and others upstairs seems an allusion to the layout of the Mileses' house. Nancy no doubt was troubled on some level by the angry, embittered, and arbitrary demand by her father, Leo, that her mother, Flo, have the kids at the door to greet him upon his arrival home from work. This demand was then double-bound by his impossible and imperious expectation that Flo control the children, allowing him some peace and quiet by keeping them with her while he ascended half a flight to watch TV in the upstairs living room.

There followed a play segment about the uncomfortable place for the driver (no real or rear seat) with the mother and daughter in the back of a toy truck. This seems to resonate with something that Flo complained about bitterly to various home visitors in the course of the study: Leo was the only one who could drive, and he would exercise his power and dominance by refusing to take his wife places on ritual Sunday drives. While many of these conflicts might strike observers as quibbling aspects of the times, there was a vehemence and ferocity to these recurrent conflicts about being housebound, husband-bound, and subject to Leo's whims and powers that raised their emotional temperature far beyond the ordinary. These were not day-to-day angers, frustrations, and petty vexations. They contained hate of object-destroying, homicidal depth. But back then, the place of positive aggression and negative hostility in the psychology of everyday life was still to be explored and developed. Once again, the play associations are overdetermined; loaded with symbolic and metaphorical meaning. Shifting from the dramatic play of the Sunday ride to the medium of painting, Nancy selects that moment to "tinkle" (the bowdlerized and castrated form of "to urinate" or "pee"). She is at pains to demonstrate that she has available a good deal of what seems to be a mixture of autonomous ego functioning and counterphobic neurotic ego function. Unlike her mother vis-à-vis the car rides, she can take care of urinating without relying on anyone else; she can even flush the toilet standing up, depressing the lever with her foot. That Molly substitutes "tinkle" for urination at that moment raises the question of whether she was defensively missing the rage or at least the opportunity to inquire about the "pissed-offness" accompanying Nancy's need to pee at that particular moment.

Nancy then mentions the panties given to her by Nana, which also seems to point to several environmental contributors to Nancy's character development. As noted, Nana, Flo's mother, was a major financial support to this ambitious but struggling family. This was a fact of life that Leo reacted to with great ambivalence. He was both appreciative and resentful, because part of the price that the family paid for her financial support was that they abided by her very strict expectations about how boys and girls dressed. These, after all, were the days of binary gender assignment. Boys will be boys and girls will be both feminine and losers. The idea of gender as a mosaic mix of biological attributes and both male and female psychological characteristics was still far in the future. Nana bought clothes accordingly. When Nancy and Eric came over to visit her on weekends, it was imperative that Nancy wear a dress, not slacks or jeans, and that her appearance be entirely feminine. Eric similarly had to be wearing masculine garb that accorded with Nana's old-world standards. This requirement seems to contribute to Nancy's overemphasis, tinged with anxiety, on the "goodness" of her psychologically degraded feminine appearance in dresses and panties, and their conformity with those of another woman of dominance, Molly, who wore dresses in earth tones.

PLAY SESSION 3: NANCY AS BOSS, SHOWING HER IDENTIFICATION WITH ERIC

In this third session, held two weeks after the second, Molly ended up once again with the formulation that Nancy was struggling with some "activation of the castration complex." In doing this she seems to be understanding the term castration complex as a neurotically fixated state rather than a possibly transient developmental constellation brought on by her brother's birth and complicated by cultural/familial emphases that could be resolved by corrective experience, therapeutic play, interpretation, and gender neutrality. The use of just two examples from a session replete with all sorts of information suggests a lack of differentiation by the clinician of what might be usual expectable developmental dynamics as well as a turning away from what potential clinical themes might be discovered that lie beyond the pale. Castration dynamics certainly may be contributing to the clinical picture—consider the missing feet and marbles in the wrong places—but there are other suggestions that Nancy's frustrations have to do with a sense of lack of wholeness that is perhaps anaclitic in nature, or to the mysteries of sources of power that are hidden or invisible, like vaginas. That she can't figure out the matching card game points to cognitive blunting: a neurotic proclivity for not understanding too much or not being understood too well. In her attempts to turn passive into active through the play of her imagination, she wants a house of her own with a mother and/or brother at her beck and call. These play themes seem to indicate that Nancy's psychological dilemmas are richer and more complex, involving narcissistic injury and deflated self-esteem in relation not just to her brother, but to her mother as well. The transference version of this appears in the play when she bosses Molly and orders her around. Her confusion at the start of the session about locating the right playroom seems more salient as one of several subtle indicators that Nancy's developmental dysphoria has infringed on her cognitive processes. Some children might respond to such ongoing traumatic stressors by becoming danger-activated, hyperalert, and sharply focused on the narrow visual and aural details of their environment. Nancy's defenses seem to work the other way, to mute and confuse her attention to her surroundings.

Around this time, Ernst Kris noted in a research meeting the interesting and paradoxical phenomenon in which the older child, Nancy, identified with her younger brother Eric and modeled her behavior after his. Is Nancy doing something similar here? With her bossy behavior toward Molly is she showing her identification with the younger but more powerful and favored brother? In another family Eric might become her ally in the family fray instead of another living reminder of her fall from grace. The whole of this session seems bracketed by the presence of another, an interloper, in the room; a proxy for Eric. She can't initially recognize her room. There are marbles that she infers don't belong there.

There are the absent and otherwise messy paints, consumed and spread around by another. It is as though she senses that intruders have been in her room and that Molly (in the maternal transference) is at some level perceived as responsible for this state of events. The implication is that Molly, like a mother, has shifted her attention to another. Nancy, turning passive into active, takes on a commanding tone toward Molly, much like a master toward a slave. Molly does not question Nancy's domineering commands that Molly build a house or that she pick up objects that Nancy has dropped. Nor does she probe for the underlying angry affect that is likely impelling these commands. Instead, Molly submits to Nancy's bidding. Currently, we might be more curious about this assigning of roles. What affect is driving the play? Is it play in the sense of being part of an unfolding psychodrama? Or is it nonplay and thus a particular form of resistance to a child's version of free association, the play process? Is Nancy turning the tables on the adult and demonstrating to Molly what it is like to be the subservient and passive child, following and identifying with a younger brother? Probably so.

In the layering of meanings in the therapeutic play process, another subtext for the session is Molly's transformation into a subservient, need-satisfying maternal object who is at daughter Nancy's beck and call. This could be termed revenge play or turning situations into their opposite; in the least very gratifying and the stuff of Hollywood. This process seems to lead to important links where feeling demoted overlaps with feelings of bodily loss and castration. These overlaps lend themselves to identifications with the aggressor, both in terms of the presenting psychological and physical depictions of the damaged self that has been wrought by the aggressor, and, more deeply, the rage, self-loathing, and violent revenge fantasies that lurk beneath the preoccupation with such a damaged and violated self.

Given the flow of the session, a technical point arises: what about asking (either inside or outside the play) what Nancy makes of Eric's role as aggressor in her world? Trying to put big marbles into small toys seems like the metaphorical expression that Nancy applies to the shrinking world with little place for her after Eric's appearance; an impossible wish to return to her solo status in infancy. Alternatively, how can she reverse life events and put Eric back into his mother's womb or, better yet, kill him? Devouring the cracker that she has assigned to Eric further underlines the forbidden, multifaceted revenge fantasies that crowd her mind. Nancy's actions of going to the bathroom by herself and flushing the toilet with her foot do not seem to work as defining evidence of a female castration dynamic. It seems more to represent that, at times anyway (perhaps in the company of a powerful, intact woman play partner), she can momentarily escape the culturally defined phallocentrism of the time and act in a relatively conflict-free manner. Then again, in this action sequence, after devouring Eric's cookie, she may be flushing Eric down the toilet in her quest for mastery, regardless of whatever the cultural proscriptions may be.

PLAY SESSION 4: LIBERATED AGGRESSION FOLLOWED BY RAGE AGAINST TWO MOMMIES

In this session, held one week later, Nancy once again seems somewhat more together. As the session ends, however, hostility erupts and she sounds the discordant notes of rage and affective diathesis. At the start of the session, she is more "there" cognitively and more affectively free than she had shown previously. She exhibits different parts of her mind in a manner that Molly finds perplexing. In this session, Nancy displayed more of the ego qualities that she had briefly flashed when finishing her sand baking in session one, and in retrieving her doll and carriage from another child during the following session. She continues to be more aggressively engaging and interactive with Molly, more spontaneous in her playing and joking. This is the Nancy who has been observed more at home than in public. She savors the absurd with the analyst. Toward the end of the session her attitude morphs into a rageful meeting with Molly and her mother. In it Nancy demonstrates her extremely conflicted ambivalence about being triangulated with her two "mommies" and having to tolerate their having their own relationship apart from her. This may be an oedipal variant that she had previously shorthanded with her comment about her aunt putting a needle into her grandmother (for her diabetes) while she looked on passively.

But Nancy's tantrum at the end of the session seems to be partly a reaction to various slights by the therapist. At the beginning of their hour together, Molly, apparently following protocol, delays engaging Nancy. After entering the nursery school, she waits for the music to end before escorting Nancy to the playroom. This is followed immediately by Nancy's report of her grandmother's being attacked by a needle and her cousin Jay's violent affront in pushing her off a chair; girls being treated roughly and badly by others. In all this, she seems more cognitively present, clearer about her colors, and better at doing puzzles; all signs of a cognitive resurgence of sorts. A transition point in the session occurs around Nancy's blurting out "Mommy." It is an ambiguous exclamation that could refer, as Molly suggests in her note, to Nancy's thoughts about taking her painting to her mother. Another more proximal alternative is that it could be making explicit the presence of Molly in Nancy's mind as the increasingly ambivalent mother; an old transference object. Nancy's insecurity about her appearance reemerges as she trolls for positive comments about her dress. In a telling sequence, she says "pretty dress" and makes an apparent parapraxis after previously getting her colors "right" by calling it "gray" rather than brown. Molly notes that she doesn't know whether this is something that Nancy says about all her dresses (or the color of her therapist's hair). That would have been an appropriate question to ask. Instead, she responds concretely as though this almost four-year-old needed an adjustment in her reality testing. She corrects Nancy, stating that the color is brown, not gray. Nancy reacts in a complex manner that is part clarification and part retaliation, but overall, a release from her general regressive passivity. As Molly notes, she turns into a dramatically different child, showing a side of herself that was previously absent in the school setting, but one that other observers had noted at home when she was carousing with Eric and in battlefield mode. A common error would be to see Nancy's actions at this particular point as regressive, rather than as an escape from regression. This gleeful, instinctual aggressive display may actually be a sign of the presence of a healthy growth potential.

As this sequence continues, Nancy tells a paradoxical joke about snow in summer as though to indicate that Molly did not get her "gray" joke; she turns a dirty poop color into something closer to Snow White. Is she also evincing guilt that in jibing with Molly she is upsetting and reversing the "natural" order of inhibition and regression? The hostile/ satirical sequence is elaborated as she sticks her tongue out at Molly. For young girls, sticking out the tongue (and in current times flashing the middle finger) is often an upward symbolic displacement that is both mocking and flaunting. It represents a disparaging display of power that carries in it signals of gendered female potency and sexuality. In the second part of the sequence she laughs uproariously before she falls off her chair. This replicates in play her earlier report of Jay's shoving her off a chair at home. The sequence continues with another passive into active trope with Nancy throwing the puzzle pieces onto the floor. She does this joyfully, "not violently," Molly notes. Molly describes here important indicators that she is in the presence of positive aggression.[3] My speculation is that Nancy is expressing developmental energies of a relatively nonneurotic, nonhostile nature that were released in the presence of a neutral but supportive analytic observer. In a flash she shows the potential that had impressed earlier investigators, particularly Provence and Coleman, before those qualities became blighted by the type of ongoing family trauma that Ernst Kris termed strain trauma. At the end, in throwing a fit in her mother's presence, Nancy targets two birds with one transference storm. She expresses an amalgam of long-bottled-up rage at her mother and more recent transferential rage toward Molly. In that era such powerful clinical determinants were still not well worked out, understood, and accepted as part of the child analytic clinical canon.[4]

MEETING WITH MRS. MILES AND MOLLY: RESISTANCES IGNORED RATHER THAN EXPLORED

In the meeting two weeks later with Mrs. Miles present, Molly once again seems somewhat emotionally oblique and relatively nonexplanatory in her approach to Nancy. This may reflect the style of the time, which was to listen, reflect, occasionally interpret, but not explain. This style may be exaggerated by the considered research posture embodied

in the participant-observation model as defined then. After acknowledging Nancy, Molly fraternizes with several other children before opening
her lap to Nancy. These days, the therapist would be more drawn to
Nancy immediately because of the appeal signaled by her smile and her
body English. In doing so the therapist would be acknowledging the
heat of Nancy's attachment and respectfully clarifying right away that
this is not a playroom day. The situation is compounded by Nancy's
insistence on a private, confidential relationship with Molly. She is quite
clear that she wants a separation of parents from the therapist. This
statement begs for an understanding to develop between therapist and
child, particularly with a child of her age who seems at times to actively
encourage not being understood. There is also some suggestion here
of a communication difficulty; that the information from home visits
is not getting transmitted to Molly but is going directly to the research
meetings or becoming submerged in the files as part of the superfluity
of data.

Nancy seems to passively accept going out to the yard. In her sub-
mitting to this directive, there is an unfortunate reinforcement of her
trends toward compliance. Granted it would have been more difficult
to support her active right to, if not veto, at least protest the meeting between Molly and Mrs. Miles. As has been speculated, participation in the
study no doubt had an exposing effect on some of the participants, both
parents and investigators. There was a heightening of anxieties about
parenting, an eliciting of fears of being judged wanting, culminating
on one side with parents imbuing the investigators with idealized wisdom that they may not have possessed. Mrs. Miles nervously lights up a
cigarette, a habit of hers that is in conflict with her husband's wishes as
well as her own mother's. (One measure of how members of the Miles
family were resolving their differences is that later on Flo states that Leo
is not criticizing her for smoking. In fact, to demonstrate his tolerance,
he buys her packs of cigarettes without protest.) Flo asks Molly about
Nancy's crying. This is a point of conflict particularly between her old-
country mother and the study investigators. Grandmother had asserted
whenever given the chance—as when the Miles family moved in with

her briefly during this time of treatment contact—that feelings were bad and it was bad for Nancy to express emotion, particularly painful affects. In other words, "Big girls don't cry."

Paints and painting at this point are associated with father. Nancy's painting now seems to be a neurotic activity expressing her conflicts about instinctual discharge, rather than a medium for creative elaborations of her inner life. There are suggestions here that Nancy is at war with both of her parents but that at times this state is quite independent of the parental conflicts. The net result is that, as she ages, Nancy's neurotic state seems to be at times resonant and at other times more separate from the storms within the family milieu. Her anxious rituals are centered around doing, undoing, and expiation; making a mess and then cleaning it up. The investigators tended to view Nancy in nursery school and in therapy as the castration-complicated victim of a brother-successor. As the material develops over the course of nine sessions, however, there is a growing suggestion that her restraint and containment at school are a reflection of her preferred mode of quiet self-containment in an atmosphere of supportive adults. On her home grounds she is the aggressor, knocking her brother around and hoarding her play money. Her mother's favoritism toward Eric is expressed ironically in Flo's conviction that Nancy has plenty of play money to share with her brother. In metaphor-speak this means that Nancy possesses plenty of power, love, and emotional supplies. In retaliation for this real loss of status, however, Nancy rejects her mother's food, and in the process, her mother and her love. She becomes "disobedient," running around the table instead of eating. Father's trying to force her to eat unconsciously increases her passive resistance. Cooking (recall the making of sand cookies in Molly's first interview) is associated with mother. We could say that at home she is in war mode, reflecting in her behavior the currents and tensions of hostility that course through the family. She gets punished for her admixture of identification with the aggressor and healthy aggression and hostility by being sent to her room. All of this only served to reinforce the mother's endorsement of Eric. A sleep disturbance ensues. Its secondary gain is that the mother's punishment is to become the emotional patch on Nancy's separation anxiety/rage as she ends up sleeping with Nancy to soothe her. It has become clearer over the years that separation anxiety is virtually inseparable from the rage at loss of love or the loved ones' emotional unavailability. The data gathered here seem to support a broader mindscape in which Nancy tries to maintain Molly as a relatively unambivalent new maternal object. She simultaneously struggles to overcome her deep ambivalence toward her own mother and to restore what Melanie Klein has termed a more stable depressive position. That is, can Nancy be rageful toward her mother and yet remain confident that her rage will not drive her mother further away? Can she remain confident that in spite of her mood her relationship to her mother will remain safe and stable? In this passage, Flo mentions that Nancy has a curtailed interest in her toys. This is the first mention made by the parents of a neurotic phenomenon that had been remarked on at the time of Nancy's developmental testing at eleven months of age. It is also the same quality that Ernst Kris commented on in a research meeting when she was in her fifth year, when he tentatively tied it in its origins to Nancy's early tendency to lose the nipple while breast-feeding.

PLAY SESSION 5: GUILT, EXPIATION, AND
DARK AND DIRTY FAMILY AFFAIRS

Much of the drama of this session seems to happen at its beginning. Nancy is playing with another child, "Pauline," whose name resonates closely with "Molly." Later it is mentioned that Pauline is seeing Al Solnit for child analysis. As I have emphasized here, the difference between child therapies may be only a matter of degree, shading, and frequency of meetings rather than of process per se. This may be particularly so within this study, given the volume of data available to fill in the blanks of a therapy and the possibility of using natural historical observation to compensate for the lesser amount of data arising from a less frequent treatment. A sibling/parent triangle is in place in the nursery school. Molly attempts to negotiate it in real life terms by telling Pauline that she can continue playing with Nancy when she returns. Nancy, however, rejects this suggestion in much the same self-assertive manner that she made Molly wait for her to finish her sand cookies play in the first session. Furthermore, in displacement she acts out a psychodramatic triumph over her sibling, Eric, when she states that she wants to play with Darla, not Pauline, upon her return.

Molly's narrative is, as usual, clear, precise, and vivid. While the meta-message of the play around arranging the doll house furniture is not forthcoming, through it Nancy indicates a preoccupation with her own housing arrangements. Around this time she became phobic about using the toilet. This manifested itself here obliquely in her preoccupation with toilets in several play sessions. Again, her need to order and structure the doll house, as well as her preoccupation with objects missing, broken, or out of place, could be easily traced back to the anxiety and confusion of her disorderly family as well as her own inner upset state. The prelude to this is her preoccupation with the cat in the box, which ultimately leads associationally to her own pet cat "Blackie," another reference to home. Nancy's fantasy play style never strays too far from the memories of actual events. Time and again she shows the limited span of her imagination. Paradoxically, this may make it difficult for Molly both to read her and to appreciate that Nancy is showing her the groundedness and fixity of fantasies characteristic of a child living amid traumatizing circumstances. Her mental stage is set and remains occupied in large part by preoccupation with her own object relations, rather than drive discharge, reminiscence, or fantasies of the future. That Molly at times seems not to "get" Nancy is a probable function of the sort of not knowing of her that her parents display around her at home. They rarely seem to "get" Nancy, bound up as they are in their own transference projections and fantasy identifications. The extensive notes from Laura Codling's social work home visits during this time are filled with the details of the Mileses' marital unrest and their frustrated, upwardly mobile social strivings. Flo and Leo were quite unhappy with their life in a split-level house in the suburbs. They both felt, Leo in particular, that they were being harassed by some neighborhood teenagers.

I read this, in part, as an externalization of their marital woes. In addition, they were looking for ways to make and save money. One rationalizing solution that they came up with was to move in with Flo's parents while they put their home up for sale. Flo was also openly missing her proximity to her own parents. She specifically felt that she was losing out in her rivalry with her older sister and her sister's husband, who lived upstairs in the same building as her parents. Transferentially, this could have influenced Flo's object parallel shift from her preference for her older child, to the younger son, Eric. This move in with her parents also amounted to a trial separation of sorts. They did this for about a month. Flo and the children slept in one room and supposedly because of space limitations, Leo slept in the attic. When their house did not sell, they reluctantly moved back to the suburbs from the inner city of New Haven. Nancy introduces these changes in her therapy play with associations around Nana's supposed visit to her house, Nancy's going for a walk with her, and the possibility that she may stay at Nana's house.

The references to toilets and their usage in this session may proclaim Nancy's anxieties about what she may have done to bring about such a dark and dirty state of family affairs. How much guilt needs assuaging in relation to her hostility toward others, whether Pauline or family members? In Nancy's mind there seems a lot of cleaning up and keeping up of appearances to be done, hence the alternations in the play between washing hands and faces, proper toileting, and bathing. The image of bread on the house coupled with her statement that her mother is feeding her good and nutritious bread and oatmeal, apparently delivered without irony, seems to further back up a sense of rapprochement between the two of them. This is another possible unarticulated effect of the working alliance between Molly and Nancy, especially given the number of interactions between the two that involve feeding and physical contact. She is in an alert and cheerful mood during this session; in a teasing manner, she confuses colors with Molly. Such shifts away from manifest and latent depression would currently warrant a comment from the therapist so as to put these shifts on the record, so to speak, and not to assume that they are obvious to the young child, or to an adult, for that matter. The session also illustrates a partial recovery from the cognitive regression that was a part of the impetus for the initial therapeutic contact. At the end of this session, Nancy is described as falling "lightly" when she is greeted while coming down from the playroom. This may be lighthearted clowning around, a further break in Nancy's depression, but it may also be a way of signaling goodbye to Molly and dramatizing through body English the dissolution of that day's play dyad. While I have speculated on the imprint that family climate, competition, and recovery from stress may have left on the play in this session, the normative developmental qualities found here are also important to summarize. At this point, Nancy seems on the way to partial recovery in terms of her mood and cognition and to a partial restitution of her ego functions. This was marked by a decrease in separation anxiety. Her immobile nursery school presence persisted. Through Molly's ministrations, in an atmosphere of relative peace and quiet, developmental processes have begun to kick back in.

PLAY SESSION 6: DADDY'S GIRL NOW

During this sixth play session, Molly is cued to Nancy's renewed separation anxiety and estrangement from her mother, and she comments directly on her sadness. Nancy's mood is probably more akin to a surfacing anaclitic depression, an affective representation of potentially permanent loss, rather than a mournful acceptance of sadness about evanescence, transition, and change. Nancy, at this time, was reluctantly negotiating a shift to her father as her primary object of affection, and away from her mother who, after her earlier mother/infant dalliance with Nancy, was so obviously involved with preferences for Eric that it added to Nancy's sense of trauma and depression. Her father, by contrast, actively courted Nancy's favor and affection. By peering out the window, anticipating her father's arrival, and making other references to him in this session, Nancy signals this growing shift. Toward the end of the session her play about "daddy" and her fantasy of having "two daddies" (probably her original paternal object and Molly in another version of the shifting transference), culminated with a play trio of two birds and the daddy doll, which most likely represent Molly, Nancy, and her father, Leo. Her rage at parental object-related shifts is presumably muted by her separation anxiety and depression, and is wrapped up in a preoccupation with her appearance. Today we might attempt to stimulate even a three-year-old child's curiosity as to why she is so focused on seeking approval and on compulsively needing to be seen as neat and tidy. The technical challenge would be to get closer to presumed underlying ambivalent feelings and fantasies of hostile aggression as well as the accompanying guilt about hostility toward love objects and "lost" objects. This tack is also suggested by her precise layering of colors on the paper followed by her washing/cleaning gesture of expiation. The emergence of Molly as a new object for Nancy is signaled again by Nancy sitting on Molly's lap early in the session. It is reinforced later on, when her painting becomes a gift to Molly. Finally, Eric emerges in transferred form, as Jerry in the session; a dominant male and study subject to whom Nancy must acquiesce as both punishment and as proof of her inferiority. The episode begins and ends with Nancy positioning herself in defensive social isolation next to another surrogate parent, Eveline Omwake, the head nursery school teacher. In this way she maintains an imaginary triad.

PLAY SESSION 7: RED SHOES, MAD MOTHERS, AND STICKING OUT TONGUES

The "overture" to this play session contains a very clear description of how the transition from the group play experience in the nursery school to the dyadic situation in the playroom sometimes occurred. First, there is the dilemma of group activity versus individual expression. Does Nancy dance like the others or perform some activity of her own? Almost simultaneously there is the problem of signaling and securing the attachment to the therapist in the presence of the group, many of whom are in treatment, some with the same therapist. (The report suggests, for instance, that Leah, like Nancy, has a therapeutic relationship with Molly.) For Nancy, as in earlier sessions, it is clear that the therapeutic encounter begins as it usually does, unbounded by doors and physical space, with the initial sighting of Molly. She signals her positive transference and working relationship with her therapist when she takes Molly's hand and insistently, albeit awkwardly, clings to it until she leaves the group and heads upstairs. "You are mine," she seems to be declaring. Also on display is an apparent conflict of loyalty represented by the dilemma of whether to include or exclude the assistance of another therapist, Al Solnit. Nancy, in her ambivalence, initially rejects him and then later accepts his help in jumping off the stairs, though she still insists on holding Molly's hand as well as Dr. Solnit's as she does this.

On arriving in the playroom, Nancy immediately expresses her continuing preoccupation with things broken, missing, or lost. Again, this seems not something to be narrowly or reductively defined as an aspect of castration anxiety. It seems instead to have deeper roots in death anxieties and a deathly dramatization of her need for company and comfort after so many abandonments in a somewhat shattered life. It is part of larger preoccupation with losing and loss; an anxious and depressive mental attitude reflecting losses of love brought on by time and tenuous family circumstances. In this session it is a door off of the sink that she gets Molly to fix. As we have seen, at other times it has been missing and broken chair legs and marbles, or other items that seem not to fit or to be faulty. A further characteristic inhibition of motor aggression, coupled with thwarted aggressive capacities for knowing and acquiring new knowledge, cause her loss of self-esteem. Nancy's tentativeness and confusion were symptomatic of the damage to her once robust primary tie to her mother; not every child's fate in such circumstances as it is here. Recall that Flo was thought by Sally Provence to be one of the three most nurturing and connected mothers in the first year of Nancy's life. Her own temperamental givens toward splitting and internalization highlight a propensity for dealing with frustrations and disappointments by internalizing her rage and hurt, and further complicate her play preoccupations about loss. In the play displacement, Molly as the agent of restitution as both the finder and the healer of lost and broken parts offers Nancy the hope that she may be similarly transformed. Molly will be her therapeutic "Santa Claus" of sorts, bringing her not sleds but security, bodily and psychological intactness, and well-being.

It is after this sequence that Nancy's anger emerges in its fullest expression, though, in keeping with the times, Molly does not pick up on it and press for further elaboration. It seems that Molly is relying on the technical precepts generally used then, which posited the therapeutic action in the treatment of young children as residing in a benign and supportive play relationship with the therapist, one that made words if not extraneous, at least immaterial, and placed interpretation in a secondary role. The play was the thing. As Erikson pointed out at the time, too many words might overburden play and lead to disruption. Now, to reverse a phrase, we assume that at any age and developmental stage one word might be worth a thousand play pictures (give or take). Interpretative comments couched in the vernacular of the child's developmental level are understood as furthering self-understanding. They maximize the effectiveness of the therapeutic contact, potentially expanding the conflict-free sphere of ego functioning and facilitating a new object relationship. Being there in that manner satisfies the child's appetite for new, novel, and refreshing relationships apart from the neurotically laden dynamics of old frozen transference objects and developmentally distorted self/other objects. As Nancy describes it, her mother gets mad at her for getting her shoes dirty (or for not eating or not sleeping, being disobedient, or otherwise acting in a hostile or "bad" fashion). Depending on the sequence, Nancy states that in her anger at her mother she either provokes her or retaliates against her by tromping in the mud and getting mother's gifted red shoes dirty. Unlike Dorothy's in the movie version of *The Wizard of Oz*, her shoes will not provide her with a talisman of magic and safety but will ground her in the despair and self/other punitiveness of her rage. As the play continues, Nancy attempts to undo her transgressions by playing out an omnipotent Prospero fantasy in which she, like Shakespeare's magician in *The Tempest*, controls everyone in the house, adding sisters and extra Erics to her assigned doll and mother and father. Her play soothes the helplessness of being little in a habitat of uncontrollable and irascible adults. The slight of the unwanted Eric is relieved as she becomes the one adding sisters and brothers to the family willy-nilly; reinforcements perhaps. It is notable that when she encounters a doll without an arm, even in the midst of these play balms, Nancy experiences a mix of heightened bodily anxiety and excitement accompanied by a pronounced shudder. Molly must once again rescue her by performing her unifying play magic, banishing the specter of permanent separation and loss. The meta-message here seems to be that such impossible aggressive wishes, awakened in the play and confounded by the inhibitions internalized in relation to her mother's prohibitions of messiness, provide the groundwork for a harsh early superego formation. The clinical manifestation of such early "sphincter morality" is seen in Nancy's physical immobility and passivity and in her inability to play freely and to extract pleasure from toys and the act of playing.

THERAPY SESSION 8: IS THE TROUBLE INSIDE, OUTSIDE, OR ON THE OTHER SIDE?

In this eighth session, held six weeks later, Nancy once again demonstrates her eager and ardent attachment to Molly. Molly, however, seems rather awkward when it comes to dealing with the strivings for her attention made by her two therapeutic charges, Leah and Nancy. This is all the more notable since it has been well established that one of the root causes of Nancy's depression has to do with her inability to adapt to a common developmental event, the arrival of a peer who becomes a competitor. Her sibling hatred of Eric and her lost competition with him remain writ large in her actions and play. Current experience with nursery school settings and day care has sensitized and alerted us to the manifold ways in which competitive issues, jealousy, and envy can insinuate themselves into the everyday lives of young children and those who care for them. Of course, it also seems a natural progression from the drama of Leah being left behind to Nancy's immediate question about the one-sided easel. Why one side rather than two? Molly's response, that only one child would be painting in the room at any one time, while factual, seems a missed opportunity to remark on Nancy's continuing sensitivity to people and things absent or missing, particularly rivals. Her preoccupation is highlighted even further by her immediately pointing out that a color is missing from the easel as well; the color red, the color associated with her anger at her mother and her shoes; the color she must blot out in anal-expressive fashion with her "mud" painting. The next sequence in the session involves a misunderstanding of Nancy's wish to sit down while she pours the red paint. Molly at first thinks that she is indicating that she wants to use the toilet. This seems a further depiction and confirmation in the play of cloaked anal dynamics that drive her red/mud play. Then, of course, she starts her painting activity by making an "N." This series of painting gestures raises the question of where Nancy is in her ambivalence toward Molly as well as her father.

Nancy's next play sequence is of falling in the water and peek-a-boo play, ending with her sticking her tongue out at Molly. Molly seems to deflect Nancy's hostile/teasing, yet erect and sensuous rebuff, when she describes this action as "stretching out her tongue." This display of potency conveys a relaxed comfort with her aggression and further suggests that departure is in the air. Molly appears and disappears through Nancy's painting movements with her hands. Nancy then shifts out of the play and moves her attention and thoughts away from Molly with her question about the dormitory going up next door. This leads to her thoughts trending home, to a central oedipal power dynamic where Nancy shares the marital bed with her parents over her mother's protest and with her father's support. In her narrative her own libidinal strivings regarding the sleeping arrangements are disavowed. The dog makes her do it. Furthermore, any guilt that she might otherwise be conscious of for going against her mother's wishes is disavowed. After all, the metaphor of the dog "Mike" knocking her mother down suggests the added strength that Nancy has acquired from Molly that is helping her deal with day-to-day family life. In fantasy she wishfully protects her mother (from herself) by locking Mike up. (Mrs. Miles hated dogs and Mike in particular.) At the end the current positive objects in Nancy's life are joined as she insists on physical contact with Molly, sitting on her lap while drawing a cutout picture to take along with her painting to her father as a gift. No apparent goodbyes are reported, but nonetheless Nancy departs from Molly as a child who at this juncture seems to have been partially psychologically resuscitated through a combination of physical contact involving feeding and sitting in Molly's lap, attentiveness if not attunement, and the provision of a therapeutic play environment by Molly, with all its built-in potentials for psychological healing.

PLAY SESSION 9: A QUIET GOODBYE

This story of a treatment contact began with Nancy cooking sand cookies and ends with her pretending to bake a clay birthday cake at Molly's suggestion. The final play session, which takes place three weeks after the eighth, is highlighted by a strong sense of purpose, if not a sort of rapture, as Nancy immerses herself in an exercise in curiosity that seems to have two parts. Part one has to do with her cold and its treatment by Dr. Coleman, and the second element is Nancy's subsequent identification with the aggressor in her play. Both Molly and Nancy were absent the previous week; Nancy because of a cold. As she is inspecting the play dishes, Molly suggests a tea party. Nancy, showing rebellion, muted sadism, and high jinx, attacks Molly's arm and leg with her needle from the doctor's kit. She delightedly injects Molly not on her bare thigh as she had wished, but through Molly's skirt. This seems to be a follow up to her sticking her tongue out at Molly in the previous session. The suggestion is that to treat her cold, Nancy received injections from Dr. Coleman. Her report of her own absence from nursery school amounts to one of the longest and clearest day-to-day conversations in her record. Part two consists of her ordering behavior such as naming the potty seat, dressing a "Negro" doll, and finally, training her curiosity on the doctor's kit and its components. At the end, Nancy makes a play stove in what seems indicative of a growing acceptance of both being a girl and things feminine in the temper of the time.

DISCUSSION

Nancy as subject and Molly as analyst came together on our analytic scene halfway through the history of analysis, which extends somewhat more than a century. We assume and hope that as analysis continues to grow and mature, our understandings of the mind will keep pace. So what did we learn, overall, from the brief contact of this subject and this analyst? Taking Molly's technique with Nancy as one typical type of therapeutic engagement, we can see that one mode was to present the child with a benign, supportive, interested adult. As noted earlier, implicit in such an approach was the realization that a child or adult could use this interpersonal stimulus to begin to construct a new, novel, hoped-for, "good" object. The relative absence of interpretations and questions in this treatment reminds me of Anna Freud and Sophie Dann's descriptions of the Bulldogs Bank children as they were revived psychologically after the Holocaust.[5] In the process of their recovery from harrowing years in the Theresienstadt concentration camp during World War II, these six children were well cared for physically and attended to emotionally. As an integral part of their recuperative process, their history and actions were never interpreted, and yet they made astonishingly speedy recoveries from their near-death infant experiences. Nancy originated in less dire circumstances. She does her own translating and interpreting of her traumatic experiences with Molly present as a witness and catalyst for her return from cognitive relapse and depression. While we have learned much in the ensuing fifty years about object constancy, how to identify transference in child therapy, object relations, and defenses, it is humbling to return to another day and view therapeutic action at work in another key. This action may not be as informed, efficient, and interactive as we now conceptualize it to be, but it nonetheless sounds a major emphasis: one thoroughgoing relationship with a troubled child, while not providing a complete formula for recovery, offers the basis for reversing regressions and reinstituting growth. Such an approach, however, is a half measure. It addresses object relations dysfunctions but not neurotic internalizations that usually require interpretative words in the context of play enactments to ameliorate. My hunch is that many adult and child analytic treatments of the day were much like that reported by Molly, long on relational dynamics and short on certain types of interpretations that address the character armor that is a secondary effect of trauma at the hands of individuals whose sacred trust should be the protection rather than the exploitation and harm of children. I am aware in making this statement that it flies in the face of much that is reported in the literature of the 1940s, 1950s, and 1960s. But I think that much of the literature was of the nature of window dressing, idealizing the psychoanalytic process as supposedly set down by Freud and glorifying abstinence while, in actuality, minimizing mutative interpretations. In present-day terms, individual treatment for Nancy would ideally be packaged with marital therapy for the parents and/or individual treatments for them, as tolerated. In the Mileses' case, in the course of the study they received a variety of indirect help for their own troubled psyches and their tormented and tormenting marital relationship. The study involvement probably saved their marriage, at least for the time being. There is certainly no evidence that the study made things worse for either Nancy or her parents. From a therapeutic point of view, it was a qualified success. It remains to be seen how much of the developmental damage that Nancy sustained was "collateral damage," secondary to her being a witness to warring parents, and how much she was a direct target of their discontents. The former would tend to lead to more transient developmental disturbances, while the latter would signify more permanent character pathology. There seems to have been some of each.

Given the early childhood time frame and the lack of follow-up data, what can we say about Nancy's future course? Nancy did continue to see a trainee after Molly's departure but that contact seems to have been static with no evidence of change in either a positive or a negative direction. While predicting future behavior is often a fool's errand, if temperament is indeed the rudder of development, then Nancy may have gone through life as a quiet, socially reserved individual who, like her parents, saved her pathology largely for home display. But we need to remember that, contrary to the tidy and somewhat romantic analytic notion that development proceeds along regular progressive lines, it is often in fact spontaneous and discontinuous. In this sense it is analogous to what we see in gene variation and transmission. What goes before may or may not be significant in accounting for or contributing to later traumas. It may take more than an infant's lack of pursuit of a stray nipple while nursing to predict future complex behavioral complexes. Traumas may emerge spontaneously from the cauldron of experience at any age. This assumes that there were no further children, that her parents remained married, and that she continued to cling anxiously to a special status with her father. The study had noted the unusual characteristic that she tended to identify with Eric as the aggressor, rather than visa versa, which would have been the more usual older-child/younger-child dynamic. After a childhood marked by passive traits, a propensity for calm (no dancing please), and submerged guilt, Nancy would reach adolescence and puberty at about the time of the Vietnam era. The conditions of the time, societal unrest, pursuit of peace and freedom in all their different forms, and the escapes provided by illegal medications could have affected her in either of several directions. They might have reinforced her tendency toward passivity, withdrawal, and quietude, or she might have become at risk for significant delinquent acting out. If the early infantile anxiety and depression, only partially resolved in her preoedipal period, reemerged as it so often does in early adolescence, Nancy would have been in for a tumultuous time, careening between breakdown and reintegration.

If we pull back at this point and take a forest rather than a tree view of the data from various sources about Nancy and her family, an interesting possibility emerges. What we may discern in the material is a historical description of "splitting" in Nancy. The discrepancy between her rough defiant behavior at home and her passive, wallflower behavior in nursery school may be better understood if we characterize it as a function of her use of splitting as both a defense and a character trait. In this way she could produce a differentiated display of energies, at certain times containing hostile, death-dealing forces and at others more relaxed, if inhibited energies similar to the libidinal schemes that infused her as an infant. In her therapy with Molly she seems to have shown both modes at various times. Certainly her parents in their relation to each other and their environment were "splitters." How they shared information was often dominated by splitting phenomena.

Whatever course she took in adolescence, perhaps Nancy's exposure to psychotherapy would sensitize her to the positive benefits of that option. As we know from experience, however, children who have been in treatment as youngsters may want to leave that option behind them, with the rest of their disparaged childhood, when they reach adolescence. In any event, it is difficult to predict outcomes on the basis of early experience except to say that early modes of character formation tend to persist. While our model of development tends to be linear, we must allow for circumlinear, spiraling ascents to maturity as well as regressive descents during adolescence. With Nancy we hope for the best, all the while remaining alert to the continuing deforming nature of early traumas and their subsequent persistence through the processes of internalization and neurotization.

POSTSCRIPT

I will conclude on an autobiographical note. As an undergraduate at Yale, I participated in a very minor way in this research project. My involvement was a major determinant in my selecting a subsequent career path as a psychoanalyst of adults, adolescents, and children. In September of 1954, I was a scholarship student at Yale College. At the time, each scholarship recipient was required to work fourteen hours a week at a job within the university. I was given the choice of working at the Yale Commons dining hall or at the Child Study Center. This turned out to be a "Hobson's choice" of sorts—that is, no choice at all. By that time I had developed an appetite for all things psychiatric and psychoanalytic. I had spent the previous two summers working as an orderly on a locked psychiatric ward of a nearby Veterans Administration hospital. At that hospital the acute psychological casualties of the Korean conflict arrived for treatment eighteen hours or so after breaking down on some battlefield near Pusan, for instance, or around the Chosan Reservoir. The psychiatric service was run by analysts on staff or in training, and during those two summers I prevailed upon them to educate me in matters psychiatric and psychoanalytic through a sort of bibliotherapy. The Child Study Center morphed into my sixth unofficial undergraduate course. One of the first papers that I duplicated for the research study group (setting aside a copy for myself) was Winnicott's magnificent work "Transitional Objects and Transitional Phenomena" from 1953.[6] It spoke to me in a way that "knocked my socks off" and led me to the naive impression that the Child Study Center was a Winnicottian outlier. When I returned to the center many years later as a fellow, I realized to my chagrin that the analytic landscape was much more as it should be, individualized and varied, hardly Winnicottian. This did not deter me from writing my first analytic paper on Winnicott's landmark 1953 paper.[7] I was inspired not only by the dynamic stream of analytic thinking that ran through the research notes, but also by the simple sight of a young Sam Ritvo and Al Solnit walking and talking with their young analytic charges as they went to explore the contents of the dog pen in the next yard. Overall, the influence of the center was such that, while upon entering I had hoped that I might become a medical doctor and a psychiatrist, upon leaving for medical school my sole intent was to join the analytic field of Kris and Kris, Provence, Ritvo, Solnit (and Winnicott!).

NOTES

1. Possible identifying data such as individual names, places, and chronological sequences have been altered in the interest of confidentiality. Care has been taken that these alterations do not measurably distort the dynamic picture of Nancy and her family.

2. Donald W. Winnicott, *The Piggle: An Account of the Psychoanalytic Treatment of a Little Girl* (Madison, CT: International Universities Press, 1977).

3. T. Wayne Downey, "Within the Pleasure Principle: Child Analytic Perspectives on Aggression," *Psychoanalytic Study of the Child* 39 (1984): 101–36.

4. Ernst Kris, "Decline and Recovery in the Life of a Three-Year-Old; or, Data on the Mother-Child Relationship," *Psychoanalytic Study of the Child* 17 (1962): 175–215.

5. Anna Freud and Sophie Dann, "An Experiment in Group Upbringing," *Psychoanalytic Study of the Child* 6 (1951): 127–68.

6. Donald W. Winnicott, "Transitional Objects and Transitional Phenomena—A Study of the First Not-Me Possession," *International Journal of Psycho-Analysis* 34 (1953): 89–97.

7. T. Wayne Downey, "Transitional Phenomena in the Analysis of Early Adolescent Males," *Psychoanalytic Study of the Child* 33 (1978): 19–46.

ABOUT THE VOLUME EDITORS

AND CONTRIBUTORS

DAVID A. CARLSON is a training and supervising analyst at the Western New England Psychoanalytic Institute and a clinical professor in the Yale Department of Psychiatry. Dr. Carlson has written about the evolution of psychoanalysis in New Haven in the time encompassed by the Yale Longitudinal Study.

JOHN DEMOS, presently retired, is the Samuel Knight Professor of History at Yale University. His most recent book is *The Heathen School: A Story of Hope and Betrayal in the Age of the Early Republic* (2014). He is also author of a number of pioneering works, beginning with *A Little Commonwealth: Family Life in Plymouth Colony* (1970); *Entertaining Satan: Witchcraft and the Culture of Early New England* (1982), Winner of the Bancroft Prize for American History by the American Historical Association in 1983; *Past, Present, and Personal: The Family and the Life Course* (1986); and *The Unredeemed Captive: A Family Story from Early America* (1994), Winner of the National Book Award and of the Ray Allen Billington Prize and the Francis Parkman Prize of the Organization of American Historians.

VIRGINIA DEMOS is a senior staff member and a past Erikson Scholar at the Austen-Riggs Institute. A clinical and developmental psychologist, infant researcher and teacher, she is assistant clinical professor of psychology in the Department of Psychiatry at Harvard Medical School. Dr. Demos has been a teacher of early development and a clinical supervisor for over twenty years in training hospitals and at the Harvard Graduate School of Education, where she was the director of the Program in Counseling and Consulting Psychology. She was also the director of a private psychotherapy clinic in Boston. Dr. Demos has published over twenty articles and book chapters on affective development in early childhood and the central role of affect in shaping psychic organization. In 1969 she published, with John Demos, a pathbreaking article in the *Journal of Marriage and the Family* entitled "Adolescence in Historical Perspective." She has also edited a book, *Exploring Affect: The Selected Writings of Silvan S. Tomkins* (1995). She has received several research fellowships and is a founding member of the International Society for Research in Emotion (ISRE). She is currently on the board of the Children's Health Program in Great Barrington, Massachusetts.

T. WAYNE DOWNEY is a child and adult psychoanalyst at the Yale Child Study Center who participated in the longitudinal study as a research assistant when he was an undergraduate at Yale.

ANDREW M. FEARNLEY is a lecturer in modern American history at the University of Manchester in the United Kingdom, with interests in the history of scientific methods, intellectual history, and the history of racial thought. He is currently working on his first book, provisionally entitled *Making Methods Work: American Psychiatry and Concepts of Race, 1880–2000.* He has also written on a number of other topics, including the history of suicide, the concept of periodization in modern American historiography, and the financial underpinnings of postwar activism.

DIANE E. KAPLAN was a senior member of the Yale Library archival staff and primarily responsible for the collection, cataloguing and maintenance of the Yale Longitudinal Study resource. She also brought considerable experience in the archiving of sensitive personal material and in considering ways to make such material available to scholars.

STEPHEN LASSONDE is dean of student life at Harvard University. He teaches courses on the history of childhood, education, family life, and aging in the United States. In 2005 he published *Learning to Forget: Schooling and Family Life in New Haven's Working Class, 1870–1940* (Yale University Press); and he served as Associate Editor of

The Encyclopedia of Children and Childhood: In History and Society (MacMillan, 2004). Since 2002 he has published, "Family and Demography in Postwar America: A Hazard of New Fortunes?"; "Ten Is the New Fourteen: Age Compression and 'Real' Childhood"; and "Age, Schooling, and Life Stages." He is currently at work on a book about changes in the ways that children in the United States have learned about and perceived authority over the course of the twentieth century.

LINDA C. MAYES is the Arnold Gesell Professor of Child Psychiatry, Pediatrics, and Psychology, Yale Child Study Center and special advisor to the dean, Yale University School of Medicine. Dr. Mayes coordinates the early childhood programs in the Center and oversees a neurobehavioral and psychophysiology laboratory at the Child Study Center. She is a member of the faculty of the Western New England Institute for Psychoanalysis and an adult and child psychoanalyst. She also coordinates the Anna Freud Centre-Yale Child Study Center Bridge Program. She has published widely in the developmental psychology, pediatrics, child psychiatry, and psychoanalytic literature. Her work focuses on stress-response and regulatory mechanisms in young children at both biological and psychosocial risk.

SAMUEL RITVO earned his medical degree from Yale School of Medicine in 1942 and was clinical professor of psychiatry at the Yale Child Study Center. He was author or coauthor of numerous publications on topics ranging from adolescent development, eating disorders, to child psychoanalysis, and the role of aggression in child development. He was a past-president of the American Psychoanalytic Association and of the Association for Child Psychoanalysis. Dr. Ritvo was one of the original therapist-researchers in the Yale Child Study Center's Longitudinal Study.

DEBORAH WEINSTEIN is assistant director of the Pembroke Center for Teaching and Research on Women at Brown University. She has published *The Pathological Family: Postwar America and the Rise of Family Therapy* (Cornell University Press, 2013).

INDEX